LATE MARX AND THE RUSSIAN ROAD

Marx and 'the peripheries of capitalism'

edited by

Teodor Shanin

LATE MARX AND THE RUSSIAN ROAD
edited by Teodor Shanin

Published in agreement with Monthly Review Press, New York
for publication and sale only in the Indian Subcontinent
(India, Pakistan, Bangladesh, Nepal, Maldives,
Bhutan & Sri Lanka)

First Published in India, 2009
Reprinted 2020

ISBN 978-93-5002-003-6

Published by
AAKAR BOOKS
28 E Pocket IV, Mayur Vihar Phase I, Delhi-110 091
Phone : 011-2279 5505 Telefax : 011-2279 5641
aakarbooks@gmail.com; www.aakarbooks.com

Printed at Sapra Brothers, Noida.

LATE MARX AND THE RUSSIAN ROAD

To Eric Hobsbawm

this book is gratefully offered
as a belated tuition fee

De omnibus dubitandum

Contents

Introduction

Books ideally speak for themselves. A lengthy explanation of contents may deflect attention from the book's goal, especially so, in a volume which includes also papers of interpretation. This introduction will be brief.

The mid-part of the book is mainly given to the drafts of Marx's 1881 discussion concerning rural Russia and some supplementary materials. The iconoclastic nature of this extraordinary piece of thinking aloud as against Marx's earlier views and later interpretations, the peculiar history of those drafts, the relevance of them for the so-called 'developing societies' of today, make these papers into one of the most important intellectual 'finds' of the century. Their first full and direct translation into English should enable the readers to judge for themselves the extent to which Marx's magnificent originality, foresight and heretical *élan* stayed with him to the very end. Bureaucrats and theologians of science in whichever camp will not like it. Good!

The book's first part offers some interpretations of Marx's work at the last stage of its development, relating directly to the drafts published. It is polemical and not of one cloth – in such matters critical doubt and debate are essential. It was Marx who chose as his favourite motto *De omnibus dubitandum* – 'doubt everything' – and the drafts below offer living proof of how much he was true to this principle. A way to honour his scholarship is to follow him in that.

The final part three of the book presents some materials which come to trace the intellectual bridges between Marx's writings on Russia and the Russian revolutionary tradition. It begins with extracts from those writings of Chernyshevskii which influenced particularly and explicitly Marx's own work. It then places before Western audiences, for once verbatim, the major programmatic and analytical statements of the People's Will – the Russian indigenous revolutionary organisation of Marx's own time, and a group to which Marx and Engels have consistently referred till the end as 'our friends'. The whole movement is remembered for its heroic defiance and bombings, which seem to have obscured its achievements in the realm of theory, namely, an alternative and highly original view of society, state and revolution within the specific social context they operated in. Also, their writings offer insight into analysis which merged, rarely acknowledged, into the thought of late Marx as well as that of Lenin. Looking at the subsequent century, one is struck by the contemporary potence of many of those statements. It is as if the global history and human society were only now catching up with many of the revolutionary considerations and illuminations of the 1880s, both those of the People's Will and Marx's own. A discussion of interdependence between Marx's analysis and the vernacular revolutionary tradition concludes both the section and the book while forming a link with the consideration of the socialisms of the twentieth century.

Even on first perusal of the book, the reader should keep in mind its assumption that the Russia of those times was a 'developing' or 'peripheral capitalist' society, in the sense attached to those terms today – arguably the first of its type. It is only in that light that the papers presented by Marx can be considered in their full contemporary relevance. In the same light one can see the fuller significance of Marx's declared wish to use Russia for the Volume III of *Capital* the way he used England in *Capital*, Volume I. Also, there are clearly different conceptions of Marxism, one of which sees itself as consistent deduction from *Capital*, Volume I using whichever empirical evidence is handy to defend its absoluteness and its universality. The text which follows should help to transform Marx's comment of the 1870s about himself 'not being a Marxist' from a sly anecdote into a major illumination of Marx's own Marxism as against that of the first generation of his interpreters.

For the rest, the book will 'speak for itself'.

Part 1
Late Marx

The first part of the book begins with an article which sets out the line of argument the book is to pursue: an historiography of Marx's thought which differs from that usually adopted, the place of Russian social data and revolution experience in it, the way it indicates Marx's developing insights into 'the peripheries' of the capitalism he was exploring in Volume I of *Capital*. The subsequent article by Wada offers a systematic textual analysis – an intellectual history – of the changes which occurred in Marx's writings since 1867 and considers their relation to the Russian scene and their direct relevance to Marx's growing awareness of the 'structure of backward capitalism'. Wada's work reflects also the very important achievement of the Japanese scholars, which was seldom given the attention and credit it deserves. The last item within Part One is a section of a larger article by Derek Sayer and Philip Corrigan which offered an early critical response to Shanin and Wada's views concerning the continuity and the change in Marx's thought. Their line of criticism is presented without being endorsed, in the spirit of the book's motto. The part of the article devoted to changes in Marx's understanding of the state, linking the experience of the Paris Commune of 1871 to his consideration of the Russian peasant commune in 1881, is presented in full as an interesting extension of the theme to which this book is devoted.

Late Marx: gods and craftsmen

Teodor Shanin

Das ist der Weisheit letzer Schluß:
Nur der verdient sich Freiheit wie das Leben
Der täglich sie erobern muß!

This is the final wisdom, ever true:
He only earns his freedom and his life
who daily conquers them anew!

Goethe, *Faust II*

Ordering change

Volume I of Marx's *Capital* was both the peak of Classical Political Economy and its most radical reinterpretation. It offered a fundamental model, built on the classical 'theory of value', of the most industrially advanced social economies of its time. It developed and placed at the centre of analysis a theory of accumulation through exploitation, and thereby of structurally determined class conflict and social transformation – the theory of 'surplus value'. It is indeed, therefore, 'the self-consciousness of the capitalist society . . . primarily a theory of bourgeois society and its economic structure',[1] but for realism's sake one must date it and place it, territorially and politically. The date is that of the pre-1870 blossoming of industrial 'private' capitalism. The place is Western Europe and its focus Great Britain. The political context is that of the socialist challenge to the *status quo*, a demand to turn the material goods and potential that industrial capitalism had produced into a base for a just society – 'to build Jerusalem in England's green and pleasant land'.[2] In the Hegelian language Marx favoured, the theoretical structure of *Capital* would be, therefore, the dialectical negation of Political Economy, a self-consciousness of capitalism turning at its highest level of accomplishment into criticism of its very root, its unmasking, and thereby its subversion and transformation.

To date and place *Capital* is also to open up a major set of questions concerning the development of Marx's thought in the period which followed. Central to it is the 1872-82 decade of Marx's life in which there was growing interdependence between Marx's analysis, the realities of Russia, and the Russian revolutionary movement – an uncanny forerunner of what was to come in 1917. The questions concern Marx's theory of social transformation – of ordering change not only within capitalism. To understand this one may well begin with *Capital* but cannot stop at that.

The strength of *Capital* lay in its systematic, comprehensive, critical, historically sophisticated and empirically substantiated presentation of the way a newly created type of economy – the contemporary capitalist economy of Great Britain – had worked on a societal level. Of paramount significance has been the more general use this model offered for other societies in which capitalism has been in manifest and rapid ascent ever since. Its limitations as well as its points of strength are 'children of their time' – the times of the breakthrough and rush forward of the 'Industrial Revolution', the rise and increasing application of science and the spread of the French Revolution's political philosophies of evolution and progress. Central to it was evolutionism – the intellectual arch-model of those times, as prominent in the works of Darwin as in the philosophy of Spencer, in Comte's positivism and in the socialism of Fourier and Saint Simon. Evolutionism is, essentially, a combined solution to the problems of heterogeneity and change. The diversity of forms, physical, biological and social, is ordered and explained by the assumption of a structurally necessary development through stages which the scientific method is to uncover. Diversity of stages explains the essential diversity of forms. The strength of that explanation lay in the acceptance of change as a necessary part of reality. Its main weakness was the optimistic and unilinear determinism usually built into it: the progress through stages meant also the universal and necessary ascent to a world more agreeable to the human or even to the 'absolute spirit' or God himself. The materialist epistemology of *Capital*, the dialectical acceptance of structural contradictions and of possible temporary retrogressions within capitalism, the objection to teleology, did not jettison the kernel of evolutionism. 'The country that is more developed industrially' was still destined 'only [to] show, to the less developed, the image of its own future'. Indeed it was a matter of 'natural laws working themselves out with iron necessity'.[3]

Yet Marx's mind was evidently far from happy with the unilinear simplicities of the evolutionist scheme. The richness of the evidence he studied militated against it and so did his own dialectical training and preferred epistemology. Also, the reason why it was the north-west corner of Europe that bred the first edition of the capitalist mode of production was still to be discovered. An admission of simple accident would be far from Marx's requirement for a science of society. In consequence and already by 1853 Marx had worked out and put to use the concepts of Oriental Despotism and of the Asiatic Mode of Production, its close synonym, as a major theoretical supplement and alternative to unilinear explanations.[4]

Marx's new societal map has assumed the global co-existence of potentially progressive social formations and of essentially static 'a-historical' ones. The nature of such static societies, of Oriental Despotism, was defined by a combination of environmental and social characteristics: extensive arid lands and hydraulic agriculture necessitating major irrigation schemes, a powerful state, and state monopoly over land and labour, multitudes of self-contained rural communities tributary to the state. Following Hegel's turn of phrase, Marx saw such societies as 'perpetuating natural vegetative existence',[5] i.e. showing cyclical and quantitative changes while lacking an inbuilt mechanism of necessary social transformation. Marx's case-list included China, Egypt, Mesopotamia, Turkey, Persia, India, Java, parts of Central Asia and pre-Columbian America, Moorish Spain etc., and also, less definitely, Russia, defined as *semi*-Asiatic.[6] The heterogeneity of global society, the differential histories of its parts, could be easier placed and explained by a heuristically richer scheme – a combination of evolutionary stages of the progressing societies and of the a-historical Oriental Despotisms, with space left between for further categories such as 'semi-Asiatic'.[7] Capitalism comes as a global unifier which drags the a-historical societies of Oriental

Despotism on to the road to progress, i.e. into the historical arena. Once that obstacle is removed the iron laws of evolution finally assume their global and universal pace.

The attitude of Marx to colonialism, for long an embarrassment to some of his adherents in the Third World, was fully consistent with those views. Marx abhorred colonial oppression, as well as the hypocrisy of its many justifications, and said so in no uncertain terms. He accepted it all the same as a possible stage on the way of progress towards world capitalism and eventually to world socialism, i.e. a fundamentally positive if terrible step on the long road to the New Jerusalem of men made free.

In the last period of his work, Marx took a further step towards a more complex and more realistic conceptualisation of the global heterogeneity of societal forms, dynamics and interdependence. The change in Marx's outlook took shape as an afterthought to *Capital* Volume I (first published in 1867), and reflected the new experience and evidence of the 1870s.

Four events stand out as landmarks in the political and intellectual background to Marx's thought in this period. First, the Paris Commune of 1871 offered a dramatic lesson and a type of revolutionary rule never known before. The very appearance of the 'dawn of' the great social revolution which will forever free mankind from the class-split society',[8] had altered the terms of establishment of a socialist society and set a new contemporaneous timetable to it. It also provided the final crescendo to Marx's activities in the first International which ended in 1872, to be followed by a period of reflection. Second, a major breakthrough within the social sciences occurred during the 1860s and 1870s – the discovery of prehistory which 'was to lengthen the notion of historical time by some tens of thousands of years, and to bring primitive societies within the circle of historical study by combining the study of material remains with that of ethnography'.[9] The captivating impact of those developments on the general understanding of human society was considerable, centreing as it did on 'men's ideas and ideals of community'[10] – then as now the very core of European social philosophy. Third, and linked with the studies of prehistory, was the extension of knowledge of the rural non-capitalist societies enmeshed in a capitalist world, especially the works of Maine, Firs and others on India. Finally, Russia and the Russians offered to Marx a potent combination of all of the above:

rich evidence concerning rural communes ('archaic' yet evidently alive in a world of capitalist triumphs) and of direct revolutionary experience, all encompassed by the theory and the practice of Russian revolutionary populism.

The relation between the new developments in Marx's thought and his Russian connections has been meticulously, yet dramatically, documented in the work of Haruki Wada, turning a variety of odd pieces of Marx's late writings, rewritings, amendments and seeming ambivalence into a consistent whole.[11] At the turn of the decade Marx became increasingly aware that alongside the retrograde official Russia, which he so often attacked as the focus and the gendarme of European reaction, a different Russia of revolutionary allies and radical scholars had grown up, increasingly engaged with his own theoretical work. It was into the Russian language that the first translation of *Capital* was made, a decade before it saw light in England. It was Russia from which news of revolutionary action came, standing out all the more against the decline in revolutionary hopes in Western Europe after the Paris Commune.

In 1870–1 Marx taught himself Russian with the purpose of approaching directly evidence and debate published in that language. In a letter to Engels, his wife complained about the manner in which he applied himself to the new task – 'he has begun to study Russian as if it was a matter of life and death.'[12] Marx proceeded with similar vigour to study Russian sources, indeed, he turned the books of the Russian radical scholars into his textbooks of language, beginning with Herzen and giving particular attention to Flerovskii and Chernyshevskii. A major library of Russian books, marked and remarked, rapidly accumulated on his shelves and their summaries increasingly entered his notes.[13]

What followed was a long relative silence, which itself calls for an explanation – Marx did not publish anything substantial until his death. Yet, the direction in which his research and thought were moving emerges from correspondence, notes and re-editions. In an 1870 letter to Engels, Marx praised Flerovskii's description of the 'labouring classes' of Russia – a major populist analysis, as 'the most substantial book since yours, *The Condition of the Working Class*. . . .'.[14] He has subsequently added to the very short list of theorists he respected and publicly applauded to a degree alloted previously only to Engels, the name of Nikolai Chernyshevskii. In

1877, Marx rebuked in a letter the 'supra-historical theorising', i.e. an evolutionist interpretation of his own writings as related to Russia, and rejected it again, much more specifically, in 1881 in relation to the Russian peasant commune. Marx's quip of those very times about himself 'not being a marxist' was coming true with particular vengeance in so far as Russia was concerned.

The Russian connection

An aside concerning Russian revolutionary populism is necessary to place Marx's new interests, insights and friends for Western audiences. The label 'populist', like that of 'marxist', is badly lacking in precision; the heterogeneity of both camps was considerable. In Russian speech a populist (*narodnik*) could have meant anything from a revolutionary terrorist to a philanthropic squire. What makes it worse is the fact that there are today no political heirs to claim and defend the heritage of Russian populism – political losers have few loyal kinsmen, while the victors monopolise press, cash and imagination. Lenin's major work, from which generations of socialists learned their Russian terminology, used 'populism' as a label for a couple of writers who stood at that time on the extreme right wing of the populists, an equivalent of using the term marxism for the so-called 'legal marxists' of Russia.[15] This made Lenin's anti-populist argument of 1898 easier, while increasing the obscurity of the populist creed to his readers of today.

Populism was Russia's main indigenous revolutionary tradition. Its particular mixture of political activism and social analysis commenced with A. Herzen and produced a long line of names well known and respected in the European socialist circles, e.g. P. Lavrov, Marx's personal friend and ally. It reached its full revolutionary potency in the writings of N. Chernyshevskii, and its most dramatic political expression in Marx's own time in *Narodnaya Volya*, i.e. the People's Will party.[16] This clandestine organisation rose to exercise considerable impact during the 1879-83 period and was finally smashed in 1887 by police action, executions and exile.

Russian populists challenged both the Slavophile belief in the innate specificity (not to say intrinsic supremacy) of Russia or its peasants and the liberal's propagation of West European capitalism as Russia's bright future.[17] Secondly, Russian populists assumed the ability and desirability of Russia 'bypassing the stage' of West-European-like capitalism on its way to a just society. That possibility resulted, however, not from Russia's uniqueness, exalted by the Slavophiles, but from Russia's situation within a global context, which had already seen the establishment of capitalism in Western Europe. The 'world-historical' analytical paradigm led to the assumption of substantively different roads along which different societies proceed toward the similar goals of a better world. In judging those roads, the 'social costs' of capitalist progress were rejected for Russia and the increase in social equality and the level of livelihood of the majority treated as the only measurestick of true social advance. A third major marker, fully expressed only by the People's Will, the tsarist state was assumed to be the main enemy of the people of Russia, both an oppressor and an economically parasitic growth. It differed from Western Europe in its ability to keep people in slavery, not only as the plenipotentiary of the propertied classes. It was the *state*, in that view, which was Russia's *main capitalist force*, both the defender and the creator of the contemporary exploitive classes.

As against the force of order, oppression and exploitation, the revolutionary populists put their trust in a class war of the Russian labouring class seen by Chernyshevskii as 'peasants, part-time workers (*podenshchiki*) and wage-workers' (this trinity became peasants, workers and working intelligentsia in later populist writings). The idea of 'uneven development' (first expressed by P. Chadayev) was to provide the theoretical core of political analysis. Uneven development was seen as turning Russia into a proletarian among nations, facing at disadvantage the bourgeois nations of the West. Internally, it polarised Russia. On the other hand, it enabled and indeed necessitated revolutionary leaps in which relative backwardness could turn into revolutionary advantage. That made an immediate socialist revolution in Russia possible. The overthrowing of tsardom by revolutionary means was to be followed by the establishment of a new regime in which an interventionist government, serving the democratically expressed needs of the people of Russia, would act in tandem with the active organisation of local popular power.

In the early debates, the revolution envisaged by the Russian populists was primarily a 'social' one, i.e. the transformation of the class nature of Russia, and not 'simply political', i.e. aiming at electoral franchise. An uprising of the peasant majority of the nation was to play a major role and other sub-groups of the labouring class and the revolutionaries of non-labouring class origin were to participate fully. Revolutionary populists turned the brunt of their propaganda firstly towards the peasants. As the attempts of the 1870s to propagate new revolutionary spirit among peasants proved disappointing, the centre of gravity shifted from rural propaganda to extra-rural action. By now a two-in-one struggle was increasingly envisaged: an attack on the state which was also the main capitalist and capitalism-inducing institution meant that political and social struggles intertwined. That made the confrontation more difficult, but also offered the opportunity, upon victory, to move with particular speed toward a combined political and social transformation. The majority in the main populist organisation, land and liberty (*Zemlya i Volya*), established in 1876, had consequently adopted a strategy of insurrection (*perevorot*), i.e. of immediate, direct and armed anti-state challenge. In 1879 the organisation split into the People's Will (*Narodnaya Volya*) majority and the Black Repartition (*Chernyi Peredel*) – a minority which opposed the militants, the new anti-state line and the growing stress on armed action. The People's Will was increasingly active in organising urban workers and even published an illegal newspaper specifically designed for them, but explained it not by the exclusive role of the proletariat, but by the tactical significance of this component of the general ('triple') labouring class, i.e. its being present at the centres of administration, where the main battle with tsardom was to be fought. The organisation operated vigorously in the army, incorporating a number of officers, and was increasingly influential with students and young intellectuals. Besides propaganda and the preparations of an uprising, the strategy of attempts at the lives of the tsar and the top officials was adopted as a major tactical weapon aiming to shake tsardom and to trigger off popular opposition and insurrection.[18]

A strong moralist and subjectivist streak was prominent within the populist *Weltanschauung*, inclusive of the writings of Chernyshevskii – a philosophical materialist and an admirer of Feuerbach. The impact of ideas was assumed and accentuated – to the populists a major determinant of the uneven development of societies and the ability of some of them to 'leap' over the stage of capitalism. The particular significance of intellectual elites as leaders and as catalysts of political action in a Russian-style society was stressed – a partial explanation of the way revolutionary populists built their organisation and chose their targets in armed action. For those reasons and also to provide the necessary cadres for the clandestine propaganda and for the armed action, exceptional stress was laid within the group on personality training, to inculcate modesty, integrity and totality of devotion. It made the People's Will organisation famous throughout Europe for its discipline as much as for the asceticism and the courage of its members.[19] The Russian image and self-image of 'professional revolutionaries' and 'party cadres' have their main origin there. More, of course, is at stake in so far as the impact of Russian revolutionary populism on the future Russian Revolution is concerned for the movement and the analysis it championed proceeded to unfold with considerable input into the revolutions of 1905-7 and 1917-20, including also what in the first decade of the twentieth century came to be called Bolshevism.

The attitude of the revolutionary populists to the Russian peasant commune was integral to their world-view. About three-fifths of the arable land of European Russia was in the hands of the peasant and cossack communes.[20] Within them, each household held unconditionally only a small plot of land, i.e. house and garden plus its livestock and equipment. The use of arable land was assigned to a family on a long-term basis by its commune, the meadows were reassigned annually and often worked collectively, the pastures and forest were in common use. The diversity of wealth within the commune was expressed mainly in differential ownership of livestock, of non-agricultural property, and in some private land bought from non-communal sources. The use of wage-labour inside the commune was limited. Many vital services were run collectively by the commune: a village shepherd, the local guards, the welfare of the orphans, and often a school, a church, a mill, etc. An assembly of heads of the households controlled and represented communal interests: decided about the services, elected its own officers, and collected its informal taxes or dues. With the exception of some areas in the West (mostly ex-Polish) the assembly also periodically redivided the arable lands in accordance with some egalitarian principle, usually in relation to the changing size of the families involved. A number of peasant communes formed a *volost*, its officers local but authorised and controlled by state authorities. Despite its surveillance by the state, the commune played (also) the role of a *de facto* peasant political organisation, a collective shield against a hostile external world of squire, policeman, tax officer, robber, intruder or neighbouring village.[21]

To the revolutionary populist the peasant commune was the proof of the collectivist tradition of the majority of Russian people, which stayed alive in spite of its suppression by the state. They were not uncritical of it, but, on balance, considered the peasant commune a major asset to their plans.[22] It was seen as a possible tool for the mobilisation of the peasants for the anti-tsardom struggle. It was to be a basic form of the future organisation of local power which would eventually rule Russia together with a democratically elected national government. For Chernyshevskii, it was also an effective framework for collective agricultural production in post-revolutionary Russia, which was to operate alongside the publicly owned industry and a minority of the private (and transitional?) enterprises. The image bears remarkable similarity to some of the realities, images and plans in Russia of the New Economic Policy period, 1921-7.

The most significant challenge to the revolutionary populism of the 1880s (and its substitution on the political map of Russia of the 1890s) was neither the Slavophiles and liberals to their 'right' nor the few Bakunist admirers of mass spontaneity to their 'left', but people who originated from the 'moderate' wing of their own conceptual fold. The main reason for the decline of revolutionary populism by the late 1880s was the defeat of their revolution, as the hope for an uprising receded, and the gallows, death in action and exile to Siberia silenced most of the People's Will activists, while their critics' voices gained in strength. A major argument against revolutionary populism came from an influential group which gathered around the journal *Russkoe Bogatsvo*, especially V. Vorontsov (who signed himself V.V.). They called for a moderate and evolutionary populism, with education as the major road forward and even with possible part-cooperation with government – a 'legal populism'. They were finding an audience and a carrier in the type of the well-meaning, highly talkative but rather ineffectual provincial intellectual – often an employee of the educational and welfare service of the local authorities and the co-operative movement. It was they who came increasingly to dominate populism in the 1890s (and once again in 1907-17 after the defeat of the Revolution in 1905-7), diluting its content, turning its revolutionary wing into a 'wild' minority, and determining the whole movement's eventual destruction. It was mostly they who 'spoke on behalf of populism' between 1887 and the end of the century.

A second attack on revolutionary populism came from the members of the Black Repartition group who parted company with People's Will in 1879 over its insurrectionist designs. The leaders of that group, Plekhanov, Axelrod, Deutch and Zasulich, emigrated to Switzerland and after failing to make any headway with their own brand of populism, reorganised by 1883 and declared for marxism, scientific socialism, the necessity of a capitalist stage and a proletarian revolution on the road to socialism. They explained the failures of People's Will accordingly.[23] The new name adopted by the group was Emancipation of Labour (*Osvobozhdenie Truda*). Their eyes were now on Germany, its economy as well as the rapid increase of the German Social Democratic Workers' Party, with an explicit expectation that Russia would follow a similar route. Their conceptual 'Europisation' and increasing conversion to 'Westernism', i.e. the type of strict evolutionism we would call today a marxisan Modernisation Theory, meant that the Russian peasant commune, and by the 1890s the peasantry *in toto*, were to them no longer an asset but a sign of backwardness and stagnation, a reactionary mass. All of that had to be first removed to clear the way for the proletariat and its revolutionary struggle, and the sooner the better. They were consequently to watch with eager anticipation the development of capitalism in Russia – once more – the sooner the better, for the advance of socialism. It was to that vision that Marx referred in 1881 derisively as that of the 'Russian capitalism admirers'.[24] His own views were moving in an opposite direction.

Archaic commune and forerunner theory

In 1881 Marx spent three weeks contemplating, one can say struggling with, an answer to a letter concerning the Russian peasant commune. It came from Vera Zasulich, made famous by her earlier attempt on the life of a particularly vicious tsarist dignitary, currently of the Black Repartition group and the future co-editor of the marxist *Iskra*. The four drafts of the reply Marx wrote testify to the immensity of work and thought which underlay it – as if the whole last decade of Marx's studies with its 30,000 pages of notes but no new major text finalised, came together. The drafts are testimony of puzzlement but also of a growing consciousness of and the first approach to a new major problem. It is a veritable display of 'the kitchen' of Marx's thought at a frontier of knowledge at which he, once more, found himself a forerunner to his own generation and friends.

The discovery of the peasant commune by the Russian intelligentsia led to a sharp debate about its nature and historiography. To its detractors, the peasant commune was a creation of the tsarist state, to police and tax the countryside, a device which conserved the backward ('archaic') characteristics of Russian agriculture and its political economy *in toto*.[25] To the populists and their academic allies, it was a survival of the social organisation of primary communism, i.e. of the pre-class society, a remnant to be sure but a positive one, both in its present function and future potential. Behind the furious debate about historiography of the commune stood fundamental political issues of strategy, of the class nature of the revolutionary camp, its enemies and even of the nature of the future (post-revolutionary?) regime. To Marx the issue of the peasant commune, significant as it was for Russia, was also a point of entry to a variety of issues of much broader significance, theoretically and politically. These were the issues of peasantry within a capitalist (capitalism-centred?) world, and the type of sub-worlds and sub-economies such 'irregularity' is bound to produce. It was also that of the socialist revolutions in the world at large, i.e. of the 'peasant chorus' without which, he said once, the proletariat's 'solo song, becomes a swan song, in all peasant countries'.[26]

Already in the *Grundrisse* (1857) Marx had undertaken extensive comparative studies of peasant agriculture and of communal landownership within the major pre-capitalist modes of production. The peasant commune was not to him (or to the revolutionary populists) exceptional to Russia. It was simply the best preserved one in Europe – persisting for sound 'materialistic' reasons and by then increasingly placed in a new international and local context of advancing capitalism. Still in 1868 in a letter to Engels he was clearly delighted with 'all that trash', i.e. the Russian peasant communal structure 'coming now to its end'.[27] During the 1870s the works of Mourer and Morgan strengthened Marx's conviction, however, as to the positive qualities of the primary-tribal communities in their ethnocentricity (i.e. their concentration on human needs rather than on production for profits), and their inherent democracy as against capitalist alienation and hierarchies of privileges. The man of capitalism – the most progressive mode of production in evidence – was not the ultimate man of human history up-to-date. The Iroquois 'red skin hunter' was, in some ways, more essentially human and liberated than a clerk in the City and in that sense closer to the man of the socialist future. Marx had no doubts about the limitations of the 'archaic' commune: material 'poverty', its parochiality and its weakness against external exploitive forces. Its decay under capitalism would be necessary. Yet, that was clearly not the whole story. The experience and excitement of the Paris Commune – to Marx the first direct experiment in a new plebian democracy and revolutionary polity – was by now part of the picture. With the evidence of what appeared as the first post-capitalist experiment Marx was more ready than before to consider the actual nature of social and political organisation in the world he strived for. To all those steeped in Hegelian dialectics, children resembled their grandparents more than their parents. The 'primary' commune, dialectically restored on a new and higher level of material wealth and global interaction, entered Marx's images of the future communist society, one in which once more the 'individuals behave not as labourers but as owners – as members of a community which also labours.'[28]

Back from the past/future to the present, the consideration of co-existence and mutual dependence of capitalist and non-capitalist (pre-capitalist?) social forms made Marx increasingly accept and consider 'uneven development' in all its complexity. New stress was also put on the regressive aspects of capitalism and on its link with the issue of the state in Russia. The acceptance of unilinear 'progress' is emphatically out. The extension of an essentially evolutionist model through the ideas of Oriental Despotism is by now insufficient. Specifically, Marx came to see the decline of the peasant commune in Western Europe and its crisis, in Russia, not as a law of social sciences – spontaneous economic process – but as the result of an assault on the majority of the people, which could and should be fought. The consideration of the Russian commune in the drafts of the 'Letter of Zasulich' brought all this to the surface. It will be best to present the essence of the message in Marx's own words.[29]

To begin with, 'what threatens the life of the Russian commune is neither historical inevitability nor a theory but oppression by the State and exploitation by capitalist intruders whom the State made powerful at the peasant's expense.' The type of society in question was singled out by its international context, i.e. 'modern historical environment: it is contemporaneous with a higher culture and it is linked to a world market in which capitalist production is predominant,' while the country 'is not, like the East Indies the prey of a conquering foreign power.' The class-coalition of peasant-destroyers – the power-block in societies with peasant numerical predominance – was defined as 'the *state* . . . the *trade* . . . the *landowners* and . . . *from within* [the peasant commune] . . . the *usery*' (italics added), i.e. state, merchant capitalists, squires and kulaks – in that order. The whole social system was referred to as a specific 'type of capitalism fostered by the state at the peasants' expense'.

To Marx the fact that the Russian commune was relatively advanced in type, being based not on kinship but on locality, and its 'dual nature' represented by 'individual' as well as 'communal land' ownership, offered the possibility of two different roads of development. The state and the specific variety of state-bred capitalism were assaulting, penetrating and destroying the commune. It could be destroyed, but there was no 'fatal necessity' for it. The corporate aspect of the commune's existence could prevail, once revolution had removed the anti-commune pressures and the advanced technology developed by Western capitalism was put to new use under the communal control of the producers. Such a solution would indeed be best for Russia's socialist future. The main limitation of the rural commune, i.e. their isolation, which facilitated a Russian edition of 'centralised despotism', could be overcome by the popular insurrection and the consequent supplementing of the state-run *volost* by 'assemblies elected by the communes – an economic and administrative body serving their own interest'. That is, shockingly, peasants running their own affairs, within and as a part of socialist society. Indeed, the Russian peasants' 'familiarity with corporate ("*artel*") relations would greatly smooth their transition from small plot to collective farming' but there is a condition to it all: 'the Russian society having for so long lived at the expense of the rural commune owes it the initial resources required for such a change,' i.e. the precise reverse of 'primitive accumulation' was now defined by Marx as the condition for successful collectivisation of the Russian peasant agriculture. Also, it would be gradual change . . . '[in which] the first step would be to place the commune under normal conditions [i.e. in a non-exploitive context] on its present basis.'

In conclusion, to Marx, a timely revolutionary victory could turn the Russian commune into a major 'vehicle of social regeneration'. A 'direct starting point of the system to which the contemporary society strives' and a grass root framework for 'large-scale co-operative labour' and the use of 'modern machinery'. Moreover, that may make some chiefly peasant countries 'supreme in that sense to the societies where capitalism rules'. That is, indeed, why 'the Western precedent would prove here nothing at all.' Morevoer, 'the issue is not that of a problem to be solved but simply of an enemy, who had to be beaten . . . to save the Russian commune one needs a Russian revolution.' Note the expression *Russian* revolution, twice repeated within the text. Finally, to understand it all 'one must descend from pure theory to Russian reality' and not be frightened by the word 'archaic', for 'the new system to which the modern society is tending will be a revival in a superior form of an archaic social type.'

The issue of the peasant commune was used by Marx also as a major way to approach a set of fundamental problems, new to his generation, but which would be nowadays easily recognised as those of 'developing societies', be it 'modernisation', 'dependency' or the 'combined and uneven' spread of global capitalism and its specifically 'peripheral' expression. There were several such components of Marx's new itinerary of topics for study and preliminary conclusions, none of which worked out in full. At the centre lies the newly perceived notion of 'uneven development', interpreted not quantitatively (i.e. that 'some societies move faster than others') but as global interdependence of societal transformations. The 'Chronological Notes', i.e. a massive conspectus of Marx written in 1880–2, is directly relevant here. As rightly noticed in an interesting contribution of B. Porshnev (who refers it to the 'last 9-12 years period of Marx's life'), it shows Marx's attention turning to 'the problem of historical interdependence of people and countries in the different period of global history, i.e. the synchronic unity of history' (and one should add to dichronic inter-societal unity).[30] Marx comes now to assume also for the future a multiplicity of roads of social transformation, within the global framework of mutual and differential impact. (Already in the *Grundrisse* he had accepted it manifestly for the pre-capitalist past.) That is indeed why the generalised application of the discussion of 'primitive accumulation' in Volume I of *Capital* is by 1877 so explicitly rejected. As is documented and argued by Wada, it meant also that Marx had begun to 'perceive the structure unique to backward capitalism'[31] – to say 'structures' would probably be to say it better. The idea of 'dependent development' is not yet there, but its foundation is laid. To sum it up bluntly, to Marx, the England he knew 'that is more developed industrially' did not and indeed could not any longer 'show to the less developed' Russia the 'image of its own future'. By one of history's ironies, a century later we are still trying to shed the opposite claim of post-1917 Russia's monopoly over revolutionary imagination, the assumption that it is Russia which is to show to all of the Englands of our time the image of their socialist futures.

Marx's new turn of mind was unmistakably recognised and acknowledged after their fashion by doctrinaire marxists. The 'Letter to the Editorial Board of *Otechestvennye Zapiski*' was left unpublished by the Emancipation of Labour group, despite promises to Engels who let them have it for publication. The 'Letter to Zasulich', written by explicit request to make Marx's views known, was not published by them either. (The first of these was initially published in 1887 by the *Messenger of People's Will*, the second only in 1924). Much psychologistic rubbish was written in Russia and in the West about how and why those writings were forgotten by Plekhanov, Zasulich, Axelrod etc. and about the 'need for specialised psychologists to have it explained'.[32] It was probably simpler and cruder. Already in Marx's own generation there were marxists who knew better than Marx what marxism is and were prepared to censor him on the sly, for his own sake.

The clearest salute to Marx's originality and to his new views was given a generation later by the most erudite of the Russian marxists of his time, Ryazanov, the first director of the Marx-Engels Institute in Moscow who published first in 1924 the four drafts of the 'Letter to Zasulich' (discovered by him in 1911). To him, the four drafts written during less than two weeks of intensive intellectual and political considerations indicated the decline of Marx's capacities.[33] On top of that hint he has added, quoting Edward Bernstein, an additional explanation for Marx's populist deviation: 'Marx and Engels have restricted the expression of their scepticism not to discourage too much the Russian revolutionaries.'[34] Poor old Marx was clearly going senile at 63 or else engaging in little lies of civility and expedience, once he departed from the 'straight and narrow' of the marxism of his epigones. (An amusing affinity – during and after the 1905-7 Revolution, Lenin was accused of leaning toward populism by some of his marxist adversaries and associates.[35] It seems that those two have had a 'deviation' in common.)

Radical backwardness and conservative revolutionaries

Three more related issues should be singled out for attention: the nature of the Russian experience, Marx's attitude to revolutionary movements and the place of Engels as Marx's most significant interpreter. Firstly, while the experience of India or China was to Marx's generation of Europeans remote, abstract and often misconceived, Russia was closer not only geographically but in the basic sense of human contact, possible knowledge of language and of availability of evidence and analysis, self-generated by the natives. It was not only the difference in extent of information which was at issue, however. The Russia of those times was marked by political independence and growing international weakness, placed on the peripheries of capitalist development, massively peasant yet with rapidly expanding industry (owned mainly by foreigners and the crown) and with a highly interventionist state. In the conceptual language of our own generation Russia was, or was rapidly turning into, a 'developing society' – a new type of social phenomenon. Newcomers are hard to recognise but Marx's conceptual 'feel in the fingers' was too good to miss entirely this first silhouette of a new shape. It had been no accident that it was from Russia and from the Russians that Marx learned new things about global 'unevenness', about peasants and about revolution, insights which would be valid in the century still to come. The triple origins of Marx's analytical thought suggested by Engels – German philosophy, French socialism and British political economy – should in truth be supplemented by a fourth one, that of Russian revolutionary populism. All that is easier to perceive when looked at in the late twentieth century, but the massive brainwashing of interpretation initiated by the second International is still powerful enough to turn it into a 'blind spot'.

To proceed with that line of argument somewhat further in order to test it, the other major departure of Marx from an evolutionist view which assumed an inexorable course of history towards capitalist centralisation, and used the index of global economic 'progress' in political judgment, was also related to a direct experience of struggle at the close 'peripheries' of capitalism *sensu strictu*. The Fenian Rebellion of the Irish made Marx write to Engels in 1868, '*I used to think* that Ireland's separation from England would be impossible. *Now* I consider it to be inevitable.' (italics added)[36] As a leader of the International he had also taken a public stand in that matter. In 1867 Marx defined Irish independence and the setting up of protective tariffs against England, together with agrarian revolution, as the country's major needs. Not only the conclusion but also the way he argued his case were important steps from the nineteenth-century ideas of progress towards the understanding of what our own generation would call 'dependent development' and its pitfalls. In the same year Marx spoke also of the way the Irish industry was being suppressed and its agriculture retarded by the British state and economy. By 1870 Marx went so far as to say that, 'The decisive blow against the ruling classes in England (and this blow is decisive for the working man's movement all over the world) is to be struck not in England but only in Ireland.'[37] With full awareness of what such a stand might mean at the very centre of metropolitan nationalism, he called British workers to support the Irish independence struggle. The beautiful phrase coined in the days of their revolutionary youth by Engels, that 'people who oppress other people cannot themselves be free',[38] came back, this time with a distinctly 'Third-Worldish' sound.

Secondly, Marx asserted his political preferences loud and clear. His sympathy was with fighters and revolutionaries, be the 'small print' of their creed as it may, and against doctrinaire marxists, especially when on theoretical grounds they rebuked revolutionary struggle. That was clear when he wrote of the Paris communards 'storming heaven' in 1871. In his *Critique of the Gotha Programme* (1875) he scorned socialists who 'keep themselves within the limits of the logically presumable and of the permissible by the police'.[39] The members of People's Will on trial for life were to him not only right in the essentials of their political stand but 'simple, objective, heroic'. Theirs was not 'tyrannicide as "theory" and "panacea" but a lesson to Europe in a "specifically" Russian historically inevitable mode of action; against which any moralising from a safe distance was offensive.'[40] In contrast he had sharply turned against their critics in Plekhanov's Black Repartition group in Geneva.[41]

It has been the way of many sophisticates of marxology to scoff at such utterances of Marx or to interpret them patronisingly as 'determined rather by . . . emotional motives'[42] (an antonym, no doubt, of 'analytical', 'scientific' or 'sound'). To understand political action, especially the struggle for a socialist transformation of humanity, as an exercise in logic or as a programme of factory building only, is utterly to misconstrue it, as Marx knew well. Also, he shared with the Russian revolutionaries the belief in the purifying power of revolutionary action in transforming the very nature of those involved in it – the 'educating of the educators'.[43] The Russian revolutionary populists' concern with moral issues found ready response in him. Moral emotions apart (and they were there and unashamedly expressed), revolutionary ethics were often as central as historiography to Marx's political judgment. So was Marx's distaste of those to whom the punch-line of marxist analysis was the adoration or elaboration of irresistible laws of history, used as the license to do nothing.

Finally, and especially after Marx's death, the difference of emphasis between Marx and Engels came to anticipate a dualism which was increasingly conspicuous within the post-Engels marxist movement. Hobsbawm's caution against the 'modern tendency of contrasting Marx and Engels, generally to the latter's disadvantage' must be kept in mind here, but also its qualification: 'the two men were not Siamese twins.'[44] The two were partners, allies and friends, while Engels's devotion to Marx and his heritage has justly become famous. On a number of issues it was Engels who led and, indeed, often taught Marx, especially in so far as political and military issues were concerned. All that is not at issue, however. In his views Engels was less inclined to move in the new directions

Marx explored in the last decade of his life. Despite Engels's warnings against treating marxism as a form of economic determinism, he had been much more than Marx a man of his own generation with its evolutionist, 'naturalist' and 'positivist' beliefs. The same is even more true for Kautsky as the later chief interpreter of Marx and for the mainstream Russian interpretation of Marx by Plekhanov.

When still working shoulder to shoulder, Marx and Engels had felt alike about the past; the medieval peasant commune in its Germanic version was to both of them 'the only kernel of popular liberty and life'[45] of that period. They agreed about the corrosive influences of capitalism on the peasant commune and that only revolution could save it in Russia. They both assumed that it was worth saving – to be integrated and transformed into the new socialist era. But to Engels, the future of the Russian commune was inevitably subject to proletarian revolution in the West, itself part of the irresistible march of 'progress'. The basic order of things could not be changed. Marx was moving away from such views (though *how far* he had moved by 1882 will be forever a matter of debate). Also, while Engels bowed to Marx's supreme knowledge of the 'East' and its peculiarities, the very heterogeneity of structure and motion round the globe were to Engels less of a problem, less of a bother and less of a trigger to new analysis.

The best way to test the differences between the two men is to consider Engels's writings after Marx's death. In mid-1884, in the space of two months, he wrote his immensely influential *The Origins of the Family, Private Property and the State*, 'in fulfilment of bequest to Marx' and using his conspectus of Morgan's study. The book was brilliant in its discussion of the 'archaic' social structures, yet in its other parts offered a virtual compendium of evolutionism with a dialectical 'happy end' to conclude. In it, and engined by the ever deepening 'division of labour', are historical stages, following each other with the precision, repetition and inevitability of clockwork, for 'what is true for nature holds good also for society.'[46] It all proceeds to progress unilinearly from the 'infancy of the human race' to 'the highest form of the state, the democratic republic in which alone the decisive struggle between proletariat and bourgeoisie is to be fought'. Then comes socialism, the 'revival in a higher form of the liberty and fraternity of the ancient gentes'.[47] Since mid-1884 not even Oriental Despotism seemed essential for historiography, and the very term disappeared from Engels's published work. In *Anti-Dühring* (1877), still written in Marx's powerful presence, Oriental Despotism spread 'from India to Russia'.[48] It is never mentioned in *The Origins of the Family, Private Property and the State*. In Engels's known correspondence the concept appears last in February 1884. As from then and until Engels's death in 1895, through the whole bulk of nearly 3,000 pages of his writings and letters, it was not mentioned even once.[49] We are back all the way to *The German Ideology* of 1846. It had been in its time a dramatic breakthrough of major illumination and a conceptual base to the *Communist Manifesto* (1848) with its immense and lasting impact. It was now a retrograde step.

Engels wrote well, his style served by his capacity to present complex issues with simplicity, strength and impeccable consistency of argument. There was a price to that clarity, however, and Engels's argument with Tkachev is a case in point.

Peter Tkachev was a Russian Jacobin, a historical materialist whose class analysis made him suspect the idealisation of the 'masses' by many of his comrades – he called for a direct use of force by a determined revolutionary minority. In his verbal assault on the Russian state Tkachev had overstated, to be sure, the extra-class, inertia-bound, 'autonomous' dimensions of tsardom – to him it was a 'state suspended in the air, so to speak, one that has nothing in common with the existing social order and that has its roots in the past'.[50] Yet as Engels was fond of saying, 'the proof of the pudding' of political theorising is 'in the eating of it'. On the point of political prediction and strategy, Tkachev had concluded, in line with Chernyshevskii's views, that Russia might benefit from the 'relative advantages of backwardness' and thereby more easily produce 'social revolution' than Western Europe. Also in his view, that potential could be lost if not taken up in time. He had suggested, impudently for 1874, that there was a chance that Russia might proceed along a revolutionary path towards socialism even earlier than the USA or Great Britain. Such a 'leap' through a 'stage' would entail the conquest and massive use of centralised state power. Tkachev had also assumed that to carry out the aims of social reconstruction, while facing enemies and a still untrustworthy majority of population, the revolutionaries should/would proceed for a time to rule 'from above' – a dictatorship of a revolutionary party. All of the European left was subsequently provided with light relief when in 1875 Engels came to exercise his wit on Tkachev. Such 'green schoolboy's views' by which Russia may do more for socialism than just to facilitate the beginning of the socialist revolution where it must actually begin, i.e. in the West, or even more outrageously, a vision of a socialist regime in muzhik-full Russia, even before industrialised Western Europe would see it, was 'pure hot-air' and only proved that it was Tkachev who was 'suspended in mid-air' and still had 'to learn the ABC of Socialism'.[51] All very funny, but with an unexpected twist when seen retrospectively, two generations after November 1917 in Russia, and a generation after October 1949 in China.

In so far as the issue of the Russian commune was concerned, Engels loyally defended to the end both the view that it may serve as a unit of socialist transformation and the provision that for that to happen a proletarian revolution in the West must show 'the retarded countries . . . by its example how it is done',[52] 'it' being the establishment of post-capitalist society. 'It should be borne in mind,' he added in 1894, 'that the far-gone dissolution of Russian communal property has [since 1875] considerably advanced.'[53] Plekhanov was by now Engels's major guide to Russia and the head of the Russian marxist organisation, involved as it was in a violent dispute about peasantry's future with the (mostly 'legal', i.e. reformist) populists of the day.[54] The Russian peasant commune was increasingly seen by Engels, accordingly, as on its last legs, with capitalism in overwhelming presence. The only thing left to those who liked it little seemed to be 'to console ourselves with the idea that all this in the end must serve the cause of human progress'.[55] As to the European peasantry, he had even more poignant things to say, in 1894, laying bare the general attitude prevailing in the second International: 'in brief our small peasant, like every other survival of the past modes of production, is hopelessly doomed . . . in view of the prejudices arriving out of their entire economic position, the upbringing and isolation . . . we can win the mass of the small peasants only if we make them a promise which we ourselves know we cannot keep'[56] – which was, of course, out of the question.

But Engels was also a revolutionary and so were many of his and Marx's intellectual heirs. It was their support of revolutionary strategies which was increasingly at odds with the theoretical doctrine. While on the level of theory Marx was being 'engelsised' and Engels, still further, 'kautskised' and 'plekhanovised' into an evolutionist mould, revolutions were spreading by the turn of the century through the backward/'developing' societies: Russia 1905 and 1917, Turkey 1906, Iran 1909, Mexico 1910, China 1910 and 1927. Peasant insurrection was central to most of them. None of them were 'bourgeois revolutions' in the West European sense and some of them proved eventually socialist in leadership and results. At the same time, no socialist revolution came in the West nor did a socialist 'world revolution' materialise. In the political life of the socialist movements of the twentieth century there was an urgent need to revise strategies or go under. Lenin, Mao and Ho chose the first. It meant speaking with 'double-tongues' – one of strategy and tactics, the other of doctrine and conceptual substitutes, of which the 'proletarian revolutions' in China or Vietnam, executed by peasants and 'cadres', with no industrial workers involved, are but particularly dramtic examples.

The alternative was theoretical purity and political disaster. Once again using personalities to pinpoint a broader issue, the end of the lives of Plekhanov and Kautsky, the 'father of Russian marxism' and the world's most erudite marxist respectively, provide to it a tragic testimony and a sign. The first died in 1918, an 'internal exile' in the midst of revolution – an embittered, bewildered and lonely foe of the experiment he fathered. The second died in 1938, an exile watching incomprehensibly and aghast the double shadow over Europe of Nazism in the industrially progressive and electorally mass-socialist Germany, and of Stalinism in the first-born socialist Russia. The terrible fate of finding oneself 'on the rubbish heap of history' had claimed its first generation of marxist theorists.

Reading Marx: gods and craftsmen

Back to Marx: what adds significance to discussion of the last stage in the development of his thought is what it teaches us about his intellectual craftsmanship and about him as a human being. The very fact of transformation in Marx's thought and not just of its logical unfolding shocks those to whom Marx is god. Was he god or human? As against gods and godlings the test of humanity is that of being context-bound, changeable in views, and fallible. Human vision reflects physical, social and intellectual environments. Human vision changes in time – we learn and discover. Humans err in perception, understanding and prediction. God's vision is unlimited, unchanging and infallible – it can only unfold what is already in it. It is also amoral, for there is no way to judge god's ethics – it is his word which is the moral code. That is one reason why the human mind has designed gods as humanity's anti-model and ever craves for their existence, as the final resort in a painfully unstable world of endless heterogeneity and surprise. Not much was changed on that score by the scientific revolution of our times.

When facing true masters of thought and deed the great temptation is to invest them with godly qualities. Surely, at least they stand above environment, history, mistake and sin, offering their worshippers and interpreters a glimpse of eternity and a link to the Absolute.

To put a case for Marx's humanity it is probably best to begin with the interpretations of his godliness. While commentary varied, the deification of Marx and of Volume 1 of *Capital* was deeply rooted in the second International. The 1917 political victory made Bolshevism into the most influential interpretation of marxism in the world. By the 1930s, stalinism had simplified it and brutalised it into a sole tool of ideological control. Stalin was right and *therefore* Lenin was right and *thereby* Marx was mostly right (or else . . .). Political expedience as defined by infallible leadership had merged with final truth and indisputable ethics of obedience. Once the 'antagonist social classes' were 'abolished' and the Communist Party put in charge, the very fact of economic advance would inevitably produce socialism followed by communism. This fundamental state legitimation has produced powerful ideological demand for unilinearity as the sole mode of explanation – a model of inevitable progress defined by every step of the most progressive regime on earth. Oriental Despotism (or indeed any multilinear model) did not fit those needs. Worst still, it could be and was used to castigate the Soviet regime itself as retrograde. Two ways to iron out these problems were toyed with in the 1920s: (a) to define Oriental Despotism as a universal stage of unilinear development (following 'primary communism' and preceding slavery) or else, a sub-stage of the pre-class 'archaic' societies; and (b) to omit Oriental Despotism altogether as unsound on scholarly grounds.[57] Stalin resolved any such doubts by cutting through them. The concept of Oriental Despotism was abolished by decree, i.e. declared un-marxist with the usual penalties attached.

To the marxists west of the USSR, the 1960s were a period of dramatic change and reassessment which, beginning with the Twentieth Congress of the Soviet Communist Party and the Hungarian uprising, culminated in the experiences of 1968: Saigon, Paris, Washington, Prague and Peking. Marx's early writings were the great find of those days.[58] The writings differed sharply from *Capital* in their immediate concern, their design and their language of exposition. More importantly, they legitimated the concern of many marxists in the post-Stalin era, with individuals facing systems of social control and repression, non-socialist as well as socialist. The discussion of the material and social determinations of human alienation offered a major and still potent analytical tool to extricate some major issues of human emancipation. That is how an unfinished and obscurely written Germanic text became an inspiration to the 1968 generation of radicals in Western and Eastern Europe.

On the face of it, the discovery of early Marx has simply meant accepting that his views developed and transformed. Amazingly, it was that very evidence of the unmistakable heterogeneity of his writings which gave yet another twist to Marx's deification. An 'epistemological rupture' was decreed in Paris, dividing between Marx of 1844 (young and part-Hegelian) and marxism, i.e. true thought of Marx (mature and pure) – a totally new rigorous and final Science of Men.[59] Marx was infallible after all; his infallibility simply began at a later age. The vision of 'epistemological rupture', i.e. Marx's leap into simultaneous maturity, scientificity and sanctity has been also used to disconnect his analysis from his goals and beliefs. 'Humanism' was declared a bourgeois concept, nothing to do with mature, i.e. scientific Marx and a survival at best of the pre-scientific thought alongside of the science.[60] 'Mature Marx' was not only absolute in truth but a-moral.

The task in the eyes of the proponents of this Science of Men was the further elaboration of and deduction from the objective and eternal Laws, uncovered in Marx's 'mature' writings. To succeed in that application one had simply to keep oneself pure and apart from the septic impact of 'bourgeois science', i.e. anything else. That is where, behind the philosophical debates about relationships between Hegel's and Marx's thought, an old and ugly face seemed to emerge. For, consequently, there could be only two truly credible explanations of failure of prediction based on absolute wisdom: (a) the misreading of what is already in the Scriptures – caused by surrender to the poison of bourgeois scholarship (that is, of course, pseudo-scholarship); and (b) wilful treason in the service of the enemies of the people. We know what were the ways of rectification for each of those. We should also know by now how immense and self-destructive the cost of it is in terms of socialist thought, deed, and blood.

Another, more sophisticated way 'to keep Marx in line' was to salvage his unilinearism by temporarily giving up his infallibility. An interesting and very erudite book by Nikoforov has done just that.[61] The author has convincingly argued out of court the attempts of his colleagues in the USSR to de-emphasise the significance of Oriental Despotism in Marx's writings. He then proceeds to demolish the concept – Marx and Engels were simply wrong on the matter. Marx's studies of prehistory and of the Russian peasant and Indian peasant communes make him see by 1879 some difficulties with that idea, but he still did not 'overcome it'. Then a most dramatic conclusion strikes one dumb. Under the impact of Morgan, in the last moments of his life Marx finally 'overcomes it', rejecting Oriental Despotism (and the mistaken theories of state attached to it) to return to unilinearism, i.e. to the belief in the 'Highway of History' (*Magisralnaya Doroga*), which all societies are bound to tread. Marx's date of divine incarnation, i.e. when he has eventually got things right and final, is 1881.[62] The proof of this lies, once again, not in Marx but in a review of *Engels*'s later writings and especially of *The Origins. . . . etc.* As a secondary proof comes the fact that in Marx's drafts of 'Letter to Zasulich' and in his conspectus of Morgan's book the term 'Oriental Despotism' did not appear. A comment by Marx related to a study of India (in the same notebook which contain the notes on Morgan), 'this ass Phear calls the organisation of the rural commune feudal', is reproduced but dismissed as inconclusive. The fact that Marx actually speaks of 'central despotism ('centralised' in further texts) in the drafts of 1881 is not even noticed.[63] There is nothing else – an outstandingly thin evidence for the size of the claim made. The happy end of Marx's return to the unilinear fold reminds one of the well-known eighteenth-century tale about Voltaire on his death bed returning to the bosom of the Catholic Church, the clergy at his bedside bearing faithful evidence to it. Engels's views are, of course,, quite another matter.

It is time to recapitulate briefly. The last decade of Marx's life was a distinctive period of his analytical endeavour: a fact recognised, if for different reasons, by a steadily growing number of scholars. Central to it was his involvement with Russian society, both as a source of fundamental data and as a vehicle of analysis and exposition of the problems of a specific type of society which differed structurally from the 'classical case of capitalism' on which *Capital*, Volume 1, was based. Already in the *Grundrisse* (1857-8) Marx had assumed the multiplicity of roads of social development in pre-capitalist societies. Hobsbawm's non-consecutive interpretation of it as 'three or four alternative routes out of primitive communal systems', each commencing in a different area, i.e. as 'analytical, though not chronological, stages in . . . evolution', is important here.[64] If accepted, it is already much more sophisticated and realistic than any simple evolutionist model would have it. Marx shifted his position further as from the 1873-4 period of extensive contacts with Russian scholars, revolutionaries and writings, but more clearly and consciously so since 1877. Marx had come now to accept the multiplicity of roads also within a world in which capitalism existed and became a dominant force. It meant (a) an anticipation of future societal histories as necessarily uneven, interdependent and multilinear in the 'structural' sense; (b) the consequent inadequacy of the unilinear 'progressive' model for historical analysis as well as for political judgments concerning the best way the socialist cause can be promoted; (c) first steps toward the consideration of the specificity of societies which we call today 'developing societies'; and, within that context, (d) a re-evaluation of the place of peasantry and its social organisation in the revolutionary processes to come; (e) a preliminary step to look anew at the ruling-class coalition and the role of the state in the 'developing societies'; and (f) a new significance given the decentralisation of socio-political power within the post-revolutionary society in which the rejuvenation of 'archaic' communes may play an important role.

Remarkably for a man who died in 1883, the Marx of those days was beginning to recognise for what they really are the nature, problems and debate concerning 'developing' and post-revolutionary societies of the twentieth century. The expression 'neo-marxist', often used for those who stepped on from *Capital*, Volume 1 in their interpretations concerning 'developing societies', is clearly misconceived. Most of the so-called neo-marxism, often treated as original or scandalous, is Marx's marxism. To understand the scope of this achievement one would have to review the three generations of conceptual blindness of the adversaries of Marx within the various 'modernisation' schools, as well as Marx's official descendants. The ground is by now littered with self-fulfilling prophecies masquerading as historical necessities and as laws of social sciences, especially so in so far as the countryside is concerned. Yet, it was Marx who laid the foundations for the global analysis of 'unevenness' of 'development', for the socialist treatment of peasantry not only as the object or the fodder of history, for the consideration of socialism which is more than proletarian, and so on. Indeed, Marx's approach to the Russian peasantry, whom he never saw, proved on balance more realistic than that of the Russian marxists in 1920 – witness the New Economic Policy. Without idealising the '*muzhik*', Marx showed better wisdom even concerning optimal parameters of collectivisation – consider contemporary Hungary. One can proceed with examples.

How does the last stage of Marx's thought fit into the general sequences of his work? To assume the very existence of that stage is to accept at least three major steps in Marx's conceptual development: early Marx of the 1840s, a middle Marx of the 1850s and 1860s (the expression 'mature' smuggles in the metaphor of 'a peak', to be necessarily followed by decline) and the late Marx of the 1870s and 1880s. Uncompleted as the last stage was left by his death in 1883, it was rich in content, laying foundations for a new approach to global capitalism, its not-so-capitalist companions of the world scene, and also the prospects for socialism – issues and doubts our own generation came to call its own. To accept that is to correct a record concerning Marx's thought. It is also to demolish the very possibility of saving Marx's godly stature by making him, or some of him, into an 'icon'. Rigid divisions into stages will not do; he often returned to an earlier piece of study to rework it and/or to incorporate it in a new way, e.g. the re-emergence of elements of the analysis of consciousness in *German Ideology* (1845–6) in the discussion of commodity fetishism in *Capital*, Volume 1 (1867), or the clear relation between the discussion of peasants and rural commune in *Grundrisse* (1857-8) and the drafts of the 'Letter to Zasulich' (1881). But it is high time to dispose of the ever recurring stupidity of discussing a synthetic 'Marx's view', while disregarding a couple of decades of intensive work and thought in between two quotations, just to discover with glee or despair 'contradictions'. He could be wrong, but for heaven's sake, he could not be unmarxist. To admit to the specificity of late Marx is (also) to see Marx in his creativity.

Finally, such an interpretation of late Marx suggests that the development in his thought was neither eclectic nor the type of zig-zag Nikoforov offered: unilinearism then something else (not quite certain what) then back to unilinearism. The movement seems much more consistent: there was (i) a sophisticated version of unilinearism with 'materialist' and dialectical assumptions forming a part of it; (ii) pre-capitalist multilinearity (bilinearity?) with a supposition that capitalism will iron it all out; and (iii) the acceptance of multidirectionality also within a capitalist-dominated (and socialism-impregnated?) world of mutual dependence, indeed, of heterogeneity resulting from that very interdependence.

Which brings us to the last question but one: was Marx human? To put it otherwise is to begin from the 'multi-dimensionality of Marx's theory which causes all but the dim-witted or prejudiced to respect and admire Marx as a thinker even when they do not agree with him',[65] and to add that we are dealing here not in pure logic only. Marx is one in his personal endeavour, ethical stand and intellectual analysis. He showed both remarkable tenacity and outstanding flexibility of mind. When, and in what way?

Since 1847, and through the trials of political defeats, factional struggles, hopes which were dashed, and extreme personal privation, Marx never deviated from the goals of serving socialist revolution the way he came to see it, as a young man. In human terms there was the winter of 1863 when underfed, with the rent unpaid, wife ill, daughters out of school for their winter shoes were with the pawnbroker, Marx carried on with his research and political action. There were more such winters yet Marx stood fast, refusing a variety of 'soft options' and offers, e.g. that of semi-governmental and well cushioned journalism. Such biographical details are inexplicable in terms of 'pure logic', yet they have a logic of their own, without which Marx's life would not make much sense.

At a more theoretical level Marx's early writings are not only clues to his personal dreams and insurrection against human poverty and oppression but also to his philosophical anthropology, his ideas about the essence of being human. It still offers the only available 'objective' base for socialist ethics, alternative to either simple political expedience, i.e. the party line as defined by a current leader, or else to theology – an issue as urgent as it is understated in socialist thought. For it is not only an issue of fine spirit and detached discourse, but of political action and of the actually existing socialisms (remember Poland).

While clearly impatient with banal sentimentality, Marx was a humanist and an heir to the culture of the Enlightenment, in which he was steeped. His scholarship was a chosen tool in the service of a grand ethical design of liberation of human essence from its alienation caused by the grip of nature as well as by the man-made worlds of class-split societies. The best evidence of that side to Marx is his unwaning appeal today, which is, after all, not like an adoration of the multiplication table. To purify 'mature' Marx from the philosophical ethics of early Marx, to divide aspects of his thought into separate boxes, or to be ashamed 'on his behalf' of the claim for the moral content of socialism, is to do him indeed 'too much honour' (by someone else's code of practice) and 'too much injury' (by that of his own).[66]

Gods remain unchanged by the process of creation and, it was said, can think only of themselves. If metaphors are to be used, Marx was not a god but a master craftsman. Craftsmen change matter while changing themselves in the process of creation. Also, if a dilettante is indeed 'a man who thinks more of himself than of his subject', Marx was professional in his analytical skills and therefore self-critical to the utmost. He was often tart in his critical comments and polemics, but for a man greatly admired by his own circle he was remarkably free from self-deification.

That is, in all probability, the root of the long public silence during the last decade of Marx's life. He was ailing, but then he was never a very healthy man. He was tired and at times depressed by the post-1871 revolutionary low in Europe, but fatigue and defeat were not new to him either. He was working on the further volumes of *Capital* but did fairly little to it. Biographers have faithfully rewritten Mehring's note that Marx's last decade was 'slow death', failing to acknowledge that even Mehring actually described this as (before 1882) 'grossly exaggerated'.[67] The subsequent discovery of 30,000 pages of notes written over ten years, as much as the quality of the work he did, militate against the solicitous remarks about Marx's failing powers. In the period directly following the publication of Volume 1 of *Capital* Marx faced critical comments and an increasing influx of 'stubborn data' which did not fully fit, and had to be digested. He was rethinking intensively, once more, his theoretical constructs, and moving into new fields. Lack of lucidity and a 'heavy pen' are often the price of depths in a path-breaking effort. Must a scholar be ill or senile not to 'rush into print', while still thinking through new theoretical thresholds?

To conclude, there was neither 'epistemological rupture' in Marx's thought nor decline or retreat but constant transformation, uneven as such processes are. His last decade was a conceptual leap, cut short by his death. Marx was a man of intellect as much as a man of passion for social justice, a revolutionary who preferred revolutionaries to doctrinaire followers. The attempts to single out as truly scientific, external and a-moral Marx from Marx the scholar, the fighter and the man, are as silly as they are false. That is why one should not 'read *Capital*' but read Marx (*Capital* included) and also Goethe, Heine and Aeschylus whom Marx admired and, together with the tale of Prometheus, made into a part of his life. To give his due to the greatest revolutionary scholar, we should see him as he was as against the caricatures and icons drawn by his enemies and his worshippers. To know him is to see him change and to see in what sense he did not. To be 'on his side' is to strive to inherit from him the best in him – his grasp of new worlds coming into being, his critical and self-critical faculty, the merciless honesty of his intellectual craftsmanship, his tenacity and his moral passion.

Acknowledgments

Thanks are given to those who by comments or help with the collection of the evidence contributed to this paper: Perry Anderson (London), Michael Barratt-Brown (Baslow), Zygmunt Bauman (Leeds), Isaiah Berlin (Oxford), Philip Corrigan (London), Arghiri

Emmanuel (Paris), Leo Haimson (New York), Harry Magdoff (New York), M. Mchedalov (Moscow), Sidney Mintz (Baltimore), Derek Sayer (Glasgow), Paul Sweezy (New York), Eric Wolf (New York), and the editorial collective of *History Workshop*.

Notes

1. Lukács defined in this way the more general but inclusive realm of 'historical materialism, in its classical form'. G. Lukács, *History and Class Consciousness*, Cambridge, Mass., 1971, p. 229. A comment by Harry Magdoff: 'This is not wrong but I would prefer in describing what *Capital* Vol. 1 is about to lay emphasis on the laws of motion of capitalism, its evolution and seeds of its transformation. . . .'
2. For those uninitiated into the British political culture, those are words of William Blake's 'Milton', still sung as an anthem at the Labour Party conventions. The New Jerusalem was Blake's anti-image to the 'dark satanic mills' of the nineteenth-century capitalism: its factories and churches.
3. K. Marx, *Capital*, Harmondsworth, 1979, vol. 1, p. 91. The same idea was expressed by Marx also as a heuristic device, specifically modelled after the natural sciences: 'Human anatomy contains a key to the anatomy of the ape . . . [which] can be understood only after the animal of the higher order is already known.' K. Marx, *Grundrisse*, Harmondsworth, 1973, p. 105 (translation slightly amended).
4. See 'The British rule in India', written in 1853, in K. Marx and F. Engels, *Selected Works*, Moscow, 1973, vol. 1. E. Hobsbawm described the concept as 'the chief innovation in the table of historical periods' introduced in the period when *Grundrisse* was written, i.e. 1857–8, for which see K. Marx, *Pre-Capitalist Economic Formations*, London, 1964, p. 32 (Introduction). See also Godelier's Preface to *Sur les Sociétés Pré-Capitalistes*, Paris, 1970, L. Krader, *The Asiatic Mode of Production*, Assen, 1975, and M. Sawyer, 'The concept of the Asiatic Mode of Production and contemporary Marxism', in S. Avineri, *Varieties of Marxism*, The Hague, 1977, and Footnote 7 below. For a good summary of the Soviet debate of that matter by a contemporary Soviet scholar, see V. Nikoforov, *Vostok i Vsemirnaya Istoriya*, Moscow, 1975, and E. Gelner, 'Soviets against Witfogel' (unpublished MS).
5. G. Hegel, *The Philosophy of History*, London, 1878, p. 168. The organic metaphor is particularly apt, for no society is assumed to be stationary in the mechanical sense, 'stagnation' meaning the overwhelming cyclicity of processes within it.
6. Russia lacked, of course, 'hydraulic' determinants. It was the impact of extensive militarisation and conquest which was assumed to have shaped Russian state and society in an 'oriental' manner.

7. The attraction of the concept of Oriental Despotism as a supplement to the dynamic model of *Capital* is still potent. For well-argued cases for and against the contempotary usage of the concept within marxist analysis, an issue which does not directly concern us here, see U. Melotti, *Marx and the Third World*, London, 1977, and P. Anderson, *Lineages of the Absolutist State*, London, 1970, Appendix B. The recent book by R. Bahro, *The Alternative in Eastern Europe*, London, 1977, has blunted the conceptual edge of the term by using it as a residual catch-all category for all which is contemporary, yet neither socialist nor capitalist. The most important explanation of Marx's attitude to heterogeneity of societal developments alternative to the one suggested is that by Hobsbawm in his Introduction to Marx's *Pre-Capitalist Economic Formations*, pp. 36–8. Hobsbawm assumes that with the singular exception of the transformation of feudalism to capitalism, Marx's 'stages' of social development have to be understood as analytical categories and not chronologically.
8. K. Marks i F. Engels, *Sochineniya*, Moscow, 1961, vol. 18, p. 51 (written by Marx in 1872).
9. R. Samuel, 'Sources of Marxist history', *New Left Review*, 1980, no. 120, p. 36. See also Nikoforov, *op. cit.*, pp. 81-103.
10. R. Nisbet, *The Social Philosophers*, St. Albans, 1973, p. 11. Nisbet described the issue of community as the main axis of the whole history of Western social philosophy.
11. H. Wada, 'Marx and revolutionary Russia' (see p. 40). Wada's achievement stands out in particular when compared with the work of analysts who 'knew it all', i.e. were aware of the evidence, yet made little of it. See, for example, the editorial comments in K. Marx and F. Engels, *The Russian Menace to Europe*, Glencoe, Illinois, 1952, and many Soviet equivalents to it, especially so in the 1930s.
12. M. Rubel and M. Manale, *Marx without Myth*, Oxford, 1975, p. 252.
13. *Marks Istorik*, Moscow, 1968, p. 373. The book offers an important contribution to the whole of the issue discussed. The most important earlier study of relevance is that of 'Marx's Russian library', written by B. Nikolaevskii and published in *Arkhiv K. Marksa i F. Engel'sa*, Moscow, 1929, vol. 4.
14. Marks i Engels, *op. cit.*, vol. 32, p. 358. Marx has clearly used the superlative 'most' referring to a type of book, i.e. the analytical descriptions of contemporary plebeian classes. Two decades later, Plekhanov was hard at work 'explaining away' as ill-informed Marx's admiring comment about this evidently populist book.
15. The book referred to is *The Development of Capitalism in Russia* and the populists selected for punishment in it were Danielson (who has signed himself Nikolai-on) and Vorontsov (the V.V.). Lenin, whose admiration of Chernyshevskii was profound, but tempered by the tactical needs of struggle against the Socialist Revolutionary Party (which claimed Chernyshevskii's heritage), solved it all by naming Chernyshevskii 'a revolutionary democrat', semantically unrelated to 'populism'. This position was often followed by official Soviet publications.

For further discussion, see A. Walicki, *The Controversy over Capitalism*, Oxford, 1969, pp. 16–22.

16. The word *volya* meant in nineteenth-century Russian both 'will' and 'liberty'.
17. For biographical details, see pp. 172-8, this volume. For a selection of relevant writings, see Part Three. For studies of the Russian populist tradition available in English, see in particular F. Venturi, *Roots of Revolution*, London, 1960, I. Berlin, *Russian Thinkers*, Harmondsworth, 1979, and Walicki, *op. cit.* See also T. Dan, *The Origins of Bolshevism*, London, 1964, chs 3, 6 and 7, and L. Haimson, *The Russian Marxists and the Origins of Bolshevism*, Boston, 1966. There is considerable Russian literature on the topic of which the most recent is the excellent study by V. Kharos, *Ideinye techeniya narodnicheskogo tipa*, Moscow, 1980. Contrary to an often held view, the Russian populists did not reject industrialisation but wanted it socially controlled and adjusted to regional needs, ideas which often bridge directly with some of the demands of the most contemporary 'environmentalists' and socialists. See Walicki, *op. cit.*, pp. 114–16, and Khoros, *op. cit.*, pp. 36–40, 220-5.
18. See Part Three, and especially the analysis by Kibalich on pp. 212-18.
19. See the last wills of members of the People's Will, pp. 239–40.
20. *Statistika zemlevladeniya 1905 g*, St. Petersburg, 1907. The figures referred to the fifty *guberya's* of European Russia, i.e. excluded Russian Poland and the Caucasus.
21. For further discussion of the Russian commune, see G.T. Robinson, *Rural Russia under the Old Regime*, New York, 1979, T. Shanin, *The Awkward Class*, Oxford, 1972, and, in Russian, V. Aleksandrov, *Sel'skaya obshchina v Rossii*, Moscow, 1976, and the general discussion by L. and V. Danilov within *Obshchina v afrike: problemy tipologii*, Moscow, 1978.
22. E.g. already Herzen spoke of the need to overcome simultaneously 'the British cannibalism', i.e. total surrender to the rules of capitalist competition, and the total immersion of the Russian peasant in his commune, to keep the personal independence of the first and the collectivist *élan* of the second.
23. See Venturi, *op. cit.*, chs 20 and 21; also Dan, *op. cit.*, chs 6, 7 and 8. For a good self-description of the Black Repartition group see L. Deutch in V. Nevskii, *Istoriko-revolyutsionyi sbornik*, Leningrad, 1924, vol. 2, pp. 280–350. For biographical details, see pp. 177-8, this volume.
24. See below, Part Two. This line of analysis has been reflected subsequently with particular strength in the works of the Russian 'legal marxists', e.g. M. Tugan Baranovskii *Russkaya fabrica*, St Petersburg, 1901, vol. 1, ch. 4.
25. Central to that line of argument were the works and views of B. Chicherin adapted in Marx's time by A. Wagner and in the latter generations by P. Miliukov, K. Kocharovskii, etc., as well as by G. Plekhanov and I. Chernyshev in the marxist camp. This view was

often referred to as the 'state school'. It was opposed by an equally impressive list of scholars and political theorists of whom N. Chernyshevskii and I. Belyaev were paramount to Marx's own generation. Marx himself spoke up sharply against Chicherin (*Marks i Engels, op. cit.*, vol. 33, p. 482). For a good historiography of the debate see Aleksandrov, *op. cit.*, pp. 3–46.

26. Marx wrote the passage in 'The Eighteenth Brumaire of Louis Bonaparte' (1852) referring to France but deleted it in the reprint of 1869. The dates are significant for reasons discussed in our text.
27. Marx and Engels, *Sochineniya, op. cit.*, vol. 32, p. 158. Relatedly in time, Marx has attacked Herzen's view in 1867 and spoke in absolute terms of the French peasantry's conservatism (e.g. in the 1871 notes on the Paris Commune, *ibid.*, vol. 17, pp. 554–7).
28. Marx, *Pre-Capitalist Economic Formations, op. cit.*, p. 68.
29. For full text, see Part Two.
30. *Marks-Istorik, op. cit.*, p. 431.
31. See below, p. 631.
32. See below, p. 129. How much all that still 'aches' can be best exemplified by a short aside from P. Konyushaya, *Karl Marx i revolyutsionnaya rossiya*, Moscow, 1975, where after a stream of invectives against the multiplicity of 'falsifiers of Marx', i.e. everybody who discussed him outside Russia, tells us that Plekhanov 'based his argument on the position formulated by Marx in his letter to "Otechestvennye Zapiski" ' (p. 357). She forgets to inform us when, where and how.
33. David Ryazanov, see below, Part Two. For contemporary Western equivalents of that view see Marx and Engels, *The Russian Menace to Europe, op. cit.*, p. 266, and on the left, J. Elster in K. Marx, *Verker i Utlag*, Oslo, 1970, p. 46.
34. See below p. 130.
35. Plekhanov's speech at the Fourth Congress of the Russian Social Democratic Workers' Party in 1906 stated it explicitly. On the other hand, the year 1905 has seen also the appeals of the Saratov Bolsheviks and of Nikodim (A. Shestakov, the chief of the agrarian section of the Bolsheviks Moscow committee) against Lenin's new agrarian programme, treated by them as 'capitulation' to the populist petty bourgeoisie.
36. Letters of 2 and 30 November 1876, Rubel and Monale, *op. cit.*, pp. 229-31.
37. *Ibid.*, p. 254. For further discussion, see the paper by K. Mohri in *Monthly Review*, 1979, vol. 30, no. 11.
38. From the 1847 speech about the independence of Poland, Marx and Engels, *Sochineniya, op. cit.*, vol. 4, p. 273.
39. *Ibid.*, vol. 19, p. 28.
40. The quotation comes from Marx's letter of 21 March 1881 to his daughter, *ibid.*, vol. 35, pp. 145–8.
41. For Marx's sharply critical view about the 'boring doctrines' of the Black Repartition, see his letter to Sorge of 5 October 1880, *ibid.*, vol.

34, p. 380. The way Marx (and in the 1880s, Engels) related their attitude to People's Will to their other contacts is interesting. The very letter of Marx, which spoke admiringly of the human qualities of the members of People's Will (11 April 1881) described Kautsky as 'mediocre, not a very able man, self-assured, the "know all" type . . . admittedly hard working, he spends much time on statistics without getting far with it, naturally belonging to the tribe of "philisters", while, on the other hand, no doubt, a decent fellow.' On 23 April 1885, Engels replied to Vera Zasulich's request to express his views about Plekhanov's book declaring his marxist creed against the Russian populists (*Nashi raznoglasiya*) refusing to pass judgment: 'My friends of *People's Will*, did not tell me of those matters', and then proceeded to defend the People's Will belief in the chances of an immediate Russian revolution.

42. W. Weitraub, 'Marx and Russian revolutionaries', *Cambridge Journal*, 1949, vol. 3, p. 501.
43. The third *Thesis of Feuerbach*, Marx and Engels, *Selected Works*, vol. 1, p. 13.
44. Marx, *Pre-Capitalist Economic Formations, op. cit.* (Introduction), p. 53. For an interesting discussion of the philosophical differences between Marx and his immediate interpreters, Engels, Kautsky, Plekhanov and Bernstein, etc., see L. Colletti, Introduction to K. Marx, *Early Writings*, Harmondsworth, 1975, pp. 7-14. See also L. Kolakowsky, *Main Currents of Marxism*, Oxford, 1981, vol. 1.
45. Marks i Engels, *op. cit.*, p. 272 (the quotation adopted from Maurer). For Engels's views see his paper 'Marka', written in 1882, Marx and Engels, *Sochineniya, op. cit.*, vol. 19, pp. 335-7.
46. See below, p. 108.
47. *Ibid.*, p. 334 (subquotation from Morgan).
48. F. Engels, *Anti-Duhring*, London 1943, p. 203.
49. Marx and Engels, *Sochineniya, op. cit.*, vols. 21-2 (publications) and 36-9 (correspondence). Thanks are due here to Professor M. Mchedlov of the Marx-Engels-Lenin Institute in Moscow for ascertaining that point. He has pointed out that, on the other hand, Engels did not remove that term from the new editions of *Anti-Duhring* in 1886 and 1894, an important point open, however, to a variety of interpretations.

    The explanation offered by Hobsbawm (Marx, *Pre-Capitalist Economic Formations, op. cit.*, p. 51) and by some Soviet scholars that the 'Asiatic Mode' is simply substituted at that stage by the broader concept of Archaic Formation does not fully meet the case, i.e. does not explain the correlation between the disappearance of the concept of Oriental Despotism from Engels's work and the date of Marx's death.
50. Quoted after Marx and Engels, *Selected Works, op. cit.*, vol. 2, p. 388. For biographical details, see below, p. 177.
51. *Ibid.*, pp. 387–8, 390, 395.
52. *Ibid.*, pp. 403–4.
53. *Ibid.*, pp. 395–412.
54. In the 1890s Plekhanov moved to a sharply 'anti-peasant' position, as

part of his growing polemic against the populists. Relentless pressure, mixing flattery and cajolery, was applied by him to enlist Engels's authority in squabbles within the Russian left, for which see *Perepiska, Marksa i Engel'sa*, Moscow, 1951, pp. 324–46. Engels had on the whole explicitly rejected those pressures, and had shown for a time considerable suspicion of Plekhanov (Walicki, *op. cit.*, pp. 181-3) but was, no doubt, influenced nevertheless, the more so as his Russian was 'rusty' by the late 1880s and by his own admission he had stopped reading any sources in that language.

55. Engels's 1892 letter to Danielson in *Perepiska, op. cit.*, p. 126.
56. Marx and Engels, *Selected Works, op. cit.*, vol. 3, pp. 460 and 469.
57. See, for discussion, Marx, *Pre-Capitalist Economic Formations, op. cit.* (Introduction), pp. 60–2.
58. Karl Marx, *Early Writings*, London, 1963.
59. L. Althusser and E. Balibar, *Reading Capital*, London, 1975. For a British version of the same see B. Hindess and P. Hirst, *Pre-capitalist Modes of Production*, London, 1975. The next step came when Althusser had discovered Hegelian traces in *Capital* itself and therefore re-timed Marx's full 'maturity' to 'The critique of the Gotha Programme', i.e. 1875 (when Marx was aged 57). L. Althusser, *Lenin and Philosophy*, New York, 1971, pp. 93–4.
60. 'Humanism is the characteristic feature of the ideological problematic (which survives alongside science). Science . . . as exposed in Marx's better work, implies a theoretical anti-humanism.' Althusser and Balibar, *Reading Capital, op. cit.*, p. 312 (translation glossary authorised by the author).
61. Nikoforov, *op. cit.*, pp. 113–35.
62. *Ibid.*, pp. 145, 149. See also, for discussion, Gellner, *op. cit.*, from which the expression 'date of incarnation' has been gratefully borrowed.
63. See below, p. 103. It seems that the only reasonable interpretation of evidence is indeed that of Hobsbawm: 'There is – at least on Marx's part – no inclination to abandon the "Asiatic Mode" . . . and quite certainly a deliberate refusal to re-classify it as feudal.' Marx, *Pre-Capitalist Economic Formations, op. cit.*, p. 58 (Introduction).
64. Marx, *Pre-Capitalist Economic Formations, op. cit.*, pp. 32 and 36–37 (Introduction).
65. Marx, *Pre-Capitalist Economic Formations, op. cit.* (Introduction), p. 16.
66. The quotation is from Marx's own words in self-defence against a unilinear interpretation of his writing, 'Letter to Otechestvennye Zapiski' (1877–8). See Part Two.
67. F. Mehring, *Karl Marx: The Story of his Life*, London, 1936 (first published 1918), pp. 501, 526. For an example of recent repetition of that view see Chapter 8 of D. McLellan, *Karl Marx: His Life and Thought*, London, 1977, from which a new generation of Anglo-Saxon students are learning about Marx.

Marx and revolutionary Russia

Haruki Wada

Introduction

In Japan since the late 1960s Marx's views of Russia in his later years have been a subject of repeated discussion. Indeed, they have been pursued with greater enthusiasm in Japan than elsewhere. Many papers have been written on the subject, and several books have appeared dealing exclusively with it, including my own, published in 1975.[1] Needless to say, the motives for taking up this matter differ from one writer to another. There have been all manner of motivations – a desire to understand the true image of the history of Russian social thought, an attempt to identify the place in this history occupied by Plekhanov, who introduced his version of 'Marxism' into Russia, a wish to discover in Marx's studies of Russia in his later years a key to the structure of underdeveloped capitalist economies, an effort to re-evaluate Russian Populism on the basis of the similarities between Marx's view of Russia in his later years and that of the Populists, a growing interest in Russian peasant communes, and even an attempt to find a recipe for rescuing the highly industrialized Japanese society from the depths of its contradictions. There has even been a heated controversy on the subject carried in the pages of non-academic magazines.

However, even the enthusiasm of today's Japanese is in no way equal to that with which the Russians at different times discussed this matter in an effort to find the best possible path of development for their own society. When we look at these debates in Russia in retrospect, we realize at the same time that Marx's theory on Russia was expressed mostly in unpublished letters or drafts of letters, and that the complexity of circumstances under which these letters or drafts were made public has made it peculiarly difficult for one to see what really was Marx's view of Russia. The writings of Marx himself from which we can infer his thesis on Russia in his later years are the 'Letter to the Editor of *Otechestvennye Zapiski*' and the 'Letter of Zasulich' and its four different drafts. Both of these manuscripts had surprisingly strange histories prior to their publication.

To begin with, the so-called 'Letter to the Editor of *Otechestvennye Zapiski*' – the manuscript of a letter that was not completed and never sent – was discovered after Marx's death by Engels who in March 1884 asked the Group for the Emancipation of Labour, which had been formed the year before, to publish it.[2] However, Zasulich and others in the group, in spite of their avowed desire to be the disciples of Marx in Russia, waited as long as seven months before responding to Engels with a promise that the letter, having been translated into Russian, would soon be printed;[3] but the promise was never fulfilled. Bent on the publication of this letter, Engels tried through N.F. Danielson to have it published in a legal Populist magazine inside Russia but was unsuccessful.[4] Finally the letter was published in *Vestnik Narodnoi Voli*, Volume 5, in December 1886, with this editorial note: 'Although we obtained a copy of this letter much earlier, we have been withholding its publication because we were informed that Friedrich Engels handed the letter to other people for publication in the Russian language.'[5] Two years later, in 1888, Marx's letter was also printed in *Yuridicheskii Vestnik*, a legal magazine published inside Russia.

The first response to the letter was made by Gleb Uspenskii, a novelist with Populist leanings, in the form of an essay entitled 'A Bitter Reproof', in which he deeply lamented the incapability of the Russian intellectuals to respond faithfully to Marx's reproof and advice.[6] Thereafter, in the 1890s, Plekhanov, Lenin and other Marxists, in opposition to the Populists who found in this letter a strong support for their line, insisted that in this letter Marx did not say anything definite about the direction in which Russian society should proceed.[7]

Somewhat similar conditions surrounded the 'Letter to Zasulich' and its draft manuscripts; that is, the recipient, Plekhanov and others close to her kept the letter's contents to themselves, and even when asked about the letter kept replying that they knew nothing about it. The draft manuscripts of this letter were discovered in 1911 by D.B. Riazanov, who with the help of N. Bukharin succeeded in deciphering them in 1913. But then the manuscripts were left for a decade. In 1923, after the Revolution was over, B.I. Nikolaevskii, a Menshevik in exile, found the letter's text in papers belonging to Aksel'rod and published it the following year. Upon reading the text, Riazanov also published the text in the same year as well as the drafts of the letter in Russian in the *Arkhiv K. Marksa i F. Engel'sa*, and in 1926, in the original French, in the *Marx-Engels Archiv*, Volume 1.[8]

Neither of the discoverers of the letter attached any special theoretical or philosophical significance to the new material. Nikolaevskii regarded the letter as a political utterance of Marx only,[9] while Riazanov said, in addition to a similar remark, that the letter and its drafts merely exemplified a decline in Marx's scholastic capability.[10] In marked contrast, Socialist-Revolutionaries in new exile enthusiastically welcomed the publication of these new materials. V. Zenzinov, for instance, insisted that the programme Marx delineated in this letter was in perfect accord with 'what has been developed by Russian revolutionary Populism' and it offered testimony to the fact that on the question of the future of peasant communes 'Marx definitely was on the side of Populism'.[11] V.M. Chernov, too, wrote that the publication of the 'letter to Zasulich which has been stored under a paperweight for more than 40 years' had brought the debate to a conclusion and that 'the programme described in this letter is exactly what forms the foundation of the S-Rs' theory of peasant revolution, agrarian demands and rural tactics.'[12]

The first person to support this letter inside the Soviet Union was A. Sukhanov who also strongly urged that the village commune should be used as a means for promoting collectivization in agriculture.[13] Several other writers offered similar arguments in the Party organ *Bol'shevik* in early 1928,[14] but in the world of historians no such opinion was heard.

It was not until 1929, the year when the collectivization issue commenced, that the letter was discussed fully on a theoretical level by M. Potash in a paper entitled 'Views of Marx and Engels on Populist Socialism in Russia'. In this paper, Potash declared that the concluding passage of Marx's letter to Zasulich – which stated that in order for the village commune to serve as 'the point of support of a social regeneration of Russia . . . the poisonous influences that attack it from all sides must be eliminated, and then the normal conditions of a spontaneous development insured' – was the passage that was 'especially wide open to question'.[15] A strong rebuttal of this view came from A. Ryndich, who maintained that Marx obtained his view of the Russian village commune as a 'result of the long and detailed studies of the primary sources on Russia after the Reform', and thus emphasized the significance of the concluding passage of Marx's letter to Zasulich.[16] However, in his rejoinder that accompanied Ryndich's paper, Potash had to say that Ryndich's piece was being printed precisely because 'it reveals the true nature of all those whose stance is that of a revision of the Leninist view.'[17] In the crucial year 1929, Potash represented the mainstream.

I

Marx's attitude towards Russian Populism at the time of the publication of Volume 1 of *Capital* in 1867 seems to have been utterly negative. In appended Footnote 9 at the end of the first German edition of *Capital*, Marx writes high-handedly:

> If, on the European continent, influences of capitalist production which destroy the human species . . . were to continue to develop hand in hand with competition in the sizes of national armies, state security issues . . . etc., then rejuvenation of Europe may become possible with the use of a whip and through forced mixture with the Kalmyks as Herzen, that half-Russian and perfect *Moskovich*, has so emphatically foretold. (This gentleman with an ornate style of writing – to remark in passing – has discovered 'Russian' communism not inside Russia but instead in the work of Haxthausen, a councillor of the Prussian Government.)[18]

Herzen's view that the Russian village commune was unique to the Slavic world was considered merely laughable by Marx at that time. Marx thought it was to be found everywhere, and was no different from what had already been dissolved in Western Europe.

> Everything, *to the minutest details*, is completely the same as in the ancient Germanic community. All that has to be added in the case of the Russians are . . . (i) the patriarchal nature . . . of

> their community and (ii) the *collective* responsibility in such matters as payment of taxes to the state. . . . These are already on their way to decay.[19]

Something like this cannot form a basis for a socialist development; this, I am sure, was the way Marx looked at the Russian peasant commune. For he wrote in the preface to the first German edition of *Capital*, 'The country that is more developed industrially only shows, to the less developed, the image of its own future!'[20] At this stage, it appears, he supposed that Russia, like Germany, would follow the example of England.

Marx's thinking, however, began to change once he mastered the Russian language and became able to pursue his Russian studies using primary sources, and especially once he came across the studies of N.G. Chernyshevskii. Needless to say, this change in Marx's attitude towards Russian Populism did not take place overnight.

Marx first wanted to study the Russian language in October 1869 when N.F. Danielson, a young Russian who asked his permission to translate *Capital* into Russian, sent him a copy of V.V. Bervi-Flerovskii's newly published book, *The Situation of the Working Class in Russia*; Marx felt he would like to read this solid book by himself. He immediately started learning Russian, and learned it very quickly; by February 1870 he managed to read as many as 150 pages of Flerovskii's book.[21] Marx found Flerovskii's book completely free from the sort of 'Russian "optimism" ' that was evident in Herzen.

> Naturally, he is caught up by fallacies such as *la perfectibilité de la proprieté perfectible de la Nation russe, et le principle providentiel de la proprieté communale dans sa forme russe.* [The perfectable property of the Russian Nation, and the providential principle of communal property in its Russian form.] This, however, does not matter at all. Examination of his writing convinces one that a dreadful social revolution . . . is inevitable and imminent in Russia. This is good news.[22]

In spite of Flerovskii's Populism, Marx thus appraised his descriptions of the social realities on Russia very highly, because they clarified the inevitability of a Russian revolution.

Having finished reading Flerovskii's work, Marx then tackled an article, 'Peasant reform and communal ownership of land (1861-1870)', which appeared in *Narodnoe Delo*, No. 2, an organ of the Russian Section of the International, the organization which, through its member Utin, once asked Marx to convey its membership application to the first International. Marx felt friendly towards Utin and his group because of their opposition to Bakunin and Herzen, but his attitude toward their Populist view of the Russian village commune was basically unchanged. While reading this paper, Marx wrote a word of rejection, 'Asinus'[!], at various points. And beside a passage where the differences in the development of communities in Russia and the West are discussed, he wrote down the following comment: 'Dieser Kohl kommt darauf heraus, daß russische Gemeineigentum ist verträglich mit russischer Barbarei, aber nicht mit bürgerlicher Civilization!' [From this rubbish, it emerges that Russian communal property is compatible with Russian barbarism, but not with bourgeois civilization.][23]

It is clear from this that at this stage Marx continued to find nothing significant in the Russian village commune.

However, his view began to change as a result of the discussions he had with German Lopatin, who visited Marx in July 1870 and who, while staying with Marx in order to work on the Russian translation of *Capital*, talked very highly of Chernyshevskii. Marx first read 'Comments on John Stuart Mill's *Principle of Political Economy*' by Chernyshevskii and found the author generally very capable.[24] He then seems to have started to read a paper of Chernyshevskii's on the peasantry, though we do not know which particular one this was. Nevertheless, there is no doubt that reading this paper was a turning point; Marx began to see Populism and the village commune of Russia in a different perspective.

This can be seen from a letter by Elizaveta Dmitrievna Tomanovskaya, a member of the Russian Section of the International, who visited Marx towards the end of 1870. In this letter dated 7 January 1871, Tomanovskaya writes:

> As regards the alternative view you hold about the destinies of the peasant commune in Russia, unfortunately its dissolution and transformation into smallholdings is more than probable. All the measures of the government . . . are geared to the sole

> purpose of introduction of individual ownership through abolition of the practice of collective guarantee.

She asked if Marx had already read the book by Haxthausen; she offered to send him a copy in case he had not. She goes on:

> This includes many facts and verified data about the organization and management of the peasant commune. In the various papers on the communal ownership of land you are reading now, you may notice tht Chernyshevskii frequently refers to and quotes from this book.[25]

This clearly shows that Marx either told or wrote to Tomanovskaya that he was reading Chernyshevskii's paper on the Russian peasant commune, and that he thought it worthwhile to consider the question raised by Chernyshevskii, that is, the Populist question, about the 'alternative': was the communal ownership of land going to be dissolved? Or was it going to survive to form the lynchpin of Russia's social regeneration? Marx's view had changed a great deal.

We do not know whether Marx at this time was given Haxthausen's book by Tomanovskaya or not, but there is no doubt that he now became interested in the conservative councillor of the Prussian government whom he had once scoffed at. It is therefore not a mere accident that Marx wrote at the end of his letter to L. Kugelmann dated 4 Februry 1871: 'Once you told me about a book by Haxthausen which deals with the ownership of land in (I presume) Westphalia. I would be very happy if you would kindly send me that same book.'[26]

However, Marx's Russian studies, which had advanced this far, were now interrupted for a considerable time by the struggle of the Paris Commune and, after its defeat, by the internal fight within the International. It was only after the Hague Congress of September 1872 that Marx returned to theory and the Russian question.

When he was able to spare time for his theoretical works again, Marx prepared the second German edition of *Capital*, Volume 1, and published it in early 1873. Except for some rearrangement of chapters and sections, there are not many major changes from the first edition. Important among these few corrections are: (1) the deletion of the exclamation mark, (!), from the passage in the preface we quoted earlier: 'The country that is more developed industrially only shows, to the less developed, the image of its own future!'; and (2) the deletion of Footnote 9 at the end of the volume in which Marx, as we saw earlier, sneered at Herzen and his 'Russian communism'. In addition to these changes, Marx in the 'Postscript to the Second Edition' paid a glowing tribute to Chernyshevskii by calling him 'the great Russian scholar and critic'.[27] The fact that Marx deleted his disdainful remark about Herzen's Populism and, furthermore, added a eulogy to the economics of Chernyshevkii clearly reveals that his attitude was undergoing a profound change.

In the period from the end of 1872 to some time in 1873, Marx read an anthology by Chernyshevskii, *Essays on Communal Ownership of Land*, published in Geneva immediately before. Of the nine articles collected in the anthology, the two most important are the review (written in 1857) of Haxthausen's book, *Studiën über die inneren Zustände, das Volksleben und insbesondere die ländlichen Einrichtungen Russlands* [*Studies on the internal conditions, the life of the people and in particular the agrarian arrangements of Russia*] and the article entitled 'Criticism of philosophical prejudices against the communal ownership of land' (1858). In these articles Chernyshevskii pointed out that the communal ownership of land in Russia was by no means a 'certain mysterious feature peculiar only to the Great Russian nature', but was something that survived till that day as 'a result of the unfavourable circumstances of historical development' in Russia which were drastically different from those in Western Europe. But anything that has a negative side ought to have a positive side as well. Among 'these harmful results of our immobility' there are some which are 'becoming extremely important and useful given the development of economic movements which exist in Western Europe', and which 'have created the sufferings of the proletariat.'[28] Among these, thought Chernyshevskii, was the communal ownership of land.

> When certain social phenomena in a certain nation reach an advanced stage of development, the evolution of phenomena up to this same stage in other backward nations can be achieved much faster than in the advanced nation. . . . This acceleration consists of the fact that the development of certain social

> phenomena in backward nations, thanks to the influences of the advanced nation, skips an intermediary stage and jumps directly from a low stage to a higher stage.[29]

On the basis of such a theoretical premise, Chernyshevskii thought that, given the development of the advanced West . . . it would be possible for Russia to leap from communal ownership of land directly to socialism. Chernyshevskii sums up his view in the following terms:

> History is like a grandmother; it loves the younger grandchildren. To the latecomers (*tarde venientibus*) it gives not the bones (*ossa*) but the marrow of the bones (*medullam ossium*), while Western Europe has hurt her fingers badly in her attempts to break the bones.[30]

Marx was deeply impressed by this view.[31] It is my contention that Marx went as far as to accept it as rational, and also to conceive it possible that, given the existence of the advanced West as a precondition, Russia could start out from its village commune and proceed immediately to socialism. Only by this inference can we reach a coherent understanding of his view in 1875.

That Marx was deeply interested in the question of the Russian village commune is evident from his letter to Danielson dated 22 March 1873, in which he asked for information on the origins of the village commune.[32] Of the books which Danielson sent to Marx in response to this request, *Materials About Artels in Russia* (1873) and a book by Skaldin, *In a Faraway Province and in the Capital* (1870), were of importance, and Marx read these two volumes earnestly.[33]

II

The new view which Marx formulated on the basis of his studies up to that time can be inferred from a correction made in the French edition of *Capital*, published in January 1875, and from an article by Engels written in April 1875, 'The social conditions in Russia'.

Let us first consider the correction made in the French edition of *Capital*. There is in Chapter 26, 'The secret of primitive accumulation', a passage which reads as follows in both the first and second German editions:

> The expropriation of the agricultural producers, of the peasant, from the soil, is the basis of the whole process. The history of this expropriation, in different countries, assumes different aspects, and runs through its various phases in different orders of succession, and at different periods. In England alone, which we take as our example, does it have the classic form.[34]

In the French edition this passage was struck out and replaced by a new one:

> At the bottom of the capitalist system is, therefore, the radical separation of the producer from the means of production. . . . The basis of this whole evolution is the expropriation of the peasants. . . . It has been accomplished in a final form only in England . . . but all the other countries of Western Europe are going through the same movement.[35]

An obvious implication of this correction is that the English form of the expropriation of the peasants is applicable only to Western Europe, or to put it differently, Eastern Europe and Russia may follow a completely different path of evolution. Thereafter Marx quotes only from the French edition whenever he refers to the passage above.

The essay by Engels was a byproduct of his polemic with P.N. Tkachev. The polemic was started by Engels when, by way of criticizing P.L. Lavrov, he took up Tkachev's pamphlet, 'The tasks of revolutionary propaganda in Russia' (1874), and ridiculed him as a 'green schoolboy'.[36] In a furious rage, Tkachev responded with the publication of a German pamphlet, 'Offener Brief an Herrn Friedrich Engels' [Open Letter to Mr Friedrich Engels] in Zurich at the end of 1874.

Upon reading this open letter by Tkachev, Marx handed it over to Engels with a brief note written on it:

> Go ahead and let him have enough of a beating, but in cheerful mood. This is so absurd that it seems Bakunin has had a hand in it. Pyotr Tka[chev] wishes above all else to prove to his readers

> that you are treating him as your opponent, and for that purpose he discovers in your argument points that do not exist at all.[37]

These words of Marx show that he found in Tkachev's open letter to Engels something reminiscent of the argument of Bakunin, and advised that Engels had better treat him as an idiotic opponent.

I deduce that Marx read Tkachev's 'The tasks of revolutionary propaganda in Russia' only *after* he read this open letter to Engels. Marx left behind him his copy of the former pamphlet in which he underlined passages here and there.[38] Reading this pamphlet he must have realized that Tkachev was fairly well versed in the social realities in Russia. In contrast to Engels, who wrote of Tkachev's assertion that he 'could not wait for a revolution' – 'Why, then, do you gentlemen keep chattering and making us sick of it? Damn you! Why don't you start one right away?[39] – Marx was more impressed by the accompanying analysis which formed the basis of Tkachev's assertion that he 'could not wait'.

> Of course, we cannot expect this social condition, which is convenient to us, to last for a long period of time. We are somehow, though stealthily and slugglishly, advancing along the path of economic development. This development now under way is subject to the same law and is in the same direction as the economic development of Western European countries. The village commune has already begun to dissolve. . . . Among the peasantry, there are being formed different classes of *kulaks* – peasant aristocrats. . . . Thus, there already exist in our country at present all the conditions necessary for the formation of the strong conservative classes of farmer-landholders and large tenants, on the one hand, and the capitalist bourgeoisie in banking, commerce and industry, on the other. As these classes are being formed and reinforced . . . the chance of success for a violent revolution grows more and more dubious. . . . Either now, or many years ahead, *or* never! Today, the situation is on our side, but ten years or twenty years from now, it definitely will become an obstacle to us.[40]

This argument of Tkachev is half way between that of Chernyshevskii and the People's Will Party. After his encounter with these views, Marx realized that anyone who wanted to debate with Tkachev would have to deal seriously with the question of the Russian village commune and present his own view of Russian society. We have thus good reason to suppose that it was because Marx gave advice of this kind that Engels's rebuttal to Tkachev took an unexpected turn in its latter half in choosing to confront the 'social conditions in Russia' in the fifth article of the series, 'Literature in Exile'. The materials as well as the logic which Engels used in the writing of this article were provided almost entirely by Marx. Although it bears the signature of Engels alone, the article's major contents consist of the conclusions which Marx and Engels would have jointly reached after discussion. Engels's article is well known for its attack upon Tkachev's supposed failure to understand that socialism was only possible once the social forces of production had reached a certain level of development, and after examining Tkachev's view of the Russian state threw this remark at him: 'It is not the Russian state which is suspended in mid-air but rather Mr Tkachev.' As far as this particular point is concerned, Engels is right in posing a question to Tkachev by asking him whether the 'suckers of the peasants' blood' and 'largely bourgeois' who are under heavy protection of the state actually have no vested interest in the continued existence of the state. The data on landholdings of the peasants and the aristocrats which Engels cites in support of his rebuttal are taken from the book by Flerovskii. And where Engels talks about the situations of the peasantry and says that the heavy burdens of redemptions and land taxes are forcing the peasants to become dependent upon the moneylender-*kulaks* and that speculators are exploiting the peasants by subleasing lands, he obviously depends on the descriptions by Skaldin. These materials are all provided by Marx.

Next, Engels attacks Tkachev's assertion that a socialist revolution is possible in Russia 'because the Russians are, so to speak, the chosen people of socialism and have *artel* and collective ownership of land.' Engels's argument about *artel* here draws heavily upon the argument of Efimenko which Marx read in the *Materials about Artels in Russia*. Engels refers also to Flerovskii.[41] It is evident that here too Engels depends on Marx. Summing up his argument about *artel*, Engels states:

> The predominance of the *artel* form of organization in Russia proves the existence of a strong drive for association among the

> Russian people but does not prove by any means that this drive makes possible a jump directly from the *artel* to the socialist society. For this to be possible it is necessary above all that the *artel* itself becomes capable of development and divests itself of its original form, in which it serves the capitalists rather than labourers (as we have seen), and at least rises to the level of the Western European co-operative associations.
>
> The *artel* in its present form is not only incapable of this, it is necessarily destroyed by large-scale industry unless it is further developed.[42]

It is indeed worthwhile to note here that Engels talks about the existence of a 'strong drive for association' among the Russian people, for this means that he recognized the two alternative destinies of the *artel*: its further development or its destruction. This conclusion, it appears, owes much to Marx.

As regards the question of communal ownership of land, Engels notes that 'in Western Europe . . . communal property became a fetter and a brake to agricultural production at a certain stage of social development and was therefore gradually abolished.' In Russia proper, however, 'it survives until today, and thus provides primary evidence that agricultural production and the corresponding conditions of rural society are here at a still very undeveloped stage.'[43] This perception has much in common with those of Marx and Chernyshevskii. Engels next maintains that the state of complete isolation of the various villages from each other is 'the natural basis of Oriental Despotism',[44] a rather general argument which is set forth even by Bakunin in Appendix A of his *Statism and Anarchy*. Engels's assertion that 'the further development of Russia in a bourgeois direction will destroy communal property gradually in this country also, without any need on the part of the Russian government to interfere with "bayonet and knout" ' is a criticism directed against the extreme assertion Tkachev made in his open letter to Engels, but is actually not much different from the argument which Tkachev set forth in 'The tasks of revolutionary propaganda in Russia'. As a matter of fact, Engels here points out Tkachev's self-contradiction by quoting a passage from the essential part of his article where it is stated that 'among the peasantry, there are being formed different classes of usurers (*kulaks*).' Where Engels points out that 'under the burden of taxes and usury, the communal property in land is no longer an advantage, but a fetter', and refers to the peasants running away as migratory workers,[45] he relies, as he indicates in a footnote, on the description by Skaldin, which was also provided by Marx. Marx might have hesitated to definitively call the rural commune a 'fetter', but it is clear that this is not a point around which Engels's argument pivots.

In conclusion of his argument, Engels makes the following statement:

> We see that communal property long ago passed its highpoint in Russia, and to all appearances is nearing its doom. Yet there exists, doubtless, the possibility of transforming this social organization into a higher form in the event that it persists until the time when circumstances are ripe for such a change, and in case the institution of communal property proves to be capable of development so that the peasants do not continue to cultivate the land individually but jointly. Society would have to be transformed into this higher form without the Russian peasants going through the intermediate step of bourgeois individual private ownership of land.[46]

It is clear that this statement, which is in agreement with the conclusion reached by Chernyshevskii (including the use of phrases such as 'higher form' and 'intermediate step'), is the joint view of Marx and Engels in 1875.

What matters is the condition required for such transformation of the Russian community. Engels underlined the importance of a 'victorious proletarian revolution' in Western Europe 'before the complete disintegration of communal property', since 'this would provide the Russian peasant with the preconditions for such a transformation of society, chiefly the material conditions which he needs, in order to carry through the necessary complementary change of his whole system of agriculture.' This too was a conclusion that could be derived from the assertion of Chernyschevskii. From what we have seen so far it is natural for us to regard this as a conclusion made jointly by Marx and Engels. This does not mean to say that they are not thinking about a Russian revolution. As a matter of fact, this article is concluded with a prophecy of the inevitability of an imminent Russian revolution 'which will be started by the upper classes in the capital, perhaps by the government itself, but which must be driven further by the peasants beyond its first constitutional phase.' What is envisaged here is clearly not a mere bourgeois revolution. It is stated furthermore that the revolution 'will be of the utmost importance for all Europe' in the sense that 'it will destroy the last, until now intact, reserve of all-European reaction with one coup.'[47] Although it is not stated explicitly, it would have been clear for both Marx and Engels that if a proletarian revolution were to become an actual issue in Europe – which in the aftermath of the defeat of the Paris Commune was as silent as the grave – it would do so only after Europe was shaken by a Russian revolution.

Engels insisted nevertheless that 'if there was anything which can save the Russian system of communal property, and provide the conditions for it to be transformed into a really living form, it is the proletarian revolution in Western Europe.' This, of course, was an exaggeration, in support of his point that 'it is pure hot air' for Tkachev to say that the Russian peasants, although 'owners of property' are 'nearer to socialism than the propertyless workers of Western Europe'.[48] It was a product of his experiences in the first International which led him to see Bakunin behind Tkachev and to stand out against Bakunin's 'Panslavism', in defence of Western European hegemony in the international proletariat movement. I believe that on this point too there was virtually no difference between Marx and Engels. Russia had two alternative paths of development to choose from; it could either follow the path of capitalist development or the route that led directly from the village commune to socialism. Chernyshevskii was well aware that Russia had embarked upon the former path, yet considered it possible for Russia to reject this path and pursue the latter course, without mentioning this precondition. Tkachev also insisted that since capitalist development was already under way in Russia, a revolution must be started at the earliest possible opportunity so as to enable it to switch paths before it became too late. Marx and Engels, accepting Chernyshevskii's assertion, came to think that it would be possible for Russia to start from its village commune and jump directly to socialism. But their treatment of Tkachev's thesis was affected both by the memory of their own struggle with Bakunin and Nechaev and by the exaggerated way in which Tkachev expressed it. They therefore argued against Tkachev that a precondition for the success of the communal path would be a victorious proletarian revolution in Western Europe and the material aid this revolution would offer. It thus seemed also that, in reaching this conclusion, Marx and Engels did not see any difference between their positions.

III

In the period from 1875 to 1876, Marx made further progress in his Russian studies. He read *Die Agrarverfassung Russlands* [*The Agrarian Constitution of Russia*] by Haxthausen, *Communal Ownership of Land in Russia* by A.I. Koshelev, Appendix A of *Statism and Anarchy* by Bakunin, an article by A.N. Engel'gardt entitled 'Various problems of Russian agriculture', a voluminous *Report of the Committee of Direct Tax*, and other materials, and made careful notes of their contents. Of these, Marx was particularly impressed by the criticisms which Bakunin directed at the patriarchal aspect and the closed character of the village communes. After a brief interruption, in the spring of 1877 Marx proceeded to read such works as *Outlines of the History of Village Communes in Russia and Other European Countries* by A.I. Vasil'chakov and *Outline of the History of Village Communes in Northern Russia* by P.A. Sokolovskii.[49]

The year 1877 saw the outbreak of the Russo-Turkish War. The desperate battles the Russian forces had to fight in its first phases led to the expectation of another Sevastopol and the hope that a revolution would follow soon after the Russian defeat. On 27 September of the same year, Marx wrote to F.A. Sorge:

> This crisis is a *new turning point* for the history of Europe. Russia – I have studied the situation in this country on the basis of official and non-official original sources in the Russian language – has for a long period been on the brink of revolution. All the factors for this are already present. The brave Turks, by the hard blow they struck against not only the Russian army and Russian finance but also the dynasty in command of the army . . . have advanced the date of explosion by a number of years. The change will begin with a constitutional comedy, *puis il y aura un beau tapage* [then all hell will break loose]. If Mother Nature is

> not extraordinarily hard on us, we will perhaps be able to live long enough to see the delightful day of the ceremony. The revolution this time starts from the East, that same East which we have so far regarded as the invincible support and reserve of counter-revolution.[50]

We see how excited Marx was at the prospect of Russian defeat in the Turkish war, followed by a Russian revolution, and then a revolution in Europe. However, these expectations were miserably disappointed. Somehow or other, Russia managed to reduce the Fort of Plevna by the end of 1877, and drove Turkey to admit its defeat in March the following year. In the face of this turn of events, Marx had to admit that 'things have turned out differently from our expectations.'[51]

According to widely accepted hypothesis, Marx is supposed to have written his so-called 'Letter to the Editor of *Otechestvennye Zapiski*' some time in November 1877. This view, however, is completely without foundation. It is much more likely that Marx wrote this letter at the end of 1878 after his hopes of an imminent Russian revolution had already been disappointed. My hypothesis is supported by Marx's letter of 15 November 1878 to Danielson, which reads in part as follows:

> As regards the polemics which B. Chicherin and several others are directing against me, I haven't seen anything other than what you sent me in 1877 (. . . an article by N.I. Ziber written as a response to Yu. Zhukovskii and another article, I guess it was, by Mikhailov – both of which appeared in the *Otechestvennye Zapiski*). Professor M.M. Kovalevskii who is staying here has told me that a fairly animated debate is going on in connection with *Capital*.[52]

The 'Letter to the Editor of *Otechestvennye Zapiski*' was written as a refutation of an article entitled 'Karl Marx before the Tribunal of Mr Zhukovskii' which Mikhailovskii published in the tenth issue of the same journal in 1877 under the signature of 'H.M.'. If Marx had actually finished writing his letter or if, after having started to write some part of it, he had chosen not to finish it and send it off, then it would have been nearly impossible for him to refer to this article inaccurately as an 'article, I guess it was, by

Mikhailov'. It would be far more logical for us to assume that he was tempted, partly perhaps stimulated by the conversations with Professor Kovalevskii, to read the article by Mikhailovskii and that only after reading the article did he feel that he should not keep silent.

Mikhailovskii in his article rejected Zhukovskii's coarse and primitive understanding of Marx's theory, while at the same time questioning the application of Marx's theory to the Russian situation. Mikhailovskii first called into question the chapter on 'The so-called primitive accumulation' in *Capital*, and considered that there Marx was expounding a 'historico-philosophical theory of Universal Progress'. In other words, Mikhailovskii took Marx to be asserting that every country must experience exactly the same process of expropriation of the peasant from the land as had been the case in England. Mikhailovskii then questioned Footnote 9 of the first German edition of *Capital* where Marx made a mockery of Herzen. Mikhailovskii criticized Marx as follows:

> Even judging solely by its overall tone, it can easily be seen what attitude Marx would take towards the efforts of the Russians to find for their country a different path of development from that which Western Europe has followed and is still following – efforts for which there is no need whatsoever to become a Slavophile or to mystically believe in the specially high quality of the Russian nation's spirit; all that is needed is to draw lessons from the history of Europe.[53]

Mikhailovskii pointed out that 'the soul of a Russian disciple of Marx' was torn apart and that 'this collision between moral feeling and historical inevitabiity should be resolved, of course, in favour of the latter.' 'But the problem,' Mikhailovskii concluded, 'is that one should thoroughly assess whether the sort of historical process that Marx described is truly unavoidable or not.'

Clearly Mikhailovskii directed his criticism against exactly those points which Marx himself had already either corrected or entirely struck out.

After reading this article by Mikhailovskii, Marx started writing the letter as he felt he should not remain silent. Since the letter was to be published in a legal journal in tsarist Russia under his own signature, Marx took the necessary precautions: he avoided talking about a revolution, chose to refer to Herzen and Chernyshevskii without explicitly mentioning their names, and on the whole talked in the 'language of Aesop'. This is why, at first glance, this letter appears equivocal. Nevertheless, anyone who is familiar with the contents of Mikhailovskii's article and the previous development of Marx's thought can easily understand what Marx is trying to say.

In the first half of the letter, Marx comments on Mikhailovskii's critique of the footnote in the *first* German edition of *Capital* in which Marx ridiculed Herzen, and points out that Mikhailovskii is utterly mistaken, since 'in no case can it serve as a key' to Marx's views on the efforts of the Russians to find for their country a path of development different from that of Western Europe. Marx then reminds Mikhailovskii that he calls Chernyshevskii a 'great Russian scholar and critic' in the postscript to the *second* edition of *Capital*, which Mikhailovskii had a chance to read; thus Mikhailovskii, argues Marx, 'might just as validly have inferred' that Marx shared Chernyshevskii's Populist views as to conclude that Marx rejected them. Reserved and brief as these statements are, Marx's reference to the second German edition – the one in which, as we have noted earlier, he deleted his words of contempt for Herzen that were present in the first edition, and included words of praise for Chernyshevskii – without doubt reveals his sympathetic attitude toward the Russian Populists. Marx goes on to say that he 'studied the Russian language, and, over a number of years, followed official and other publications that dealt with this question', and reached this conclusion: 'If Russia continues along the road which it has followed since 1861, it will forego the finest opportunity that history has ever placed before a nation, and will undergo all the fateful misfortune of capitalist development.'[54] This is the story told in 'the language of Aesop'. From 1861 Russia started to follow the path of capitalist development; should it continue to follow the same path, the peasant commune would be destroyed and with it the possibility of proceeding directly towards socialism based on the rural community. Therefore, dear people of Russia, Marx pleads, don't dare to 'forego the finest opportunity that history has ever placed before a nation', the opportunity that is too precious to be wasted. Throughout the period of the Russo-Turkish War, Marx kept looking forward to a Russian revolution which, he expected, would come on the heels of Russia's defeat in the war, and after the failure of his expectations he felt as if the revolution had just slipped through the people's fingers. This is exactly why he felt compelled here to remind the Russian people that they should not leave things as they were and thus lose for good the great chance of regeneration. This amounts to an appeal to the Russians to start a revolution right away.

In the second half of his letter, Marx quotes from the French edition of *Capital*, explains that the chapter on primitive accumulation only traces the path followed in Western Europe, and thus clarifies for the first time what really was his motivation when he revised this chapter in 1875. Marx further maintains that if this historical sketch were to be applied to Russia, the following two points must be made:

> (1) If Russia attempts to become a capitalist nation, like the nations of Western Europe . . . it will not succeed without having first transformed a good part of its peasants into proletarians, and afterwards, (2) once it has crossed the threshold of the capitalist system, it will have to submit to the implacable laws of such a system, like the other Western nations.

It may be possible for us to interpret the second point above as suggesting that if Russia does not cross the threshold of the capitalist system, it need not submit to the implacable laws of capitalism. If our interpretation is correct, then the second point above is not much different from Mikhailovskii's 1872 interpretation of the preface to *Capital*.[55] On closer reading of *Capital*, however, Mikhailovskii later began to wonder if he was actually doing justice to Marx's theory. Marx takes advantage of this wavering in Mikhailovskii's interpretation and accuses him of twisting his own theory. 'For him', asserts Marx, 'it is absolutely necessary to change my sketch of the origin of capitalism in Western Europe into an historico-philosophical theory of a Universal Progress, fatally imposed on all peoples, regardless of the historical circumstances in which they find themselves, ending finally in that economic system, which assures both the greatest amount of productive power of social labour and the fullest development of man.' Marx says that 'this is to do me both too much honour and too much discredit.' However, the reproach which Marx aims at Mikhailovskii is evidently wide of the mark and irrelevant, for Mikhailovskii's interpretation cannot be regarded as totally mistaken. It is rather Marx himself who underwent a significant change after he wrote the first German edition of *Capital*.

Before concluding the letter, Marx emphasized that 'events which were strikingly analogous, but which took place in different historical environments, led to entirely dissimilar results.' When Marx made this remark, he had clearly in his mind the opportunity open to the Russian village community in the prevailing historical conditions, in particular the existence of the advanced West and the crisis of capitalism there.

This letter which contains Marx's second conclusion on the Russian question was not to be sent. Engels later reasoned that Marx chose not to send it because he was 'afraid that his name would be enough of a threat to the continued existence of the journal' which was going to print the letter. The true reason, I suppose, was rather that Marx, after reading his letter again, saw something wrong with his critique of Mikhailovskii.

IV

The Russian victory in the war with Turkey, after all, reinforced the power of tsarism inside Russia. In a country whose modern history was literally a series of defeats in wars that resulted either in drastic internal changes or in revolutions, this was the only war that ended in victory. And this very fact seems to have been one of the important factors that precipitated the contest between tsarism and revolutionary Populism. But let us for the time being go back to the days when the result of the struggle between tsarism and Populism was still unknown.

Even before the end of the war, the revolutionary Populists were markedly stepping up their efforts. In February 1879 when Engels heard the news of the assassination of Governor Kropotkin of Kharkov, he found a positive meaning in the incident, stating that political assassination was the only means of self-defence available to the Russian intellectuals, and that the movement was 'just about to explode'.[56] His expectations of a Russian revolution were thus brought to life again. They were further enhanced when the Executive Committee of People's Will came into being in the summer of the same year and began its activities. Engels wrote in his New Year's letter to Wilhelm Liebknecht dated 10 January 1880: 'I offer you and all of you my congratulations on the New Year and on the *Russian Revolution* which is most likely to take place during it.'[57]

In contrast, Marx in this period did not put into words any expectations of this sort; but it seems safe to say that he was in the same state of mind as Engels. When, for instance, Leo Hartman visited London in February 1880 as a representative of People's Will, Marx received him very warmly, showed hearty affection for him, and offered to help him as much as possible.[58]

In the months of May to July, Hartman wrote to N. Morozov saying that Marx was reading the 'Programme' which Morozov sent him, that he was critical toward the Black Repartition group (*Chernyi Peredel*) led by Plekhanov and supported the programme of the 'Russian Terrorists', and also that Marx, in spite of his sympathy toward the terrorists, was unwilling to write for their publications as he found their programme something other than that of socialists.[59] We cannot, however, hastily conclude from these observations of Hartman that such was indeed the attitude which Marx finally adopted towards the People's Will.

Five months later, in November of the same year, Marx received a message from the 'Executive Committee of the Russian Social Revolutionary Party' as well as the programme which People's Will prepared for its working-class party members.[60] That Marx read the programme of the worker-members of People's Will very carefully, underlining it here and there, is an indication of how highly he evaluated it. As a matter of fact, ever since his encounter with this programme, Marx stopped calling this party the 'Terrorist Party'. On the other hand, his feeling of antipathy toward the members of the Black Repartition, who were taking refuge in Geneva, grew deeper. Marx spoke of them thus:

> These gentlemen are against all political-revolutionary action. Russia is to make a somersault into the anarchist-communist-atheist millenium! Meanwhile they are preparing for this leap with the most tedious doctrinairism, whose so-called principles have been hawked about the street ever since the late Bakunin.[61]

Meanwhile Marx advanced his Russian studies a step further. In the fall of 1879, he read M.M. Kovalevskii's new book, *Communal*

Ownership of Land – The Causes, Process and Consequences of its Dissolution, Part I (Moscow, 1879) and left a very detailed note of it.[62] By comparing Marx's note with the corresponding passage of the original text of the book, we can clearly see that Kovalevskii's resentment towards the land policy of colonizers who accelerated the dissolution of communal ownership of land was emphasized even more strongly by Marx. Take, for instance, the following pair of excerpts:

> *Kovalevskii*: Relying on their testimonies [i.e. testimonies of the government officials in India], the British critics took a calm attitude toward the dissolution of this social form which appeared archaic in their eyes. If some of them on some occasions expressed their regret about its decaying too fast, they did so simply out of considerations of an academic nature . . . it occurs to nobody that the British land policy should be regarded first of all as the offender responsible for the dissolution of communal ownership of land.[63]

> *Marx*: British officials in India, as well as critics like *Sir Henry Maine* who rely on them, describe the dissolution of communal ownership of land in Punjab as if it took place as an inevitable consequence of the *economic progress* in spite of the affectionate attitude of the British toward this archaic form. The truth is rather that the British themselves are the *principal* (and active) *offenders* responsible for this dissolution. . . . [emphasis original][64]

At about the same time as he read Kovalevskii's book, Marx read an article by N.O. Kostomarov, 'The revolt of Sten'ka Razin', and made a very detailed note on it.[65] It may be that he turned to this article hoping to find out about the potential capabilities of the Russian peasants. Important among other Russian books which Marx read around that time is *Collection of Materials for Studies on the Rural Land Commune*, Volume 1, published jointly by the Free Economic Society and the Russian Association of Geography in 1880. Out of this book, Marx made a note only on the article by P.P. Semenov. This note has attracted the attention of scholars in the Soviet Union since, commenting on the social differentiation of peasant households, Marx ironically states: 'The consequence of communal ownership of land is splendid!'[66] What is still more important about Semenov's article is that in passages beyond the point where Marx's note ends, Semenov talks about communal use of land.[67] Semenov notes that in most cases the Russian peasants practise a collective form of production in the meadowlands and distribute the grass mowed there equally among themselves. This description by Semenov left a profound impression on Marx, as can be inferred from his 'Letter to Zasulich'.

Marx's theory of Russian capitalism took shape in this period through his discussions with Danielson. To be more précise, Marx wrote a well-known letter on 10 April 1879, in reply to Danielson who in his long letter (dated 17 February 1879) pointed out to Marx that the peasants, because of the heavy burden of taxes, were forced to sell the cereals necessary for their own subsistence, and that railways and banks were accelerating these grain transactions, thereby further impoverishing the peasants.[68] In his letter of response, Marx elaborates on Danielson's description of the destructive functions of railways and generalizes this as a phenomenon characteristic of capitalist development in backward countries everywhere.[69] We might suggest that this shows that Marx was beginning to perceive the structure unique to backward capitalism.

Encouraged by the support he received from Marx, Danielson further developed his idea into an article, 'Outlines of our country's society and economy after reform', which was printed in the October 1880 issue of the *Slovo*. Marx's assessment of this article as a whole was quite high, even though he was not satisfied with Danielson's assessment of the abolition of serfdom or with his thesis on the absolute crisis of Russian capitalism.[70] There is no denying that Marx owed much to Danielson.

As to the circumstances in which Zasulich wrote her letter to Marx of 16 February 1881, asking for his opinion about the destinies of the rural commune, L. Deich left his own account. According to him, a debate took place around the end of 1880 or the beginning of 1881 in connection with an article by V.P. Vorontsov, printed in an issue of the *Otechestvennye Zapiski*, which asserted that Russia lacked a foundation for capitalist development; and it was decided that Zasulich should write a letter to Marx asking for his opinion on this question.[71] This account of Deich was at variance with what Zasulich herself says in her letter to Marx dated 16 February where she asks for Marx's opinion about the assertion, frequently made by the people who call themselves his special disciples, that the village commune is 'an archaic form', condemned to perdition.[72] If we were to attribute any significance to the recollection of Deich, it is perhaps only by assuming that Deich and his group started a debate in connection with an article by Vorontsov, as he claims, as well as in connection with an article by Danielson which was published immediately before and which caused some stir. My assumption, therefore, is that Deich and his group called into question Danielson's assertion that a 'capitalist current' was already predominant in Russia and was inducing the decay of the communal utilization of land.[73] If we bear in mind that Danielson's position in the 1880s was not very different from that of Vorontsov, it is not at all surprising that Deich should have confused Vorontsov with Danielson. Furthermore, Danielson was at the same time well known as a disciple of Marx: he quotes Marx very frequently in his own work.

What should also be noticed about Zasulich's letter to Marx is that she not only asked for Marx's opinion but for an answer that could be made public in the name of the group, the Black Repartition.

Marx received this letter on either 18 or 19 February. 19 February 1881 was the day when Marx, having just finished reading an article by Danielson, was on the point of writing to him about his impression of the article. A few days later, on 22 February, he wrote a reply to Ferdinand Domela Niuwenhuis, in Holland, after one and a half months' delay.

It was after writing these letters that Marx set about working on his reply to Zasulich. Marx, who supported People's Will, might at first have felt reluctant to comply with the request from the Black Repartition which he held in contempt. However, he felt obliged to confront the criticism that his disciples were expounding a thesis on the inevitable dissolution of the village commune.

There is no room for doubt that the so-called fourth draft of his 'Letter to Zasulich' was written last. However, the three earlier drafts were written not in the order of Riazanov's numbering, but in the order, draft two, draft one, draft three. Hinada Shizuma, a Japanese scholar, has made a careful re-examination of the four drafts,[74] and I completely agree with his conclusions. The fact that the concept '*commune agricole*' which is absent from the second draft begins to be employed abruptly in the middle of the first, while in the third draft it is used from the outset, obliges us to reason that the three drafts were written in the order mentioned above.

To begin with, in 'Second Draft', Marx first makes clear that his discussion of primitive accumulation in *Capital* is not applicable to Russia. He then goes on to discuss matters such as 'historical environments' which decide the destinies of the village commune, the place which the Russian village commune occupies in the historical chain of 'archaic organizations of society', the dualism inherent in the structure of the Russian commune, and the alternative paths of development. He concludes the draft by touching upon the troubles which actually beset the Russian commune. Although Marx brings out all the relevant points in this draft, his thought on the question is still not fully shaped.

'First Draft', which was written next, is not written in a flowing style; obviously Marx's pen often halts and limps while writing it. His thought, however, is far better developed in this draft than in the second draft. Paying attention to the two major characteristics of the agrarian commune, i.e. collectivism and individualism, Marx asserts that this 'dualism' may become the germ of its decomposition, but at the same time it may also permit that aspect of the commune favouring collectivism to overcome that aspect favouring private property. He further maintains that which of the two alternative directions is followed depends entirely on the 'historical environment in which the commune finds itself'. On the basis of this general consideration, Marx also deals with the Russian case. His argument may be roughly summarized as follows:

(1) In Russia, village communes have been preserved on a vast nationwide scale.

(2) Structural characteristics of the Russian commune: (i) the communal ownership of the soil offers the Russian commune a natural basis for collective production and collective appropriation; (ii) the Russian peasants' familiarity with the *artel* would greatly facilitate the transition from agriculture by individual plot to collective agriculture; and (iii) in the exploitation of the jointly owned meadowlands the Russian peasants already practise a form of communal production.

(3) 'Historical environments': (i) the transition from agriculture by individual plot to co-operative labour is vital for rescuing Russian agriculture from its crisis, but the material conditions of this transition are already available in the form of technological

achievements of the capitalist system; (ii) 'Russian public' – meaning the educated, privileged sector of society – which for such a long time has existed at the expense and cost of the village commune, owed it the first advances which are necessary for introducing mechanical cultivation; and (iii) the development of the village commune along such a path is exactly what the historical currents of the time were calling for, and the ready proof of this is in the 'fatal crises' that are shaking capitalist production in Europe and America.[75]

There is no mention of a proletarian revolution in Western Europe here. Obviously the whole of Marx's argument is developed, as previously, along lines similar to that of Chernyshevskii. However, there is a marked change in his perception of the way in which the advanced West serves as a precondition for a Russian revolution. Whereas previously he expected that a victorious proletarian revolution in Western Europe and material help from this revolution would constitute a major precondition for a revolution in Russia, he now finds an essential precondition in the technological achievements of capitalism as well as in the crises of capitalist production.

Another important point in the first draft of Marx's letter to Zasulich is that he sees as a weakness of the Russian commune its characteristic of being a 'localized microcosmos'. Marx writes for the first time that all that is necessary to get rid of this weakness is to abolish the *volost*, a government institution, and to establish in its place 'une assemblée de paysans [an assembly of peasants]' which is chosen by the communes themselves, and capable of serving as an economic and administrative institution for the protection of the interests of those communes.[76] This is the proposal Marx made on the question of what policies should be devised and carried out from above by the revolutionary forces. Placed in the perspective of later events, i.e. from the time of the 1905 Revolution, the Russian peasants united together on a village commune basis and began to collide with chiefs of the *volost*; and in the 1917 Revolution they abolished the *volost* chiefs and created their own *volost* committees; the proposal of Marx appears to have closely approximated to the social realities. At another point in the first draft, he takes up this issue once again and he wrote at one stage that the village commune's characteristic of being a 'localized microcosmos' could be broken only during a 'massive uprising', but later erased this passage.[77] Later, in the third draft, however, Marx chose to reintroduce this dynamic concept and drop the rather static proposal about *volost* committees.[78] Marx thus emphasizes the ability of the peasants to change themselves spontaneously.

Marx's analysis of the realities of the Russian village commune and the 'tragedies' which inflict pain upon it[79] depends on Kovalevskii's analysis in its emphasis on the fact that since the time of the emancipation of the peasants the state, by means of its policies of oppression and exploitation, had aggravated conflicts of interests within the commune, and had rapidly developed the seeds of its decomposition; Marx also relies on Danielson's analysis when he asserts that 'the state has helped in the enrichment of a new capitalist pest which is sucking the already thin blood of the "village commune".'

At the end of the draft Marx argues, in opposition to the attempts to find a way out of the prevailing crisis through the destruction of the commune and the employment of a new method of exploitation, that 'a Russian revolution is required, if the Russian commune is to be saved.'

Marx writes:

> If the revolution occurs in time, if it concentrates all its forces . . . , to insure the free flowering of the rural commune, then the latter will develop itself before long as an element in the regeneration of Russian society, as a point of advantage when compared to the nations enslaved by the capitalist system.[80]

(At the point of the ellipsis (. . .) in the foregoing quotation, Marx wrote: 'and if the intelligent sector of Russian society, the Russian intellect, concentrates all the living forces of this country', and then crossed it out.)

Here, Marx anticipates that even if a Russian revolution were victorious and the regeneration of Russian life took place on the basis of the village commune, these would not immediately be followed by revolutions in other countries in Europe. This seems closely related to the pessimistic view which Marx then held about the possibility of a German revolution at the time of Bismarck's law outlawing socialism.[81]

The viewpoint which Marx presents in 'First Draft' is also the conclusion he arrived at in his Russian studies in the 1870s, as well as the expression of the hope he pinned on People's Will. Needless to say, he does not describe what the process of the social regeneration based on the village commune would be like in actuality. Here, he tries to face the reality with a 'scientific insight' supplemented by '*Traum* [dream]' as he always does. Marx writes in his letter of 22 February 1881 to Niuwenhuis as follows:

> But was there a single Frenchman in the eighteenth century who sensed even a bit, beforehand and a priori, the way by which the demands of the French bourgeoisie were carried through? A purely theoretical, and thus inevitably fantastic, prophesy of the programme of actions for a future revolution would simply turn people's attention away from the present struggle. The fancy that the collapse of the world was imminent let the primitive Christians stand up in the war against the world empire of Rome and gave them confidence in their victory.[82]

Let us now turn to 'Third Draft'. Hoping to complete his letter of reply by putting his 'First Draft' in better order, Marx started this draft with the remark that, while it was impossible for him to deal with the question thoroughly: 'I hope that even this succinct explanation which I am having the honour of offering you would suffice to wipe away all the misunderstandings about my so-called theory.'[83] But Marx abruptly stops writing any further when he is half-way through with his discussion of the 'historical environments'. This is very strange indeed. I am sure that the reason for this abrupt interruption is political. For one reason or another, Marx must have come to think that he, a supporter of People's Will, should not give a different organization, the Black Repartition, such an important statement on his own and let them publish it in their name. I make this assumption on the basis of the content of the fourth and last draft of Marx's letter to Zasulich.

Marx starts this draft with an apology for the delay in his reply due to a nervous illness from which he had been suffering for the past ten years, and writes: 'I am sorry, but I cannot send you a succinct explanation, which could be published. . . . Two months ago I promised a work on the same subject to the St. Petersburg Committee.'[84] If this excuse were really true, Marx might as well have written so from the outset without taking trouble to prepare four drafts. So far no confirmation had been discovered by People's Will and its allies to the effect that the Executive Committee of this party actually made such a request to Marx. According to the *Chronological Record of Marx* which was published by the Marx-Engels-Lenin Institute in the Soviet Union, Morozov, who visited Marx at the end of 1880, made such a request to him.[85] This, however, is very hard to believe in view of the fact that neither of the two memoirs which Morozov wrote, one before the publication of the *Chronological Record of Marx* and the other after, makes any mention of such a request.[86] I assume that Marx referred to a promise which did not actually exist, for the sake of emphasizing his political position as a supporter of People's Will, refusing to give Zasulich's group, the Black Repartition, a manuscript for publication.

After this refusal to prepare a statement for publication, Marx says that 'a few lines will suffice' to clear up misunderstandings about his theory, and offers the gist of his view. The letter that was actually sent is extended to about twice the length of 'Draft Four'. In this letter, he points out that the analysis of primitive accumulation presented in *Capital* cannot be applied to Russia; he concludes the letter with the assertion that in order for the commune to serve as the 'point of support of a social regeneration of Russia', 'the poisonous influences that attack it from all sides must be eliminated, and then the normal conditions of a spontaneous development insured.'[87] This conclusion is the most clear-cut elaboration of his thought which was presented in 'First Draft'.

V

Marx and Engels were excited over the assassination of the tsar, Alexander II, in March 1881. They thought that this incident would 'in the end certainly lead to the establishment of the Russian Commune, even if it is by way of fierce struggle'.[88] At the end of March, Engels wrote in his letter to A. Bebel: 'The revolutionary global conditions for the overall crisis which have long been anticipated, are ripening.'[89] Marx, for his own part, was trying to put his ideas about the emancipation of serfs in Russia into shape during the same month. In a letter addressed to his daughter Jenny Longuet on 11 April, he applauded the attitude which Zhelyabov and Perovskaya showed in the court room: 'Being strong-hearted people through and through, they are without a melodramatic pose, but are simple, *sachlich* [matter-of-fact] and heroic. Screaming and action are the mutually irreconcilable opposites.' In the same letter, he also commented on the letter which the Executive Committee of People's Will sent to Alexander III with a remark that it was 'a well refined declaration of "moderation" '.[90]

Despite Marx's expectations, the assassination of Alexander II neither induced the state power to make concessions nor gave rise to any sort of popular movements except for a wave of anti-Semitic pogroms in the south. Mass arrests had decimated the People's Will. By the end of 1881, Marx was completely exhausted mentally and physically; his beloved wife passed away on 2 December and he was himself sick in bed. Towards the end of the year he visited Ventnor for a change of air. While staying there he did not make any response to what Engels wrote to him about the political situation in Russia, as if he were not interested in those matters any more.

Upon his return to London on 16 January 1882, Marx found there waiting for him a letter from P.L. Lavrov asking him and Engels to write a new preface to the Russian edition of the *Communist Manifesto* which was soon to be published.[91] Marx decided that this request must be complied with.

The manuscript of the preface marked 'London, 21 February 1881' was drafted entirely by Engels, with Marx doing nothing other than making one very minor correction and affixing his signature.[92] In view of the fact that the manuscript we have today has a passage towards the end which was written once, crossed out, and then rewritten, it is impossible to regard it as a clean copy which Engels transcribed from yet another manuscript. All these factors lead us to infer that Marx, who was in low spirits at the time, asked Engels to make a draft, and put his signature to it. That Marx was not entirely satisfied with the manuscript can be guessed from the letter which he sent to Lavrov along with the manuscript: 'If this piece, which is meant for translation into Russian, were to be published as it is in German, it still needs finishing touches to its style.'[93]

This famous preface to the Russian edition of the *Communist Manifesto* has this to say on the destinies of the Russian commune:

> The only possible answer to this question at the present time is the following: If the Russian revolution becomes the signal for a proletarian revolution in the West, so that the two can supplement each other, then present Russian communal land

> ownership can serve as a point of departure for a communist development.[94]

The prospect offered here is different from that in Marx's 'Letter to Zasulich' and its drafts in that it postulates as a precondition for a Russian regeneration the occurrence of a proletarian revolution in the West. Engels continued to believe firmly that a Russian revolution, once started, would be sure to be followed by a German revolution. Indeed, one month later, Engels wrote in his letter of 22 February to Bernstein:

> We have in Germany a situation which is certain to move toward a revolution at an increasing speed and push our Party to the forefront within a short period of time. . . . One thing we want is an immediate impact from without. It is the situation in Russia that will provide this for us.[95]

It seems clear, therefore, that the 'Preface to the Russian Edition' written under the joint signature of Marx and Engels expresses the opinion of Engels more directly than that of Marx.

In 1882 Marx read the book by Vorontsov, *The Destinies of Capitalism in Russia*[96] On 14 December of the same year, Marx wrote to his daughter Laura Lafargue as follows:

> Some *recent Russian publications*, printed in Holy Russia, not abroad, show the great run of my theories in that country. Nowhere is my success more delightful to me; it gives me the satisfaction that I damage a power, which, besides England, is the true bulwark of the old society.[97]

Here Marx did not talk of a Russian revolution. He has only seen consolation in the fact that his theories found a receptive audience and were damaging the reactionary power. Three months later on 14 March 1883, Karl Marx died.

Notes

1. Wada Haruki, *Marukusu, Engerusu to Kakamei Roshia* (*Marx, Engels and Revolutionary Russia*), Tokyo, 1975.
2. Karl Marx-Friedrich Engels, *Werke* (hereafter abbreviated *MEW*), Berlin, 1953-, vol. 36, p. 121.
3. *K. Marks, F. Engels i Revoliutsionnaia Rossiia*, Moscow, 1967, p. 504.
4. *Ibid.*, pp. 521-2.
5. 'Pis'mo Karla Marksa', *Vestnik Narodnoi Voli*, no. 5, Geneva, 1886, p. 215.
6. G. Uspenskii, 'Gor'kii uprek', *Sobranie Sochinenii*, vol. 9, Moscow, 1957, p. 172.
7. V.I. Lenin, *Polnoe Sobranie Sochinenii*, vol. 1, pp. 273–4; G.B. Plekhanov, *Sochineniia*, vol. 7, pp. 263–4.
8. *Arkhiv K. Marksa i F. Engel'sa*, vol. 1, Moscow-Leningrad, 1924, pp. 265–6; *Marx-Engels Archiv*, vol. 1, Frankfurt-am-Main, 1926, pp. 309–10. See Part Two of the present work.
9. B. Nikolajewski, 'Marx und das russische Problem', *Die Gesellschaft*, vol. 1, no. 4, July 1924, pp. 362, 364.
10. *Archiv K. Marksa i F. Engel'sa*, vol. 1, 1924, pp. 266–7.
11. V. Zenzinov, 'Propavshaia gramota', *Sovremennie Zapiski*, book 14, Paris, 1925, pp. 399, 401.
12. V. Chernov, *Konstruktivnyi Sotsializm*, Prague, 1925, p. 128.
13. N. Sukhanov, 'Obschina v sovetskom agrarnom zakondatel'stve', *Na Agrarnom Fronte*, no. 11-12, 1926, p. 110.
14. A Suchkov, 'Kak ne nado rassmatrivat' vopros o formakh zemlpol'zovanieisa', *Bol'shevik*, no. 2, 1928.
15. M. Potash, 'Marks i Engel's o narodnicheskom sotsializme v Rossii', *Proletarskaia Revoliutsiia*, no. 12, 1929, p. 41.
16. A. Ryndich, 'Marks, Engel's i Lenin o narodnichestve', *Proletarskaia Revoliutsiia*, no. 5, 1930, pp. 177, 178.
17. M. Potash, 'Kak ne sleduet pisat' o revoliutsionnom narodnichestve i narodovol 'chestve', *Proletarskaia Revoliutsiia*, no. 5, 1930, p. 208.
18. K. Marx, *Das Kapital, Kritik der Politischen Ökonomie*, 1st edn, vol. 1, Hamburg, 1867, p. 763. For biographical details concerning Herzen and other figures of the Russian scene particularly relevant to the article, see pp. 172-8 below.
19. *MEW*, vol. 32, p. 197.
20. Marx, *Das Kapital*, vol. 1, p. ix.
21. *MEW*, vol. 32, p. 437.
22. *MEW*, vol. 32, p. 659.
23. B. Nikolaevskii, 'Russkie knigi v bibliotekakh K. Marksa i F. Engel'sa', *Archiv K. Marksa i F. Engel'sa*, vol. 4, Moscow-Leningrad, 1929, p. 380.
24. In various passages of this book, Marx writes such criticisms as 'not true', 'stupid', 'error' (Nikolaevskii, *Arkhiv*, bk 4, pp. 385-9).

However, this, I think, is not necessarily inconsistent with Lopatin's account that Marx thought very highly of this book. See *Russkie Sovremenniki o K. Markse i F. Engel'se*, Moscow, 1969, p. 46.
25. *K. Marks, F. Engels i Revoliutsionnaia Rossiia*, pp. 186–7.
26. *MEW*, vol. 33, p. 183.
27. K. Marx, *Das Kapital, Kritik der Politischen Ökonomie*, vol. 1, 2nd edn, Hamburg, 1872, p. 817.
28. N.G. Chernyshevskii, *Stat'i ob Obschinnom Vladenii Zemlei*, Geneva, 1872, pp. 40–2; N.G. Chernyshevskii, *Polnoe Sobranie Sochinenii*, Moscow, 1939-71, vol. 4, p. 341.
29. Chernyshevskii, *Polnoe Sobranie Sochinenii*, vol. 5, pp. 288-389. See Part Three below.
30. *Ibid.*, p. 387. See pp. 187–8.
31. Nikolaevskii, 'Russkie knigi', pp. 390–1.
32. *MEW*, vol. 33, p. 577.
33. Nikolaevskii, 'Russkie knigi', pp. 403–4.
34. Marx, *Das Kapital*, vol. 1, 1st edn, p. 701; *Das Kapital*, 2nd edn, Hamburg, 1872, pp. 744–5.
35. K. Marx, *Le Capital*, ed. Lachâtre, Paris, 1872-5, p. 315.
36. *MEW*, vol. 18, pp. 540–1.
37. *MEW*, vol. 34, p. 5.
38. R. Koniushaia, *Karl Marks i Revoliutsionnaia Rossiia*, Moscow, 1975, p. 331.
39. *MEW*, vol. 18, p. 541.
40. P.N. Tkachev, *Izbrannie Sochineniia na Sotsial'nopoliticheskie Temy*, vol. 3, Moscow, 1933, pp. 69-70.
41. *MEW*, vol. 18, pp. 560–1.
42. *Ibid.*, pp. 561-2. For definition of *artel* see below p. 125 fn. 5.
43. *Ibid.*, p. 563.
44. *Ibid.*
45. *Ibid.*
46. *Ibid.*, p. 565.
47. *Ibid.*, p. 567.
48. *MEW*, vol. 18, p. 565.
49. See Nikolaevskii, 'Russkie knigi', pp. 409-12.
50. *MEW*, vol. 34, p. 296.
51. *MEW*, vol. 34, p. 317.
52. *MEW*, vol. 34, p. 359.
53. N.K. Mikhailovskii, *Polnoe Sobranie Sochinenii*, vol. 4, St. Petersburg, 1909, pp. 167–8, 171.
54. *MEW*, vol. 19, p. 108.
55. *MEW*, vol. 19, p. 111. Marx wrote in the preface to the first German edition of *Capital*, Volume 1, as follows: 'Auch wenn eine Gesellschaft dem Naturgesetz ihrer Bewegung auf die Spur gekommen ist . . . kann sie naturgemässe Entwicklungsphasen weder überspringen noch wegdekretieren.' (Marx, *Das Kapital*, vol. 1, 1st edn, p. x.) In English this passage means: 'Even if a society has got on the track of discovering the natural laws of its movement . . . it can neither clear

by bold leaps nor remove by legal enactment the successive phases of its normal development.'

When Danielson translated this passage into Russian, he skipped the word 'auch' (even) with the result that his translation reads: 'Kogda kakoenibud' obshchestvo napalo na sled estestvennogo zakona svoego razvitiya. . . .' (Marks, *Kapital*, vol. 1, St. Petersburg, 1872, p. xii.) Here, the phrase 'napalo na sled' means 'has discovered the track'; however, with the omission of the word 'auch', the meaning of the whole passage became unclear.

In his review of this Russian edition of *Capital*, Volume 1, therefore, Mikhailovskii quoted the passage by correcting 'napalo' into 'popalo', i.e. he interpreted the sentence in the following sense: 'When a society has got on the track of the natural laws of its movement, it can clear by bold leaps. . . .' In other words, he interpreted Marx as insisting here that 'if a society has not entered the track of the natural laws of its movement, it can clear by bold leaps . . . the successive phases of its normal development' (Mikhailovskii, *Polnoe Sobranie Sochinenii*, vol. 10, St. Petersburg, 1913, p. 10).

56. *MEW*, vol. 19, p. 149.
57. *MEW*, vol. 34, p. 437.
58. See below, p. 173. The intimate relations between Marx and Hartman surprised socialists in the West; see Henry Hyndman, *The Record of an Adventurous Life*, London, 1911, p. 280; E. Bernstein, 'Karl Marks i russkie revol'iutsionery', *Minuvshie Gody*, November 1908, p. 21..
59. *Russkie Sovremenniki o K. Markse i F. Engel'se*, p. 180; S.S. Volk, 'Karl Marks, Fridrikh Engel's i "Narodnaia volia" ', *Obshchestvennoe Dvizhenie v Poreformennoi Rossii*, Moscow, 1965, p. 51. For the debate between the People's Will and the Black Repartition, see pp. 10 and 13 of the present work.
60. See pp. 231-7.
61. *MEW*, vol. 34, p. 477.
62. The note is presented in *Sovetskoe Vostokovedenie*, no. 3, 1958, pp. 3-13; no. 4, pp. 3-22; no. 5, pp. 3-28; *Problemy Vostokovedeniia*, no. 1, 1959, pp. 1-17; *Narody Azii i Afriki*, no. 2, 1962, pp. 3-17 (recently published in English by L. Krader).
63. M. Kovalevskii, *Obshchinnoe Zemlevladenie, Prichiny, Khod i Posledstviia ego Razlozheniia*, pt 1, Moscow, 1879, p. 184.
64. *Sovetskoe Vostokovedenie*, no. 5, 1908, p. 20.
65. The note is presented in 'K. Marks, Sten'ka Razin', *Molodaia Gvadriia*, bk 1, 1926, pp. 104-23.
66. *Arkhiv K. Marksa i F. Engel'sa*, vol. 12, p. 128.
67. *Sbornik Materialov dlya Izucheniia Sel'skoi Pozemel'noi Obshchiny*, vol. 1, St. Petersburg, 1880, pp. 123-4.
68. R. Koniushaia, *K. Marks, F. Engel's i Revoliutsionnaia Rossiia*, pp. 357-73.
69. *MEW*, vol. 34, pp. 372-4.
70. *MEW*, vol. 34, pp. 35, 155.
71. *Gruppa 'Osvobozhdenie Truda*, no. 2, p. 218.

72. *Marx-Engels Archiv*, vol. 1, pp. 316–17.
73. The article written by Danielson in 1880 is included in the first part of his book published in 1893. Nikolai-on, *Ocherki Nashego Poresgormennogo Obshchestvennogo Khoziaistva*, St. Petersburg, 1893, p. 71.
74. Hinada Shizuma, 'On the meaning in our time of the drafts of Marx's letter to Vera Zasulich (1881)', *Suravu Kenkyu* (*Slavic Studies*), no. 20, 1975.
75. *Marx-Engels Archiv*, vol. 1, pp. 323–6.
76. *Ibid.*, vol. 1, p. 324.
77. *Ibid.*, vol. 1, p. 325.
78. *Ibid.*, vol. 1, p. 339.
79. *Ibid.*, vol. 1, pp. 326–7.
80. *Ibid.*, vol. 1, p. 329.
81. In 1880, Marx explained his view of the situations in European countries to Swinton, an American journalist. He talked with much 'hope' about the 'dynamic fermentation of the intellect' taking place in Russia, but with regard to Germany he simply commented 'philosophically' about the 'development of the mental aspects'. See Koniushaia, *Karl Marks i Revoliutsionnaia Rossiia*, p. 379.
83. *MEW*, vol. 35, pp. 160–1.
83. *Marx-Engels Archiv*, vol. 1, p. 334.
84. *Ibid.*, p. 340.
85. *Karl Marx: Chronik seines Lebens in Einzelndaten*, Moscow, 1934, p. 381.
86. N. Morozov, 'Karl Marks i "Narodnaia Volia" v nachale 80-kh godov', *Katorga i ssylka*, no. 3, pp. 145–7; N. Morozov, 'U Karla Marksa', *Izvestiia*, 7 November 1935, p. 5.
87. *Marx-Engels Archiv*, vol. 1, p. 342.
88. *MEW*, vol. 19, p. 244.
89. *MEW*, vol. 35, p. 175.
90. *MEW*, vol. 35, p. 179.
91. Koniushaia, *K. Marks, F. Engel's i Revoliutsionnaia Rossia*, pp. 457–8.
92. The photocopy of this manuscript is presented in 'K 75-letiiu "Kommunisticheskogo Manifesta" ', *Byloe*, no. 22, 1927, pp. 314–15.
93. *MEW*, vol. 35, p. 262.
94. *MEW*, vol. 19, p. 296.
95. *MEW*, vol. 35, p. 283.
96. Koniushaia, *K. Marks, F. Engel's i Revoliutsionnaia Rossiia*, pp. 430–1.
97. *MEW*, vol. 35, p. 408.

Late Marx: continuity, contradiction and learning[1]

Derek Sayer and Philip Corrigan

Shanin's and Wada's essays put the distinctiveness and importance of 'late Marx' beyond dispute. But there are still questions to be raised about the generality of this period of Marx's work and its implications for our understanding of his legacy as a whole. We believe Shanin and Wada bend the stick too far and yet not far enough. Too far, in that in their eagerness to establish late Marx's novelty they concede too much to dubious orthodoxies regarding the evolutionism of Marx's previous writings. And not far enough, in that they fail sufficiently to relate Marx's late writings on Russia to other equally striking developments in his thinking after *Capital*.

Marx, evolutionism and capitalism

At times Marx certainly adopted an evolutionist idiom in the presentation of his general conclusions, as in the 'progressive epochs in the economic formation of society' of the 1859 Preface.[2] He had obvious enough reasons for claiming scientific status for his theories and for drawing attention to their affinities with theories in natural science which also upheld the mutability of the world and the role of struggle in advancement. In this sense Marx saw *The Origin of Species* as a book which 'supports the class struggle in history from the point of view of natural science'.[3] But whether, as Shanin maintains, *Capital* and other works by the 'mature' Marx rest on an *essential* kernel of evolutionism in any stronger sense than this is a more difficult question.

To begin with, it is important to note that Darwin (the only evolutionist Marx had time for; his opinion of Comte was unprintable) did *not* in fact believe in 'necessary development through pre-ordained stages'. In Darwin's theory species survive because they have acquired characteristics which enable them to adapt to their environments; they do not acquire such characteristics in order so to adapt. The relevant mutations are fortuitous, not preordained; there is no *necessity* involved. This matters here because what Marx celebrated in Darwin's book was precisely that 'it deals the death-blow to teleology in the natural sciences.'[4] This forms part of a long-standing hostility on Marx's part to teleological explanations in history, which dates back at least to the text which first proclaimed the fundamentals of historical materialism, *The German Ideology* of 1845–6. There any idea that 'later history is the goal of earlier history' is ridiculed as a 'speculative distortion': 'what is designated by the words "destiny". "goal", "germ" or "idea" of earlier history is nothing but an abstraction from later history.'[5] Marx was later to attack both Proudhon and the Political Economists on similar grounds.[6] *The German Ideology*'s hostility to 'historico-philosophical theory' and the advocacy of empirical method is every bit as pronounced as that of Marx's letter to *Otechestvennye Zapiski* of more than thirty years later.

Turning to *Capital*, one can certainly question Shanin's reading of the notorious '*De te fabula narratur*!' ['the tale is told of you!'] passage from the *Preface* to the first edition. What Marx actually says is this:

> . . . England is used as the chief illustration in the development of my theoretical ideas. If, however, the German reader shrugs his shoulders at the condition of the English agricultural and industrial labourers, or in optimistic fashion comforts himself with the thought that in Germany things are not nearly so bad, I must plainly tell him, '*De te fabula narratur*!'
>
> Intrinsically, it is not a question of the higher or lower degree of development of the social antagonisms that result from the *natural laws of capitalist production*. It is a question of these laws themselves, of these tendencies working with iron necessity towards inevitable results. The country that is more developed industrially only shows, to the less developed, the image of its own future. . . .
>
> And even when a society has got upon the right track for the discovery of the natural laws of its movement – and it is the ultimate aim of this work, to lay bare the economic law of motion *of modern society* – it can neither clear by bold leaps, nor remove by legal enactments, the obstacles offered by the successive phases of its normal development.[7]

At first sight this is incontrovertible evidence for the 'mature' Marx's evolutionism. But is it?

Marx is publishing, in Germany in 1867, a treatise illustrated mainly with English data. He is understandably concerned to establish its relevance to German conditions. Since Germany is a society in which capitalism has taken root already, its 'normal development' can reasonably be expected to follow an 'English' path. But this in no way implies any necessity for societies in which capitalist production is *not* already established to do the same. We will see shortly that what Marx wrote at the time on Ireland and India suggests he thought otherwise. But in any case the only 'iron necessity' he speaks of in this passage is that of 'the natural laws of capitalist production' taking their course once the latter is present. And the only 'phases of development' he refers to are those of 'modern society', i.e. capitalism itself. Nothing said here bears on the wholly *separate* issue of whether capitalism as such is a necessary stage of historical development through which all societies must pass, or whether indeed there are any such necessary stages in history at all. This was, of course, exactly what Marx was to make clear in his letter of 1877 or 1878 against Mikhailovskii's interpretation of *Capital*:

> . . . what application to Russia could my critic make of this historical sketch? Simply this: *If* Russia wants to become a capitalist nation after the example of the West European countries . . . *then, once drawn into* the whirlpool of the capitalist economy, she will have to endure its inexorable laws like other profane nations.[8]

Textual evidence can never conclusively resolve such disagreements since the interpretation of texts is often precisely what is at issue. Clearly Marx did make some pronouncements of an evolutionist character as in the 1859 Preface. Equally clearly there is much in his work prior to 1870 which casts doubt on the contention that evolutionism was its 'essential kernel'. Our view is that Shanin overstates the degree to which the Marx of *Capital* was a consistent evolutionist and therefore the extent of the break between 'late Marx' (on whom we mostly agree) and what went before. In so far as they were present at all, evolutionist 'arch-models' served Marx as summary devices to present conclusions rather than as essential tools or premises of analysis. As so often, posterity has violently abstracted the summaries and treated them as fundamentals. It is less the totality of what Marx wrote than the deadweight of received interpretation from late Engels onwards which makes the evolutionist reading of Marx the 'obvious' one and thereby renders texts like the drafts of the letter to Zasulich so utterly startling. We cannot be said to have established these contentions here. But the possibility ought at least to be entertained that Marx's late texts represent not so much a radical break as a *clarification* of how his 'mature' texts should have been read in the first place. This is not to deny specific shifts of view in connection with Russia, where we broadly agree with Wada.

Nor is it for a moment to deny that for Marx socialism presupposed levels of social production that only capitalism (hitherto) had proved capable of attaining. But it cannot plausibly be argued that 'late Marx' changed his views on this. Two problems in Wada's argument are worth remarking in this connection. First, Wada practically ignores Marx's 1874 notes on Bakunin's *Statism and Anarchy*, written after Marx had read Chernyshevskii. Here Marx continues to insist that 'a radical social revolution . . . is only possible where with capitalist development the industrial proletariat occupies at least an important position among the mass of the people', and derides Bakunin for expecting 'the European social revolution, premised on the basis of capitalist production, to take place at the level of the Russian or Slavic agricultural and pastoral peoples'.[9] Second, Wada's claim that by 1881 Marx had abandoned his view that an *obshchina*-based Russian socialism required a revolution in the West is extremely dubious. Wada's only evidence for this is Marx's failure explicitly to reiterate this requirement in the drafts of the letter to Zasulich, while he cavalierly dismisses Marx's later endorsement of his previous position in the 1882 *Manifesto* Preface on the highly speculative grounds that Marx was too grief-stricken by his wife's death to know or care what he was doing. What we know of Marx's reading for January 1882 (it included extensive Russian materials) and his correspondence suggest otherwise.[10] The reservations Wada quotes from Marx's letter to Lavrov clearly concern style alone. This is special pleading with a vengeance.

Although Marx saw some features of capitalism as historically progressive, he was equally aware of the contradictory character of capitalist development. This is not a feature of his late writings alone either, as Wada and Shanin's comments may imply – though these late texts undoubtedly take his insights furthest. Marx knew that capitalist development could sustain, strengthen and even create oppressive and unproductive 'archaic' social forms on its peripheries long before the 1870s. In 1847, for instance, he argued: 'Direct slavery is just as much the pivot of bourgeois industry as machinery, credits, etc. Without slavery you have no cotton; without cotton you have no modern industry. . . . Slavery is an economic category of the greatest importance.'[11] Marx reiterated this in his writings of 1861-2 on the American Civil War: the slave South 'grew and developed simultaneously with the monopoly of the English cotton industry on the world market.' The same articles severely qualify the 'progressivist' conclusions of Marx's 1853 articles on India:

> England pays now, in fact, the penalty for her protracted misrule of that vast Indian empire. The two main obstacles she has now to grapple with in her attempts at supplanting American cotton by Indian cotton are the want of means of communication and transport throughout India, and the miserable state of the Indian peasant, disabling him from improving favourable circumstances. Both these difficulties the English have themselves to thank for.[12]

Shanin mentions Ireland. By 1867 Marx knew well that England 'struck down the manufactures of Ireland, depopulated her cities, and threw her people back on to the land'; 'every time Ireland was about to develop industrially, she was crushed and reconverted into a purely agricultural land', one 'forced to contribute cheap labour and cheap capital to building up "the great works of Britain" '[13] The same manuscript documents the underdevelopment of Irish agriculture itself consequent upon English absentee landlordism. *Capital* indeed goes beyond this to generalise as follows:

> as soon as people, whose production still moves within the lower forms of slave-labour, corvee-labour, &c., are drawn into the whirlpool of an international market dominated by the capitalist mode of production, the sale of their products for export becoming their principal interest, the civilised horrors of overwork are grafted on to the barbaric horrors of slavery, serfdom, &c.[14]

Ironically enough, Marx illustrates the point with a Russian example. Later on in *Capital* he suggests a *systematic* unevenness in capitalist development:

> A new and international division of labour, a division suited to the requirements of the chief centres of modern industry springs up, and converts one part of the globe into a chiefly agricultural field of production, for supplying the other part which remains a chiefly industrial field.[15]

This does not amount to a worked-out theory of dependent development, but nor do Marx's deeper insights in his late texts. What is clear, however, is that far from the latter coming from out of the blue to shatter a secure progressivist unilinear evolutionism, they extend apprehensions as to 'the specific structure of backward capitalism' which were already well established. Again, our general point is to remark both the complexity of Marx's work and his openness to learning.

Capitalism, socialism and the State

Let us now turn to another major dimension of Marx's thought after *Capital*. We will begin with the Paris Commune of 1871, which, as Shanin notes, deeply influenced Marx's thinking in his last decade. Its immediate product was a body of material as important, as neglected, and as subversive of much 'Marxism' as the writings on Russia published in this volume and ultimately related to its themes: the text and even more the two drafts of *The Civil War in France*.[16] This work is especially important for its theorisation of the State, in relation to both capitalism and socialism – the one area where Marx thought *Capital* to be in need of his personal supplementation.[17] As in Marx's late writings on Russia, there is genuine development here, leading at times to explicit self-criticism. But again we need to beware of too simple a periodisation. For not the least interesting feature of 'late Marx' is his re-engagement, albeit in a very different context, with themes central to his thought in the early and mid-1840s. What we witness here is the re-animation of concerns which are for the most part subordinated in *Grundrisse* and *Capital* and marginalised by later

Marxists and commentators.

For Marx the Commune was 'the greatest revolution of this century'.[18] What impressed him was not so much its measures, which he saw as having 'nothing socialist in them'[19] but its potentialities *as a political form* – 'the political form at last discovered under which to work out the economical emancipation of labour'.[20] Marx argued in 1859 that 'political forms . . . originate in the material conditions of life',[21] and here warns that except as a vehicle for such emancipation the Commune 'would have been an impossibility and a delusion.'[22] But more novel, and less often remarked in these texts is the extension of Marx's materialism to assert the *contrary* dependence: the Commune 'affords the rational medium through which that class struggle can run through its various phases in the most rational and humane way.'[23] 'The economical emancipation of labour' in other words presupposes political forms which are *themselves* emancipatory. Marx drew an unambiguous conclusion from this:

> the working class cannot simply lay hold on the ready-made state-machinery and wield it for their own purpose. The political instrument of their enslavement cannot serve as the political instrument of their emancipation.[24]

Marx thought this conclusion not only highly important but also sufficient of a change in his views for him to advertise the fact. Not only is it urgently reiterated throughout the second draft of *The Civil War* and included in the final text; Marx also quotes it as self-criticism in the 1872 Preface to the *Manifesto*, against the 'revolutionary measures' in the latter which had hinged precisely upon 'centralisation . . . in the hands of the State'.[25] Engels similarly qualified his and Marx's calls in 1850 for 'the really revolutionary party [in Germany] to carry through the strictest centralisation', writing in 1885 that this had been 'based on a misunderstanding' of French history.[26]

Quite simply, for Marx the Commune was a rational form for the emancipation of labour because and to the extent that it was *not* a State, and this was the lesson of 1871 he chose to emphasise most. He is absolutely clear on this:

> This was . . . a Revolution not against this or that, legitimate,

> constitutional, republican or Imperialist form of State Power. It was a Revolution against the *State* itself, of this supernaturalist abortion of society, a resumption by the people for the people of its own social life. It was not a revolution to transfer it from one faction of the ruling classes to another, but a Revolution to break down this horrid machinery of class domination itself. . . . The Second Empire was the final form of this State usurpation. The Commune was its definite negation, and, therefore, the initiation of the social Revolution of the 19th century.[27]

Behind this antithesis lies an implicit theory of the modern State. In part Marx presents this in the text's historical sketch of the rise of the French State, in part it can be inferred from what he writes, by way of contrast, about the Commune.

In brief, the modern State is 'the creation of the middle class, first a means to break down feudalism, then a means to crush the emancipatory aspirations of the producers, the working class'.[28] Its roots (in the French case)[29] lie in the period of Absolutism, when 'the checkered (partycoloured) anarchy of medieval powers' was superseded by 'the regulated plan of a statepower, with a systematic and hierarchic division of labour'. The 1789 Revolution extended the 'circumference and attributes' of the State and with it its 'independence, and its supernaturalist sway of real society'; 'with its task to found national unity (to create a nation), it 'had to break down all local, territorial, townish and provincial independence.'[30] Marx notes that national unity, 'if originally brought about by political force', became a 'powerful coefficient of social production'.[31] The first Napoleon perfected this 'parasitical [excrescence upon] civil society', subjugating popular liberties at home and creating 'more or less states after the image of France' abroad.[32]

The second aspect, suppression of the working class, now comes to the fore in Marx's account. As 'the modern struggle of classes, the struggle between labour and capital, assumed shape and form' the State increasingly 'develop[ed] its character as the instrument of class despotism, and political engine forcibly perpetuating the social enslavement of the producers of wealth by its appropriators, of the economic rule of capital over labour.'[33] The revolutions of 1830 and 1848 served only to transfer power from one faction of the ruling class to another and in each case 'the repressive character of the state power was more fully developed and more mercilessly used.'[34] So was the 'second exploitation' of the financial burden of the State on the people.[35]

The French Second Empire was for Marx the 'last triumph of a *State* separate of and independent from society'.[36] It is important how we understand this. 'At first view, apparently [another formulation is "to the eye of the uninitiated"[37]] the usurpatory dictatorship of the governmental body over society itself, rising alike above and humbling all classes, it has in fact, on the European Continent at least, become the only possible stateform in which the appropriating class can continue to sway it over the producing class.'[38] In one sense the State indeed had 'grown so independent of society itself that a grotesquely mediocre adventurer with a hungry band of desperadoes behind him sufficed to wield it.'[39] The Empire 'divested the state power from its direct form of class despotism.'[40] But in substance it remained bourgeois: 'Apparently the final victory of the governmental power over society . . . in fact it was only the last degraded and the only possible form of that class ruling.'[41] This amounts to a critique of the model of 'Bonapartism', habitually drawn from Marx's *Eighteenth Brumaire*, of a really autonomous State explained by a stalemate of classes. Here the State's formal independence is itself a form through which the bourgeoisie rules.

That the State is an instrument – or better, a form of organisation – of class power is a common enough theme in Marxist theory. Other themes in this analysis are less so. The Marxist mainstream follows *Anti-Dühring*[42] in identifying the State with government of people (as opposed to administration of things) in general, and sees States as coextensive with class society. Marx's usage here is much more historically specific. The State he analyses here is a modern phenomenon: it is a form of organisation of the class power of the *bourgeoisie*, created in struggles against feudalism and perfected in struggles against the proletariat. Since coercive government manifestly antedates the bourgeoisie, Marx evidently must have something more particular in mind when he refers here to the State. The other side of this is equally important. These texts make clear that for Marx State formation was inseparable from the making of the capitalist mode of production and the State remains an essential relation of bourgeois society rather than a mere 'superstructure' in any meaningful sense of the term.[43] As Marx put it in *The German Ideology*, *bürgerliche*

Gesellschaft – the German translates as either bourgeois or civil society – 'must assert itself in its external relations as nationality and internally must organise itself as State.'[44]

What gives the State in the sense Marx uses the term here its historical specificity is its *separation* from 'civil society'. The novelty of the bourgeois organisation of its collective class power lies in the exercise of this power through a distinct polity, or arena of the 'general interest', which is counterposed to a 'non-political' civil society which is held to be the realm of particular, individual and private interests. Marx had identified this constitutive relation of bourgeois civilisation as early as 1843:

> the political constitution as such is brought into being only where the private spheres have won an independent existence. Where trade and landed property are not free and have not yet become independent, the political constitution too does not yet exist. . . . The abstraction of the *state as such* belongs only to modern times, because the abstraction of private life belongs only to modern times. The abstraction of the *political state* is a modern product.[45]

State formation is the other side of that monumental transformation in which, as *Capital* puts it, 'property . . . receives its purely economic form by discarding its former political and social embellishments and associations',[46] becoming free and disposable. This separation of the State from civil society – and it is instructive that Marx chooses to resurrect the latter concept in *The Civil War in France* – is central both to the analysis of the State in his late writings and also to the way we understand his injunction to smash it. It is not merely the State in so far as it is a bourgeois instrument, but (to quote another late text) '*the state insofar as it forms through the division of labour a special organism separate from society*'[47] that Marx wishes to smash. What is new in Marx's writings of the 1870s as against those of the 1840s is their stronger focus on this division of labour.

What is also new in 'late Marx', generalising the experience of the Paris Commune, is the urgency and detail in which he poses the State as a problem for *socialist* strategy. One reading of *The Civil War in France* is simply as a manifesto for extreme political democracy.[48] Marx does indeed welcome the Commune's achievement of real representation ('Never were elections more sifted, never delegates fuller representing the masses from which they had sprung'[49]) and genuine public accountability in the political sphere, ensured by the openness of the Commune's sittings, publication of its proceedings and revocability of its delegates. But the major thrust of his analysis lies elsewhere. Again the continuities with his texts of the early 1840s are important. In his 1843 essay on the Jewish question Marx had developed a highly germane critique of merely political democracy, arguing that since the very existence of a separate political sphere represents an alienation of human social powers, it must of necessity remain a very partial emancipation:

> Only when man has recognised and organised his '*forces propres*' as *social* forces, and consequently no longer separates social power from himself in the shape of *political* power, only then will human emancipation have been accomplished.[50]

States as such presuppose relations between individuals within which the latter *cannot* collectively control the conditions of their real lives in 'civil society'. The problem for socialism is therefore not only the class content of political power but its State form. What is needed is not simply political emancipation but emancipation from politics, understood as a particularised set of activities, occasions and institutions. This is why Marx hails the Commune as 'a Revolution against the *State* itself . . . a resumption by the people for the people of its own social life'.

We are not arguing that Marx turned anarchist in his old age or ever thought the State could simply be decreed away. On the contrary, he is insistent that long class struggles, for which the communal form was only the 'rational medium', would be required for labour to free itself from the 'muck of ages'[51] including the State/civil society separation. Indeed his emphasis on the protractedness – he draws an explicit parallel in *The Civil War in France* drafts with the transformations from slavery to feudalism and feudalism to capitalism[52] – and complexity of socialist revolution is a marked feature of his late texts. But nor did he endorse the view that a 'proletarian State' could be used to make the revolution and then 'wither away' or be 'thrown away'.[53] Sixty years after the October Revolution, is it not time socialists abandoned this amiable but murderous fantasy? For Marx the Commune was an appropriate form of labour's self-emancipation because and to the extent that it constituted a *material* and *present* challenge to those relations through which labour is subordinated. Attacking the State/civil society separation was not one of communism's remote objectives but part of any practical *means* for its attainment.

The Commune's extension of the principles of election and revocability to administrative and juridical as well as political functionaries,[54] for instance, represented an extension of the *sphere* of social control beyond the realm of the polity within bourgeois society. So did the Commune's infractions upon the 'private jurisdiction' of employers in 'their' factories, one of the few measures Marx sees as being 'for the working class'.[55] The Critique of the Gotha Programme (1875) extends this awareness of the need for despotic inroads on bourgeois right.[56] More generally Marx celebrated the fact that 'the initiative in all matters of social life [was] to be reserved to the Commune'.[57] What saves this from being a blueprint for totalitarian aggrandisement of a strengthened central State is that the forms through which such social control were to be exercised were themselves neither centralised nor State-like, but part of a wider revolution in civil society against any such alienation of social powers. The extension of purely political democracy was part of this, but not the whole story. Marx is clear that the Commune stood for a once-and-for-all reduction in the cost, scale and power of *any* central societal authority. It prefigured 'all France organised into self-working and self-governing communes . . . [with] the army of stateparasites removed . . . [and] the state-functions reduced to a few functions for general national purposes'.[58]

We have left the most important feature of Marx's account until the end. The *means* through which this revolution was possible were a sustained attack on the *divisions of labour* that render administrations and government 'mysteries, transcendent functions only to be trusted to the hands of a trained caste'.[59] It is of the utmost importance, first, that Marx brands this unequivocably as 'a delusion',[60] and second, that it is a delusion he insists can and must be *materially* challenged now, in the very way socialism is made, not in the communist hereafter. The Commune *was* such a challenge, and this is why Marx celebrated it in the moment of its defeat as a social discovery of such immense significance for the emancipation of labour:

The whole sham of state-mysteries and state-pretensions was done away [with] by a Commune, mostly consisting of simple working men . . . doing their work publicly, simply, under the most difficult and complicated circumstances, and doing it . . . for a few pounds, acting in broad daylight, with no pretensions to infallibility, not hiding itself behind circumlocution offices, not ashamed to confess blunders by correcting them. Making in one order the public functions – military, political, administrative – *real workmen's functions*, instead of the hidden attributes of a trained caste. . . . Whatever the merits of the single measures of the Commune, its greatest measure was its own organisation . . . proving its life by its vitality, confirming its theses by its action . . . giving body to the aspirations of the working class of all countries.[61]

The 'Russian road' in context: continuity and discovery

Against this background, what is most striking in the drafts of Marx's letter to Zasulich is an *exactly* parallel concern with the centrality of the State to capitalist development, on the one hand, and the appropriateness of the *obshchina* as a communal form through which labour can further its own emancipation, on the other. Marx is again counterposing commune against State. He fastens upon a contradictory *dualism* within the Russian village community, between private and collectivist tendencies, which permits alternative possibilities for its social development depending entirely upon the historical environment. One possibility is towards socialism:

The historical situation of the Russian 'rural commune' is without parallel! . . . While it has in common land ownership the [natural] basis of collective appropriation, its historical context – the contemporaneity of capitalist production – provides it with ready-made material conditions for huge-scale common labour. It is therefore able to incorporate the positive achievements of the capitalist system without having to pass under its harsh tribute. . . . It may thus become the *direct*

> *starting-point* of the economic system towards which modern society is tending.[62]

The starting-point for this development, importantly, is to re-establish the commune in its normal state.[63] The basis for socialist transformation is there in present social relations (and the personal experiences they sustain); in particular, in the peasants' familiarity with the *artel* and the collective forms of cultivation already practised in the meadows and other areas of general interest.[64]

Against this, 'what threatens the life of the Russian commune is neither a historical inevitability nor a theory; it is state oppression, and exploitation by capitalist intruders whom the state has made powerful at the peasants' expense'.[65] The State has acted as a 'hothouse'[66] for capitalist development in Russia. It was the State which, after 1861, 'placed the Russian commune in abnormal economic conditions', its tax demands which transformed the commune into 'a kind of inert matter easily exploited by trade, landowners and usurers', its 'oppression from without' which precipitated conflicts of interest within the commune. It was the State which fostered a form of capitalist enterprise which, 'in no way developing the productive premises of agriculture, are the best suited to facilitate and precipitate the theft of its fruits by unproductive middlemen. In this way, it helped to enrich a new capitalist vermin which is sucking the already depleted blood of the rural commune'.[67] What is needed is therefore first and foremost a revolution against this 'conspiracy of powerful interests':

> If the revolution takes place in time, if it concentrates all its forces . . . to ensure the unfettered rise of the rural commune, the latter will soon develop as a regenerating element of Russian society and an element of superiority over the countries enslaved by the capitalist regime.[68]

The major parallels between these two seminal (and equally neglected) moments in Marx's later writings need no further labouring. Given space, these and related themes could be further explored in other works of Marx's last decade. What in our view 'late Marx' has to offer is above all a sustained reflection – the culmination of a lifetime's reflection informed by a deep involvement in the political struggles of the day – on *appropriate forms for socialist transformation*. A search, on the one hand, for social forms within present modes of life and struggle which are *capable* of advancing the emancipation of labour – prefigurative forms, as we nowadays call them, not in any Utopian sense but as the only material and effective means for furthering socialism. And a sober identification, on the other hand, of the myriad social forms and relations – going well beyond manifest property relations: State, division of labour, forms of social classification and identity 'encouraged' by complex modes of moral and legal regulation – which fetter that emancipation. This is not, of course, a concern of Marx's post-*Capital* writings alone, but it is at its sharpest and most developed here.

'Late Marx', then, is a major and scandalously neglected resource for socialists today. Partly this is for the reasons given by Shanin, partly for those reasons we have developed here. Marx's late writings contain much that is new and extremely *un*orthodox, not to say pertinent to our own situation. Having said that, it would be a great pity if Shanin's claims for late Marx (coupled, perhaps, with E.P. Thompson's recent labelling of *Grundrisse* and *Capital* as an 'anti-political economy')[69] were to have the kind of negative effects on evaluations of *Capital* as Althusser's periodisation had for a time on evaluations of Marx's early writings. To argue a fundamental continuity in Marx's work, from the 1840s to the 1880s, is not to deny discovery or development. Marx was supremely good at learning. It is to assert a continuity of *concern*, and the real import of Marx's late writings lies in helping us see where this lies.

For us, the late writings are a testament, as for Shanin, to the empirical, historical, anti-speculative core of Marx's work. We would say this is true of *The German Ideology* and *Capital* too, and that the importance of Marx's last texts in this context is the support they offer for an anti-evolutionist reading that can already be amply defended. But they are also a testament to something no less important: the centrality to the end of Marx's days of what are too readily dismissed as youthful and idealistic elements in his thought, about the State, about the division of labour, and about their overcoming. Marx was never a writer of socialist Utopias, still less an anarchist. He fought bitter battles with the anarchists in the 1870s, denouncing what he called 'political indifferentism' – the rejection of working-class action in the arena of official politics – with deep irony. But nor was he an instrumentalist, a

'*Realpolitiker*'.[70] He was as passionate a critic of Lassalle's 'State socialism' as he was of Bakunin or Proudhon. Political indifferentism does not advance the emancipation of labour because it does not engage with the facts of bourgeois power. But *Realpolitik* only appears to do so, because the means it employs are themselves forms of bourgeois domination. In our times, the latter seems the more pertinent lesson. We can learn a lot from Marx's attention to *forms*.

Notes

1. A fuller version of this chapter, together with an extended biographical and bibliographical chronology of Marx's last fifteen years, will appear as *Working Paper no. 4*, Glasgow University, Department of Sociology, 1984. Some problems relevant to the questions discussed here are further explored in our work with Harvie Ramsay, *Socialist Construction and Marxist Theory*, London and New York, 1978, or in our joint papers in *Radical Philosophy*, no. 12, 1975, and in B. Fryer *et al.* (eds), *Law, State and Society*, London, 1981. Individually, see D. Sayer, *Marx's Method*, Brighton, 1979 and 1983, and P. Corrigan, 'On the politics of production' *Journal of Peasant Studies*, 1975 and 'Feudal relics or capitalist monuments?', *Sociology*, 1977.
2. 1859 Preface to *A Contribution to the Critique of Political Economy*, London, 1971.
3. Letter to Lassalle, 16 January 1861, in Karl Marx and Friedrich Engels, *Selected Correspondence*, Moscow, 1975 (hereafter cited as *MESC*), p. 115.
4. Ibid.
5. *The German Ideology*, in Karl Marx and Friedrich Engels, *Collected Works*, London, Moscow and New York, 1975 onwards (hereafter cited as *MECW*), 5, p. 50.
6. See, for example, *MECW*, 6, pp. 173–4; K. Marx, *Grundrisse*, Harmondsworth, 1973, p. 106.
7. K. Marx, *Capital* I, London, 1970, pp. 8, 10.
8. 'Letter to *Otechestvennye Zapiski*', *MESC*, pp. 291–4.
9. *The First International and After*, Harmondsworth, 1974 (hereafter cited as *FI*), pp. 334-5.
10. In January 1882 Marx's reading included works by Semevsky, Issayev, Mineiko and Vorontsov (see M. Rubel, *Marx: Life and Works*, London, 1980, p. 121). His MS 'Remarks on the 1861 reform and Russia's post-reform development' dates from late 1881/early 1882 (in Marx/Engels *Werke*, Berlin, 1953 onwards, vol. 19, pp. 407-24). Jenny Marx died on 2 December 1881. Marx's letters, for example to Engels of 5 and 12 January 1882, do not suggest that grief completely obliterated Marx's interest in politics (in Marx/Engels *Werke* vol. 35).

11. *MECW* 6, p. 167.
12. K. Marx, *The Civil War in the United States*, New York, 1974, pp. 84, 19.
13. *Ireland and the Irish Question*, Moscow, 1978, pp. 139, 142, 143; see also the letters and speeches in *FI*, pp. 158–71.
14. *Capital* I, p. 236.
15. Ibid., p. 451.
16. The drafts were first published in *Archiv K. Marksa i F. Engel'sa*, 3(8), Moscow, 1934. They first became widely available in English in the Peking Foreign Languages Press edition of *The Civil War in France* (1966). The source used here is H. Draper (ed.), *Writings on the Paris Commune* (hereafter cited as *WPC*) New York, 1971. Marx wrote the two drafts in English, which we have not altered even when it is agrammatical or otherwise linguistically peculiar (as is sometimes the case). Marx's *Notebook on the Paris Commune*, containing press cuttings etc., from which he compiled the drafts, is also now published (ed. H. Draper, Berkeley, 1971).
17. Letter to Kugelmann, 28 December 1862, in *Letters to Dr. Kugelmann*, London, n.d.
18. *WPC*, p. 147.
19. Ibid., p. 162.
20. Ibid., p. 76.
21. 1859 Preface to *A Contribution to the Critique of Political Economy*, p. 20.
22. *WPC*, p. 76.
23. Ibid., p. 154.
24. Ibid., p. 196.
25. *Manifesto of the Communist Party*, Moscow, 1973, pp. 7-9 (Preface), pp. 74–5 (the 'revolutionary measures' criticised).
26. *MECW* 10, pp. 285–6 (fn).
27. *WPC*, pp. 150–1.
28. Ibid., p. 150.
29. Marx sees the French case as 'classical' (*WPC*, p. 75), at the same time noting English 'historical peculiarities' which allowed completion of 'the great central State organs by corrupt vestries, jobbing councillors, and ferocious poor-law guardians in the towns, and virtually hereditary magistrates in the counties'.
30. *WPC*, p. 148.
31. Ibid., p. 75.
32. Ibid., p. 149.
33. Ibid., p. 197.
34. Ibid.
35. Ibid., p. 149.
36. Ibid., p. 151.
37. Ibid., p. 150.
38. Ibid., p. 196.
39. Ibid., p. 149.
40. Ibid., p. 198.
41. Ibid., p. 150.

42. *Herr Eugen Dühring's revolution in science* [*Anti-Dühring*] (New York, 1972) pp. 306–8. We do not deny that Marx uses the term 'State' more broadly too in other texts; but the issue here is the substance of the analysis rather than the semantics of the term.
43. For development of this point see P. Corrigan, H. Ramsay and D. Sayer, 'The State as a relation of production', in P. Corrigan (ed.), *Capitalism, State Formation, and Marxist Theory*, London, 1980; and P. Corrigan and D. Sayer, 'How the law rules', in Fryer *et al.*, *Law, State and Society*.
44. *MECW* 5, p. 89.
45. *MECW* 3, p. 32; see also pp. 167, 197-9.
46. *Capital* III, Moscow, 1971, pp. 617-18.
47. 'Critique of the Gotha Programme', in *FI*, p. 356.
48. We would argue that this is Lenin's reading in *State and Revolution*. See the fuller version of this paper as cited in Note 1 above.
49. *WPC*, p. 147.
50. *MECW* 3, p. 168.
51. See *WPC*, p. 154; the 'muck of ages' image is Marx's, *MECW* 5, p. 53.
52. *WPC*, pp. 154–5.
53. 'Withering away' is Engels's formulation in *Anti-Dühring*, loc. cit., being 'thrown away' is Lenin's in his 1919 lecture on the state (*Collected Works* 29, Moscow 1965, p. 488).
54. See *WPC*, pp. 140, 153, 200.
55. *WPC*, p. 138.
56. *FI*, pp. 334–7; cf Corrigan and Sayer, 'How the law rules'.
57. *WPC*, p. 200.
58. Ibid., p. 154.
59. Ibid., p. 153.
60. Ibid.
61. Ibid.
62. See pp. 111-12, this volume.
63. Ibid.
64. See p. 110.
65. See pp. 104–5.
66. See p. 115. Marx employed the same image in *Capital* I, p. 751, in a well-known passage which concludes that (State) force 'is itself an economic power'.
67. See pp. 114–15.
68. See pp. 116–17.
69. See E.P. Thomson, *The Poverty of Theory and Other Essays*, London, 1978, pp. 249f.
70. See Marx's letter to Kugelmann of 23 February 1865 (in *FI*).

Part II
The Russian Road

The core of Part Two consists of writings representing Marx's analysis of the Russian peasant commune and of related issues, triggered off by a letter from Vera Zasulich. The letter of Zasulich, dated 16 February 1881, is followed by four drafts of reply which Marx prepared and which are translated fully from the French original discovered in 1911 by D. Ryazanov, transcribed in the following years by himself and N. Bukharin but first published only in 1924. The drafts are followed by the reply actually despatched by Marx in March 1881, yet published only in 1923, after a delay of forty-two years. Those texts are preceded by Ryazanov's introduction to their first full publication, which tells the peculiar tale of their discovery in the words of the man who found most of them. It also offers a major example of the way they were understood by the Russian Marxists trained in Plekhanov's school of interpretation.

The further items of Part Two are Marx's letter to *Otechestvennye Zapiski*, the 'Introduction' by Marx and Engels to the second Russian edition of the *Communist Manifesto* and Marx's half-jocular 'Confessions', the relevance of which was considered in Part One. Two biographical notes bring Part Two to completion. The first, illustrating Marx's life in the period directly related to the content of our volume, offers relevant evidence as well as a conclusive answer to 'the slow death' interpretation of Marx's long silence of the last decade in his life. The last item is a brief note concerning Russian scholars and revolutionaries who persistently appear in the pages of our book.

Marx–Zasulich correspondence: letters and drafts

This set of documents concerning Marx's exchange of letters with Vera Zasulich in February/March 1881, and first published in Russia in 1924 in *Arkhiv K. Marksa i F. Engel'sa*, Volume 1, represents a discovery, the profound intellectual significance of which has not yet been fully acknowledged. Their lasting importance lies as much in the uncovering of the 'kitchen' of thought of a theorist whose impact has been paramount as in the essence of the topic tackled – the problems of social transition in the societies which our generation has misnamed 'developing'. An introduction by D. Ryazanov to the first publication of Marx's text which follows offers direct evidence of the way those writings of Marx came to public knowledge. The text of Zasulich (for whose biographical details see p. 178) holds some particular relevance of its own. Her initial letter bears testimony to Marx's influence upon the radical intelligentsia as far as the Russian verge of Europe. It also shows how much the question she posed and Marx answered was not only that of the Russian peasants but also, much more broadly, of socialists facing non-proletarians and pre-capitalist social structures in a world in which capitalism had already made its powerful appearance.

Both the Marx/Zasulich letters and Marx's own drafts were translated from the French original in *Marx-Engels Archiv*, Frankfurt, 1925, Volume 1, pp. 316–42 by Patrick Camiller who was assisted at the stage of verification by Perry Anderson, Derek Sayer and Teodor Shanin. The division into text and page footnotes follows the one adopted in the first 1925 publication. The chapter notes are by myself, Teodor Shanin. The order of presentation in which the 'Second Draft' appears before the 'First Draft', is explained in Note 1 below.

Vera Zasulich: A letter to Marx

16 Feb. 1881,
Genève,
Rue de Lausanne, No. 49,
L'imprimerie polonaise.

Honoured Citizen,

You are not unaware that your *Capital* enjoys great popularity in Russia. Although the edition has been confiscated, the few remaining copies are read and re-read by the mass of more or less educated people in our country; serious men are studying it. What you probably do not realise is the role which your *Capital* plays in our discussions on the agrarian question in Russia and our rural commune. You know better than anyone how urgent this question is in Russia. You know what Chernyshevskii thought of it. Our progressive literature – *Otechestvennye Zapiski*, for example – continues to develop his ideas. But in my view, it is a life-and-death question above all for our socialist party. In one way or another, even the personal fate of our revolutionary socialists depends upon your answer to the question. For there are only two possibilities. Either the rural commune, freed of exorbitant tax demands, payment to the nobility and arbitrary administration, is capable of developing in a socialist direction, that is, gradually organising its production and distribution on a collectivist basis. In that case, the revolutionary socialist must devote all his strength to the liberation and development of the commune.

If, however, the commune is destined to perish, all that remains for the socialist, as such, is more or less ill-founded calculations as to how many decades it will take for the Russian peasant's land to pass into the hands of the bourgeoisie, and how many centuries it will take for capitalism in Russia to reach something like the level of development already attained in Western Europe. Their task will then be to conduct propaganda solely among the urban workers, while these workers will be continually drowned in the peasant mass which, following the dissolution of the commune, will be thrown on to the streets of the large towns in search of a wage.

Nowadays, we often hear it said that the rural commune is an archaic form condemned to perish by history, scientific socialism and, in short, everything above debate. Those who preach such a view call themselves your disciples *par excellence*: 'Marksists'. Their strongest argument is often: 'Marx said so.'

'But how do you derive that from *Capital*?' others object. 'He does not discuss the agrarian question, and says nothing about Russia.'

'He would have said as much if he had discussed our country,' your disciples retort with perhaps a little too much temerity. So you will understand, Citizen, how interested we are in Your opinion. You would be doing us a very great favour if you were to set forth Your ideas on the possible fate of our rural commune, and on the theory that it is historically necessary for every country in the world to pass through all the phases of capitalist production.

In the name of my friends, I take the liberty to ask You, Citizen, to do us this favour.

If time does not allow you to set forth Your ideas in a fairly detailed manner, then at least be so kind as to do this in the form of a letter that you would allow us to translate and publish in Russia.

With respectful greetings,
Vera Zassoulich

My address is: Imprimerie polonaise,
Rue de Lausanne No. 49,
Genève.

K. Marx: Drafts of a reply (February/March 1881)

The 'Second'[1] Draft

I. I have shown in *Capital* that the [transformation] metamorphosis of *feudal production into capitalist production* had its starting-point *in the expropriation of the producers*; and, in particular, that '*the expropriation of the agricultural producer, of the peasant, from the soil is the basis of the whole process*' (p. 315 of the French edition).[2] I continue: 'Only in England has it (the expropriation of the agricultural producer) been accomplished in a radical manner. . . . *All the other countries of Western Europe* are following the same course' (*loc. cit.*).[3]

Thus [in writing these lines] I expressly restricted [the development in question] this 'historical inevitability' to '*the countries of Western Europe*'. So that there should not be the slightest doubt about my thinking, I say on p. 341: 'Private property, as the antithesis to social, collective property, exists only where . . . *the external conditions of labour* belong to private individuals. But according to whether these private individuals are workers or non-workers, private property has a different character.'[4]

Thus the process I [described] analysed, substituted a form of private, fragmented property of the workers – capitalist property[(a)] of a tiny minority (*loc. cit.*, p. 342), *substituted one kind of property for another*. How [would it apply] could it apply to Russia, where the land is not and never has been the private property of the agricultural producer? [In any case, those who believe that the dissolution of communal property is a historical necessity in Russia cannot, at any event, prove such a necessity from my account of the inevitable course of things in Western Europe. On the contrary, they would have to provide new arguments quite independent of the course I described. The only thing they can learn from me is this:] Thus, the only conclusion they would be justified in drawing from the course of things in the West is the following: If capitalist production is to be established in Russia, the first step must be to abolish communal property and expropriate the peasants, that is, the great mass of the people. That is anyway the wish of the Russian liberals [who wish to naturalise capitalist production in their own country and, quite consistently, to transform the great mass of peasants into simple wage-labourers], but does their *wish* prove more than Catherine II's wish [to graft] to implant the Western medieval craft system in Russian soil?

[Since the Russian peasants' land is their common property and has never been their private property. . . .]

[In Russia, where the land is not and never has been the peasant's

(a) This sentence is heavily corrected. The original text reads as follows: 'Thus the process of which I speak eventually transforms private, fragmented property – into capitalist property, transforms one kind of property into another.'

'private property', the {transformation} metamorphosis {of this} of such private property into capitalist property {has no sense} {is impossible} is therefore out of the question. {The only} conclusion one might draw is that. . . . {All that can be concluded from the Western data. . . .} {If one wishes to draw some {indication} lesson from the (Western) data. . . .}]

[The most simple-minded observer could not deny that these are two quite distinct cases. In any case, the Western process. . . .]

Thus [the process I have analysed] the expropriation of the agricultural producers in the West served 'to transform the fragmented private property of workers' into the concentrated private property of capitalists. But it was always the substitution of one form of private property for another form of private property. [How, then, could this same process apply {to the land in Russia} to the Russian agricultural producers {whose land is not and never has . . .} whose property in land always remained 'communal' and has never been 'private'. {The same historical process which [I analysed] such as it was realised in the West. . . .}] In Russia, on the contrary, it would be a matter of substituting capitalist property for the communist property [of the tillers of the land – a process that would evidently be quite . . .].

Yes indeed! If capitalist production is to establish its sway in Russia, then the great majority of peasants – that is, of the Russian people – will have to be transformed into wage-labourers, and hence be expropriated through the prior abolition of their communist property. But in any event, the Western precedent would prove nothing at all [about the 'historical inevitability' of this process].

II. The Russian 'Marxists' of whom you speak are completely unknown to me. As far as I am aware, the Russians with whom I do have personal links hold altogether opposite views.

III. From a historical point of view, the only serious argument [that may be invoked] in favour of the *inevitable dissolution* of communal property in Russia is as follows: *Communal property existed everywhere in Western Europe, and it everywhere disappeared with the progress of society*; [why should its fate be different in Russia?] how, then, could it escape the same fate in Russia?[(b)]

(b) This paragraph reappears later in the draft in the following form: 'From a historical point of view, there is only one serious argument in favour of the inevitable *dissolution* of Russian communist property. It is as follows: Communist

First of all, in Western Europe, the death of communal property [and the emergence] and the birth of capitalist production are separated by a [centuries-long] huge interval which covers a whole series of successive economic revolutions and evolutions, [The death of communal property did not give birth to capitalist production,] of which capitalist production is but [the last] the most recent. On the one hand it has marvellously developed the social productive forces, but on the other it has betrayed [its transitory character] its own incompatibility with the very forces it generates. Its history is no longer anything more than one of antagonisms, crises, conflicts and disasters. Lastly, it has unveiled its purely transitory character to all except those who have an interest in remaining blind. The peoples among which it reached its highest peak in Europe and [the United States of] America seek only to break its chains by replacing capitalist with co-operative production, and capitalist property with a *higher form* of the archaic type of property, that is, [collective] communist property.

If Russia were isolated in the world, it would have to develop on its own account the economic conquests which Western Europe only acquired through a long series of evolutions from its primitive communities to the present situation. There would then be no doubt whatsoever, at least in my mind, that Russia's communities are fated to perish with the development of Russian society. However, the situation of the Russian commune is absolutely different from that of the primitive communities in the West [in Western Europe]. Russia is the only European country in which communal property has maintained itself on a vast, nationwide scale. But at the same time, Russia exists in a modern historical context: it is contemporaneous with a higher culture, and it is linked to a world market in which capitalist production is predominant.

[It is therefore capitalist production which enables it to achieve results without having to pass through its. . . .]

Thus, in appropriating the positive results of this mode of production, it is able to develop and transform the still archaic form of its rural commune, instead of destroying it. (I would remark in passing that the form of communist property in Russia is the most

---

property existed everywhere in Western Europe, and it everywhere disappeared with the progress of society. Why should it escape the same fate only in Russia?'

modern form of the archaic type which has itself gone through a whole series of evolutionary changes.)

If the admirers of the capitalist system in Russia deny that such a combination is possible, let them prove that Russia had to undergo an incubation period of mechanical production in order to make use of machinery! Let them explain to me how they managed, in just a few days as it were, to introduce the machinery of exchange (banks, credit companies, etc.) which was the work of centuries in the West.

[Although the capitalist system is past its prime in the West, approaching the time when it will be no more than {a social regime} {a regressive form} an 'archaic' formation, its Russian admirers are. . . .]

IV. The archaic or primary formation of our globe itself contains a series of layers from various ages, the one superimposed on the other. Similarly, the archaic formation of society exhibits a series of different types [which together form an ascending series], which mark a progression of epochs. The Russian rural commune belongs to the most recent type in this chain. Already, the agricultural producer privately owns the house in which he lives, together with its complementary garden. This is the first element unknown to older types which dissolves the archaic form [and which may serve as a transition from the archaic form to. . .]. On the other hand, these older types all rest upon natural kinship relations between members of the commune, whereas the type to which the Russian commune belongs is emancipated from that narrow bond. For this very reason, it is therefore capable of broader development. The isolation of the rural communes, the lack of connection between the lives of different communes – this localised microcosm [which would have constituted the natural basis of a central despotism] does not everywhere appear as an immanent characteristic of the primitive type. But wherever it is found, it leads to the formation of a central despotism above the communes. It seems to me that in Russia [the isolated life of the rural communes will disappear] this isolation, originally imposed by the country's huge expanse, may easily be overcome once the government fetters have been removed.

This brings me to the heart of the matter. One cannot disguise from oneself that the archaic type, to which the Russian rural commune belongs, conceals an inner dualism which, given certain historical conditions, may bring on its ruin [its dissolution]. There is common land ownership, but [on the other hand, in practice the work of cultivation or production is done on small peasant plots] each peasant cultivates and works [his plot, reaps the fruits of his field] his field on his own account, like the small Western peasant.

Communal property and small-plot cultivation: this combination [which used to be a (fertilising) element of progress, the development of farming], useful in more distant times, becomes dangerous in our own epoch. On the one hand movable property, playing an ever more important role in agriculture itself, gradually differentiates the commune members in terms of wealth and gives rise to a conflict of interests, above all under state fiscal pressure; on the other hand, the economic superiority of communal property – as the basis of co-operative and combined labour– is lost. It should not be forgotten, however, that the Russian peasants already practise the collective mode in the cultivation of their joint meadows (prairies indivises); that their familiarity with the *artel* relationship[5] could greatly facilitate their transition from small-plot to collective farming; that the physical configuration of the Russian land makes it suitable for large-scale and combined mechanical farming [with the aid of machines]; and finally, that Russian society, having for so long lived at the expense of the rural commune, owes it the initial funds required for such a change. What is involved, of course, is only a gradual change that would begin by creating normal conditions for the commune on its *present* basis.

V. Leaving aside all questions of a more or less theoretical nature, I do not have to tell you that the very existence of the Russian commune is now threatened by a conspiracy of powerful interests. A certain type of capitalism, fostered by the state at the peasants' expense, has risen up against the commune and found an interest in stifling it. The landowners, too, have an interest in forming the more or less well-off peasants into an agricultural middle class, and in converting the poor farmers – that is, the mass – into mere wage labourers – that is to say, cheap labour. How can a commune resist, pounded as it is by state exactions, plundered by trade, exploited by landowners, and undermined from within by usury!

What threatens the life of the Russian commune is neither a

historical inevitability nor a theory; it is state oppression, and exploitation by capitalist intruders whom the state has made powerful at the peasants' expense.

The 'First'[6] Draft

(1) In discussing the genesis of capitalist production, I said [that the secret is] that there is at bottom 'a complete separation of . . . the producer from the means of production' (p. 315, column I, French edition of *Capital*)[7] and that '*the expropriation of the agricultural producer* is the basis of the whole process. Only in England has it been so far accomplished in a radical manner. . . . *But all the other countries of Western Europe* are following the same course' (*loc. cit.*, column II).[8]

Thus I *expressly* restricted the 'historical inevitability' of this process to the countries of Western Europe. Why did I do this? Please refer to the argument in Chapter XXXII;

'The transformation of the individualised and scattered means of production into socially concentrated means of production, the transformation, therefore, of the dwarf-like property of the many into the giant property of the few, this terrible and arduously accomplished expropriation of the mass of the people forms the pre-history of capital. *Private property*, founded on personal labour . . . is supplanted by *capitalist private property*, which rests on exploitation of the labour of others, on wage-labour' (p. 340, column II).[9]

In the last analysis, then, *one form of private property is transformed into another form of private property*; (the Western course). Since the Russian peasant lands have never been *their private property*, how could this tendency be applied to them?

(2) From a historical point of view, only one serious argument has been given for *the inevitable dissolution* of the Russian peasant commune: If we go far back, it is said, a more or less archaic type of communal property may be found everywhere in Western Europe. But with the progress of society it has everywhere disappeared. Why should it escape the same fate only in Russia?

My answer is that, thanks to the unique combination of circumstances in Russia, the rural commune, which is still established on a national scale, may gradually shake off its primitive characteristics and directly develop as an element of collective production on a national scale. Precisely because it is contemporaneous with capitalist production, the rural commune may appropriate all its positive achievements without undergoing its [terrible] frightful vicissitudes. Russia does not live in isolation from the modern world, and nor has it fallen prey, like the East Indies, to a conquering foreign power.

Should the Russian admirers of the capitalist system deny that such a development is *theoretically* possible, then I would ask them the following question. Did Russia have to undergo a long Western-style incubation of mechanical industry before it could make use of machinery, steamships, railways, etc.? Let them also explain how they managed to introduce, in the twinkling of an eye, that whole machinery of exchange (banks, credit companies, etc.) which was the work of centuries in the West.

If, at the time of the emancipation, the rural commune had been initially placed under conditions of normal prosperity, if, moreover, the huge public debt, mostly financed at the peasants' expense, along with the enormous sums which the state (still at the peasants' expense) provided for the 'new pillars of society', transformed into capitalists – if all these expenses had served for the further development of the rural commune, no one would be dreaming today of the 'historical inevitability' of the annihilation of the commune. Everyone would see the commune as the element in the regeneration of Russian society, and an element of superiority over countries still enslaved by the capitalist regime.

[The contemporaneity of capitalist production was not the only factor that could provide the Russian commune with the elements of development.]

Also favourable to the maintenance of the Russian commune (on the path of development) is the fact not only that it is contemporary with capitalist production [in the Western countries], but that it has survived the epoch when the social system stood intact. Today, it faces a social system which, both in Western Europe and the United States, is in conflict with science, with the popular masses, and with the very productive forces that it generates [in short, this social system has become the arena of flagrant antagonisms, conflicts and periodic disasters; it makes clear to the blindest observer that it is a transitory system of production, doomed to be eliminated as soc(iety) returns to. . .]. In short, the rural commune finds it in a state of crisis that will end only when the social system is eliminated through the return of modern societies to the 'archaic' type of communal property. In the words of an American writer[10] who, supported in his work by the Washington government, is not at all to be suspected of revolutionary tendencies, ['the higher plane'] 'the new system' to which modern society is tending 'will be a revival, in a superior form, of an archaic social type.' We should not, then, be too frightened by the word 'archaic'.

But at least we should be thoroughly acquainted with all the historical twists and turns. We know nothing about them.[(c)] In one way or another, this commune perished in the midst of never-ending foreign and intestine warfare. It probably died a violent death when the Germanic tribes came to conquer Italy, Spain, Gaul, and so on. The commune of the archaic type had already ceased to exist. And yet, its *natural vitality* is proved by two facts. Scattered examples survived all the vicissitudes of the Middle Ages and have maintained themselves up to the present day – e.g. in my own home region of Trier. More importantly, however, it so stamped its own features on the commune that supplanted it (a commune in which arable land became private property, while the forests, pastures, waste ground, etc., remained communal property), that Maurer was able to reconstruct the archaic prototype

(c) At this point, the following section is appended to p. 13 of the draft:

The history of the decline of the primitive communities has still to be written (it would be wrong to put them all on the same plane; in historical as in geological formations, there is a whole series of primary, secondary, tertiary and other types). So far, only very rough sketches have been made. Still, the research is sufficiently advanced to warrant the assertion that: (1) the primitive communities had incomparably greater vitality than the Semitic, Greek, Roman and *a fortiori* the modern capitalist societies; and (2) the causes of their decline lie in economic factors which prevented them from going beyond a certain degree of development, and in historical contexts quite unlike that of the present-day Russian commune.

[A number of bourgeois writers – mainly of English extraction, like Sir Henry Maine – above all seek to demonstrate the superiority and sing the praises of capitalist society, the capitalist system. People enamoured of this system, unable to understand the. . .].

One has to be on one's guard when reading the histories of primitive communities written by bourgeois authors. They do not shrink [from anything] even from falsehoods. Sir Henry Maine, for example, who enthusiastically collaborated with the English government in its violent destruction of the Indian communes, hypocritically tells us that all the government's noble efforts to maintain the communes succumbed to the spontaneous power of economic laws!

while deciphering the commune [of more recent origin] of secondary formation. Thanks to the characteristic features inherited from the prototype, the new commune which the Germans introduced into every conquered region became the only focus of liberty and popular life throughout the Middle Ages.

We know nothing of the life of the [Germanic] [rural] [archaic] commune after Tacitus, nor how and when it actually disappeared. Thanks to Julius Caesar, however, we do at least know its point of departure. In Caesar's time, the [arable] land was already distributed on an annual basis – not yet, however, among individual members of a commune, but among the gentes [Geschlechter] and tribes of the [various] Germanic confederations. The agricultural *rural commune* therefore emerged in Germania from a more archaic type; it was the product of spontaneous development rather than being imported ready-made from Asia. It may also be found in Asia – in the East Indies – always as the *final term* or last period of the archaic formation.

If I am [now] to assess the possible destinies [of the 'rural commune'] from a purely theoretical point of view – that is, always supposing conditions of normal life – I must now refer to certain characteristics which differentiate the 'agricultural commune' from the more archaic type.

Firstly, the earlier primitive communities all rested on the natural kinship of their members. In breaking this strong yet narrow tie, the agricultural commune proved more capable of adapting and expanding, and of undergoing contact with strangers.

Secondly, within the commune, the house and its complementary yard were already the farmer's private property, whereas the communal house was one of the material bases of previous communities, long before agriculture was even introduced.

Finally, although the arable land remained communal property, it was periodically divided among the members of the agricultural commune, so that each farmer tilled on his own behalf the various fields allocated to him and individually appropriated their fruits. In the more archaic communities, by contrast, production was a common activity, and only the final produce was distributed among individual members. Of course, this primitive type of collective or co-operative production stemmed from the weakness of the isolated individual, not from socialisation of the means of production.

It is easy to see that the dualism inherent in the 'agricultural commune' may give it a sturdy life: for communal property and all the resulting social relations provide it with a solid foundation, while the privately owned houses, fragmented tillage of the arable land and private appropriation of its fruits all permit a development of individuality incompatible with conditions in the more primitive communities. It is just as evident, however, that the very same dualism may eventually become a source of disintegration. Apart from the influence of a hostile environment, the mere accumulation over time of movable property, beginning with wealth in livestock and even extending to wealth in serfs, combines with the ever more prominent role played by movables in agriculture itself and with a host of other circumstances, inseparable from such accumulation, which would take me too far from the central theme. All these factors, then, serve to dissolve economic and social equality, generating within the commune itself a conflict of interests which leads, first, to the conversion of arable land into private property, and ultimately to the private appropriation of forests, pastures, waste ground, etc., already no more than communal appendages of private property.[(d)] Accordingly, the 'agricultural commune' everywhere presents itself as *the most recent type* of the archaic formation of societies; and the period of the agricultural commune appears in the historical course of Western Europe, both ancient and modern, as a period of transition from communal to private property, from the primary to the secondary formation. But does this mean that the development of the 'agricultural commune' must follow this route in every circumstance [in every historical context]? Not at all. Its constitutive form allows of the following alternative: either the element of private property which it implies gains the upper hand

(d) These considerations reappear in only slightly altered form on p. 12 of the draft: '[Apart from any action by a hostile environment, the gradual development, the growth of movable property belonging not to the commune but to individual members – e.g. wealth in the form of livestock, and sometimes even serfs or slaves. . . . The ever more marked role of movable property within the rural economy, such accumulation may alone serve to dissolve. . . .] Apart from the reaction of any other harmful element, of a hostile environment, the gradual growth of movable property in the hands of individual families – e.g. their wealth in livestock, and sometimes even slaves or serfs – such private accumulation is in the long run sufficient by itself to dissolve the primitive economic and social equality, and to foster at the very heart of the commune a conflict of interests which cuts into communal ownership, first of the arable land, and ultimately of the forests, pastures, waste ground, etc., having already converted them into a *communal appendage* of private property.'

over the collective element, or the reverse takes place. Everything depends upon the historical context in which it is situated. . . . Both solutions are *a priori* possibilities, but each one naturally requires a completely different historical context.

(3) Coming now to the 'agricultural commune' in Russia, I shall leave aside for the moment all the evils which weigh upon it, and only consider the capacities for further development permitted by its constitutive form and its historical context.

Russia is the only European country in which the 'agricultural commune' has maintained itself on a national scale up to the present day. It is not, like the East Indies, the prey of a conquering foreign power. Nor does it live in isolation from the modern world. On the one hand, communal land ownership allows it directly and gradually to transform fragmented, individualist agriculture into collective agriculture [at the same time that the contemporaneity of capitalist production in the West, with which it has both material and intellectual links . . .], and the Russian peasants already practise it in the jointly owned meadows; the physical configuration of the land makes it suitable for huge-scale mechanised cultivation; the peasant's familiarity with the *artel* relationship (*contrat d'artel*)[11] can help him to make the transition from augmented to co-operative labour; and, finally, Russian society, which has for so long lived at his expense, owes him the credits required for such a transition. [To be sure, the first step should be to create normal conditions for the commune *on its present basis*, for the peasant is above all hostile to any abrupt change.] On the other hand, the *contemporaneity* of Western [capitalist] production, which dominates the world market, enables Russia to build into the commune all the positive achievements of the capitalist system, without having to pass under its harsh tribute.

If the spokesmen of the 'new pillars of society' deny that it is *theoretically* possible for the modern rural commune to follow such a path, then they should tell us whether Russia, like the West, was forced to pass through a long incubation of mechanical industry before it could acquire machinery, steamships, railways, and so on. One might then ask them how they managed to introduce, in the twinkling of an eye, the whole machinery of exchange (banks, credit companies, etc.) which was the work of centuries [elsewhere] in the West.

One debilitating feature of the 'agricultural commune' in Russia is inimical to it in every way. This is its isolation, the lack of connection between the lives of different communes. It is not an immanent or universal characteristic of this type that the commune should appear as a *localised microcosm*. But wherever it does so appear, it leads to the formation of a more or less central despotism above the communes. The federation of North Russian republics proves that such isolation, which seems to have been originally imposed by the huge size of the country, was largely consolidated by Russia's political changes of fortune after the Mongol invasion.[12] Today, it is an obstacle that could be removed with the utmost ease. All that is necessary is to replace the '*volost*',[13] a government institution, with a peasant assembly chosen by the communes themselves – an economic and administrative body serving their own interests.

Historically very favourable to the preservation of the 'agricultural commune' through its further development is the fact not only that it is contemporaneous with Western capitalist production [so that it] and therefore able to acquire its fruits without bowing to its *modus operandi*, but also that it has survived the epoch when the capitalist system stood intact. Today it finds that system, both in Western Europe and the United States, in conflict with the working masses, with science, and with the very productive forces which it generates – in short, in a crisis that will end through its own elimination, through the return of modern societies to a higher form of an 'archaic' type of collective ownership and production.

It is understood that the commune would develop gradually, and that the first step would be to place it under normal conditions *on its present basis*.

[The historical situation of the Russian 'rural commune' is without parallel! Alone in Europe, it has preserved itself not as scattered debris (like the rare and curious miniatures of an archaic type that were recently to be found in the West), but as the more or less dominant form of popular life spread over a vast empire. While it has in common land ownership the {natural} basis of collective appropriation, its historical context – the contemporaneity of capitalist production – provides it with ready-made material conditions for huge-scale common labour. It is therefore able to incorporate the positive achievements of the capitalist system, without having to pass under its harsh tribute. The commune may gradually replace fragmented agriculture with large-scale, machine-assisted agriculture particularly suited to the physical configuration of Russia. It may thus become the *direct starting-point* of the economic system towards which modern society is tending; it may open a new chapter that does not begin with its own suicide. Indeed, the first thing to do would be to place it under normal conditions.] [But it is not enough to eliminate the dualism within the rural commune, which it could eliminate by. . . .]

It is confronted, however, by landed property, which controls nearly half the land, and the best at that, not to mention the state holdings. In this respect, the preservation of the 'rural commune' through its further development merges with the general course of Russian society: it is, indeed, the price for its regeneration.

[Even from an] Even from a purely economic point of view, Russia can break out of its agricultural. . . . ? . . . .[c] through the evolution of its rural commune; it would try in vain to find a way out through [the introduction of] English-style capitalised farming, against which [the totality] all the rural conditions of the country would rebel.

[Thus, only a general uprising can break the isolation of the 'rural commune', the lack of connection between the lives of different communes, in short, its existence as a localised microcosm which denies it {any} the historical initiative.]

[Theoretically speaking, then, the Russian 'rural commune' may preserve its land – by developing its base of common land ownership, and by eliminating the principle of private property which it also implies. It may become a *direct starting-point* of the economic system towards which modern society is tending; it may open a new chapter that does not begin with its own suicide; it may reap the fruits with which capitalist production has enriched humanity, without passing through the capitalist regime which, simply in terms of its possible *duration*, hardly counts in the life of society. But it is necessary to descend from pure theory to Russian reality.]

If we abstract from all the evils now weighing down upon the Russian 'rural commune' and merely consider its constitutive form and historical context, it is immediately apparent that one of its fundamental characteristics, common land ownership, forms the

(c) An illegible word: perhaps cul-de-sac. In the 'Third Draft', the word *impasse* appears in the corresponding place.

natural basis of collective production and appropriation. Furthermore, the Russian peasant's familiarity with the *artel*[14] relationship would facilitate the transition from fragmented to collective labour, already practised to some extent in the jointly owned meadows for the drying of grass and other ventures of general interest. If in agriculture proper, however, collective labour is to supplant fragmented labour (the form of private appropriation), then two things are necessary: the economic need for such a transformation; and the material conditions for its realisation.

The economic need would make itself felt in the 'rural commune' as soon as it is placed under normal conditions – that is to say, as soon as its burdens are lifted and its land for cultivation expands to a normal size. The time has passed when Russian agriculture required no more than land and tillers of parcellised holdings armed with rather primitive instruments [and the fertility of the soil]. . . . That time has passed all the more quickly in that the oppression of the farmer has infected and sterilised his fields. He now needs co-operative labour, organised on a large scale. Moreover, since the peasant does not have what is necessary to till his three desyatins, would he be any better off if he had ten times the number of desyatins?[15]

But where is the peasant to find the tools, the fertiliser, the agronomic methods, etc. – all the things required for collective labour? This is precisely where the Russian 'rural commune' is greatly superior to archaic communes of the same type. For, alone in Europe, it has maintained itself on a vast, nationwide basis. It is thus placed within a historical context in which the contemporaneity of capitalist production provides it with all the conditions for co-operative labour. It is in a position to incorporate the positive achievements of the capitalist system, without having to pass under its harsh tribute. The physical configuration of the Russian land is eminently suited to machine-assisted agriculture, organised on a large scale and [in the hands] performed by co-operative labour. As for the initial expenses, both intellectual and material, Russian society owes them to the 'rural commune' at whose expense it has lived for so long and in which it must seek its 'regenerative element'.

The best proof that such a development of the 'rural commune' corresponds to the historical trend of our epoch, is the fatal crisis undergone by capitalist production in those European and American countries where it reached its highest peak. The crisis will come to an end with the elimination of capitalist production and the return of modern society to a higher form of the most archaic type – collective production and appropriation.

(4) [In descending from theory to reality, no one can disguise the fact that the Russian commune now faces a conspiracy by powerful forces and interests. Not only has the state subjected it to ceaseless exploitation, it has also fostered, at the peasant's expense, the domiciliation of a certain part of the capitalist system – stock exchange, bank, railways, trade. . . .]

Life is the first requirement for development, and no one can hide from themselves that, here and now, the life of the 'rural commune' is in peril.

[You are perfectly aware that the very existence of the Russian commune is now threatened by a conspiracy of powerful interests. Overburdened by direct state exactions, fraudulently exploited by intruding capitalists, merchants, etc., and the landed 'proprietors', it is also being undermined by village usurers and the conflict of interests in its midst aroused by the situation in which it has been placed.

In order to expropriate the agricultural producers, it is not necessary to drive them from the land, as happened in England and elsewhere; nor to abolish communal property by some ukase. If you go and take from the peasants more than a certain proportion of the product of their agricultural labour, then not even your gendarmes and your army will enable you to tie them to their fields. In the last years of the Roman Empire some provincial decurions, not peasants but actual landowners, fled their homes, abandoned their land, and even sold themselves into bondage – all in order to be rid of a property that had become nothing more than an official pretext for exerting quite merciless pressure over them.

After the so-called emancipation of the peasantry, the state placed the Russian commune in abnormal economic conditions; and since that time, it has never ceased to weigh it down with the social force concentrated in its hands. Exhausted by tax demands, the commune became a kind of inert matter easily exploited by traders, landowners and usurers. This oppression from without unleashed the conflict of interests already present at the heart of the commune, rapidly developing the seeds of its disintegration. But that is not all. [At the peasant's expense, it grew as in a hothouse those excrescences of the capitalist system that can be most easily acclimatised (the stock exchange, speculation, banks, share companies, railways), writing off their deficits, advancing profits to their entrepreneurs, etc., etc.] At the peasant's expense, the state [lent a hand to] grew in hothouse conditions certain branches of the Western capitalist system which, in no way developing the productive premises of agriculture, are the best suited to facilitate and precipitate the theft of its fruits by unproductive middlemen. In this way, it helped to enrich a new capitalist vermin which is sucking the already depleted blood of the 'rural commune'.

. . . . In short, the state [came forward as middleman] lent a hand in the precocious development of the technical and economic instruments best suited to facilitate and precipitate the exploitation of the farmer – Russia's greatest productive force – and to enrich the 'new pillars of society'.

(5) [One can see at a glance the combination of these hostile forces which are favouring and precipitating the exploitation of the farmers, Russia's greatest productive force.]

[One can see at a glance that unless there is a powerful reaction, this combination of hostile forces will inevitably bring about the ruin of the commune through the simple pressure of events.]

Unless it is broken by a powerful reaction, this combination of destructive influences must naturally lead to the death of the rural commune.

It may be asked, however: why have all these interests (and I include the big government-protected industries) found an advantage in the present situation of the rural commune? Why should they knowingly conspire to kill the goose that lays the golden eggs? Precisely because they feel that 'this present situation' is no longer tenable, and that the present mode of exploiting it [is not tenable either] is therefore no longer in vogue. The land, infected by the farmer's poverty, is already growing sterile. Good harvests [which favourable weather conditions sometimes draw from the land] are matched by periods of famine. Instead of exporting, Russia has to import grain. The average results of the last ten years reveal a level of agricultural production that is not only stagnant but actually declining. For the first time, Russia has to import grain instead of exporting it. And so, there is no longer any time to lose. And so, an end must be made to the situation. The more or less well-off minority of peasants must be formed into a rural middle class, and the majority simply converted into proletarians [into wage-labourers]. – To this end, the spokesmen of the 'new pillars of society' denounce the very evils weighing upon the commune as so many natural symptoms of its decrepitude.

Since so many different interests, particularly the new 'pillars of society' constructed under Alexander II's benevolent empire, find an advantage in *the present situation* of the rural commune, why should they knowingly conspire to bring about its death? Why do their spokesmen denounce the evils weighing upon it as irrefutable proof of its natural decay? Why do they wish to kill the goose that lays the golden eggs? Quite simply, the economic facts, which it would take me too long to analyse, have uncovered the secret that *the present situation of the commune is no longer tenable*, and that, through mere force of circumstances, the present mode of exploiting the popular masses will go out of fashion. Thus, something new is required; and this something new, insinuated in the most diverse forms, always comes down to the abolition of communal property, the formation of the more or less well-off minority of peasants into a rural middle class, and the straightforward conversion of the majority into proletarians.

[One cannot disguise from oneself that] On the one hand the 'rural commune' is almost at its last gasp; on the other, a powerful conspiracy is waiting in the wings to finish it off. To save the Russian commune, there must be a Russian Revolution. For their part, those who hold the political and social power are doing their best to prepare the masses for such a catastrophe. While the commune is being bled and tortured, its lands sterilised and impoverished, the literary flunkeys of the 'new pillars of society' ironically refer to the evils heaped on the commune as if they were symptoms of spontaneous, indisputable decay, arguing that it is dying a natural death and that it would be an act of kindness to shorten its agony. At this level, it is a question no longer of a problem to be solved, but simply of an enemy to be beaten. Thus, it is no longer a theoretical problem; [it is a question to be solved, it is quite simply an enemy to be beaten.] To save the Russian commune, there must be a Russian Revolution. For their part, the Russian government and the 'new pillars of society' are doing their best to prepare the masses for such a catastrophe. If the revolution takes place in time, if it concentrates all its forces [if the intelligent part of Russian society] [if the Russian intelligentsia (*l'intelligence russe*) concentrates all the living forces of the country] to ensure the unfettered rise of the rural commune, the latter will soon develop as a regenerating element of Russian society and an element of superiority over the countries enslaved by the capitalist regime.

The Third Draft

Dear Citizen,

In order to examine in depth the questions raised in your letter of 16 February, I would have to enter into the relevant details and interrupt some urgent work. I do hope, however, that the brief account which I have the honour of sending you will suffice to clear up any misunderstanding about my so-called theory.

(I) In analysing the genesis of capitalist production, I said: 'At the heart of the capitalist system is a complete separation of . . . the producer from the means of production . . . the expropriation of *the agricultural producer* is the basis of the whole process. Only in England has it been accomplished in a radical manner. . . . *But all* the other countries of Western Europe are following the same course.' (*Capital*, French edition, p. 315.)[16]

The 'historical inevitability' of this course is therefore expressly restricted to *the countries of Western Europe*. [Next, the cause.] The reason for this restriction is indicated in the following passage from Ch. XXXII:

> '*Private property*, founded on personal labour . . . which is personally earned . . . is supplanted by *capitalist private property*, which rests on exploitation of the labour of others, on wage-labour.'[17]

In the Western case, then, *one form of private property is transformed into another form of private property*. In the case of the Russian peasants, on the contrary, *their communal property would have to be transformed into private property*. Whether or not one believes that such a transformation is inevitable, the reasons for and against have nothing to do with my analysis of the genesis of the capitalist system. At the very most, it might be inferred that, given the present condition of the great majority of Russian peasants, their conversion into small landowners would merely be a prologue to their swift expropriation.

(II) The most serious argument used against the Russian commune comes down to the following:

If you go back to the origins of Western societies, you will everywhere find communal ownership of the land; with the progress of society, it everywhere gave way to private ownership; it cannot therefore escape the same fate in Russia alone.

I shall consider this line of reasoning only in so far as it [concerns Europe] is based upon European experiences. As regards the East Indies, for example, everyone except Sir H. Maine and his like is aware that the suppression of communal land ownership was nothing but an act of English vandalism which drove the indigenous population backward rather than foward.

Primitive communities are not all cut according to the same pattern. On the contrary, they form a series of social groups which, differing in both type and age, mark successive phases of evolution. One of these types, conventionally known as *the agrarian commune* (*la commune agricole*), also embraces *the Russian commune*. Its equivalent in the West is the very recent *Germanic commune*. This did not yet exist in the time of Julius Caesar, and no longer existed when the Germanic tribes came to conquer Italy, Gaul, Spain, etc. In the time of Julius Caesar, the cultivable land was already distributed on an annual basis among different groups, the *gentes* and the *tribes*, but not yet among the individual families of a commune; probably the land was also worked by groups, in common. In the Germanic lands themselves, this more archaic type of community changed through a natural development into the *agrarian commune* described by Tacitus. After then, however, it fell out of sight, disappearing in the midst of constant warfare and migration. Perhaps it died a violent death. But its natural vitality is proved by two indisputable facts. A few scattered examples of this model survived all the vicissitudes of the Middle Ages and may still be found today – for example, in my home region of Trier. More importantly, however, we find the clear imprint of this 'agrarian commune' so clearly traced on the new commune which emerged from it that Maurer was able to reconstruct the former while working to decipher the latter. The new commune – in which cultivable land is *privately owned* by the producers, while the forests, pastures, waste ground, etc., still remain *communal property* – was introduced by the Germans to all the countries they conquered. Thanks to certain features borrowed from its prototype, it became the only focus of popular life and liberty throughout the Middle Ages.

The 'rural commune' may also be found in Asia, among the Afghans, etc. But it everywhere appears as *the most recent type* – the last word, so to speak, in *the archaic formation* of societies. It was to emphasise this point that I went into some detail concerning the Germanic commune.

We must now consider the most characteristic features differentiating the 'agrarian commune' from the more archaic communities:
(1) All the other communities rest upon blood relations among their members. No one may join unless they are a natural or adopted relative. These communities have the structure of a genealogical tree. The 'agrarian commune' was[f] the first social group of free men not bound together by blood ties.
(2) In the agrarian commune, the house and its complementary yard belong to the individual farmer. By contrast, *communal housing* and *collective habitation* were an economic base of the more primitive communities, long before the introduction of agricultural or pastoral life. To be sure, there are some agrarian communes in which the houses, though no longer sites of collective habitation, periodically change owners. Personal usufruct is thus combined with communal ownership. Such communes, however, still carry their birth-mark, being in a state of transition from a more archaic community to the agrarian commune proper.
(3) The cultivable land, inalienable and common property, is periodically divided among the members of the agrarian commune, so that each on his own behalf works the fields allocated to him and privately appropriates their fruits. In the earlier communities, work was done in common, and after a portion had been set aside for reproduction, the common product was distributed in accordance with consumption needs.

(f) Using a blue pencil, Marx corrected the last sentence and the beginning of this sentence to read as it does above. The original text is as follows: 'These organisms have the structure of a genealogical tree. By cutting the umbilical cord which attached them to nature, the 'agrarian commune' became etc. . . .'

Clearly, the *dualism* inherent in the constitution of the agrarian commune was able to endow it with a vigorous life. Emancipated from the strong yet narrow ties of natural kinship, the communal land ownership and resulting social relations provided a solid foundation; while at the same time, the house and yard as an individual family preserve, together with small-plot farming and private appropriation of its fruits, fostered individuality to an extent incompatible with [the structure] the framework of the more primitive communities.

It is no less evident, however, that this very dualism could eventually turn into the seeds of disintegration. Apart from all the malignant outside influences, the commune bore within its own breast the elements that were poisoning its life. As we have seen, private land ownership had already crept into the commune in the shape of a house with its own country-yard that could become a strong-point for an attack upon communal land. But the key factor was fragmented labour as the source of private appropriation. It gave rise to the accumulation of movable goods such as livestock, money, and sometimes even slaves or serfs. Such movable property, not subject to communal control, open to individual trading in which there was plenty of scope for trickery and chance, came to weigh ever more heavily upon the entire rural economy. Here was the dissolver of primitive economic and social equality. It introduced heterogeneous elements into the commune, provoking conflicts of interest and passion liable to erode communal ownership first of the cultivable land, and then of the forests, pastures, waste ground, etc. Once converted into *communal appendages* of private property, these will also fall in the long run.

As [the most recent and] the latest phase in the [archaic] primitive formation of society, the agrarian commune [naturally represents the transition] is at the same time a phase in the transition to the secondary formation, and therefore in the transition from a society based on communal property to one based on private property. The secondary formation does, of course, include the series of societies which rest upon slavery and serfdom.

Does this mean, however, that the historical career of the agrarian commune is fated to end in this way? Not at all. Its innate dualism admits of an alternative: either its property element will gain the upper hand over its collective element; or else the reverse will take place. Everything depends upon the historical context in which it is located.

Let us, for the moment, abstract from the evils bearing down upon the Russian commune and merely consider its evolutionary possibilities. It occupies a unique situation without any precedent in history. Alone in Europe, it is still the organic, predominant form of rural life in a vast empire. Communal land ownership offers it the natural basis for collective appropriation, and its historical context – the contemporaneity of capitalist production – provides it with the ready-made material conditions for large-scale co-operative labour organised on a large scale. It may therefore incorporate the positive achievements developed by the capitalist system, without having to pass under its harsh tribute. It may gradually replace small-plot agriculture with a combined, machine-assisted agriculture which the physical configuration of the Russian land invites. After normal conditions have been created for the commune in its present form, it may become the direct *starting-point* of the economic system towards which modern society is tending; it may open a new chapter that does not begin with its own suicide.

[It is confronted, however, by landed property, which has in its clutches nearly half the land {the best part, not to mention the state holdings}, and the best part at that. In this respect, the preservation of the rural commune through its further development merges with the general course of Russian society: it is, indeed, the price for its regeneration. {Even from a purely economic point of view. . . .} Russia would try in vain to break out of its impasse through English-style capitalist farming, against which all the social conditions of the country would rebel. The English themselves made similar attempts in the East Indies; they only managed to spoil indigenous agriculture and to swell the number and intensity of famines.]

The English themselves made such attempts in the East Indies; they only managed to spoil indigenous agriculture and to swell the number and intensity of famines.

But what of the anathema which strikes the commune – its isolation, the lack of connection between the lives of different communes, that *localised microcosm* which has so far denied it all historical initiative? It would vanish in the general upheaval of Russian society.[18]

The Russian peasant's familiarity with the *artel* would particularly facilitate the transition from fragmented to co-operative labour – a form which, to some extent [in the jointly owned meadows and a few ventures of general interest], he already applies in such communal activities as tossing and drying the hay. A wholly archaic peculiarity, which is the bugbear of modern agronomists, also points in this direction. If you go to any region in which the cultivable land exhibits a curious dismemberment, giving it the form of a chessboard composed of small fields, you will have no doubt that you are confronted with the domain of a dead agrarian commune. The members, without studying the theory of ground-rent, realised that the same amount of labour expended upon fields with a different natural fertility and location would produce different yields. In order to [secure the same economic benefits] equalise the chances for labour, they therefore divided the land into a number of areas according to natural and economic variations, and then subdivided these areas into as many plots as there were tillers. Finally, everyone received a patch of land in each area. It goes without saying that this arrangement, perpetuated by the Russian commune to this day, cuts across agronomic requirements [whether farming is on a collective or a private, individual basis]. Apart from other disadvantages, it compels a dispersion of strength and time. [But it has great advantages as the starting-point for collective farming. Extend the land on which the peasant works, and he will reign supreme.] Still, it does favour [as a starting-point] the transition to collective farming, however refractory to the objective it may appear at first sight. The small plot. . . .

The Fourth Draft

8 March 1881

Dear Citizen,

A nervous complaint which has periodically affected me for the last ten years has prevented me from answering your letter of 16 February [which you did the honour of sending me].

I regret that I am unable to give you a concise account for publication [of the problems] of the question which [you kindly] you did me the honour of asking. Two months ago, I already promised a text on the same subject to the St. Petersburg committee.[19] Still, I hope that a few lines will suffice to leave you in no doubt [about the conclusions that have been] about the way in which my so-called theory has been misunderstood.

(1) The analysis in *Capital* therefore provides [nothing] no reasons that might be used either for or against the vitality of the Russian commune.

[My personal opinion concerning the Russian commune, which I have studied for many years in the original sources, is as follows.]

[After studying (for many years) the Russian commune in the original sources for.]

[In order to have a definitive view on the possible destinies of the Russian commune, one must have more than vague historical analogies. One must study it.] [I have studied it for many.] [I have made a study of it.]

[My personal opinion on the possible fate of the Russian commune.]

The special studies I have made of it, including a search for original source-material, have [led me to the conclusion] convinced me that the commune is the natural [starting-point] fulcrum for social regeneration in Russia [for the regeneration of Russian society]. But [the first step must, of course, be to place it in conditions . . .] in order that it might function as such, the harmful influences assailing it on all sides must first be eliminated, and it must then be assured the conditions for spontaneous development.

Karl Marx: The reply to Zasulich

8 March 1881
41, Maitland Park Road, London N.W.

Dear Citizen,

A nervous complaint which has periodically affected me for the last ten years has prevented me from answering sooner your letter of 16 February. I regret that I am unable to give you a concise account for publication of the question which you did me the honour of raising. Some months ago, I already promised a text on the same subject to the St. Petersburg Committee.[20] Still, I hope that a few lines will suffice to leave you in no doubt about the way in which my so-called theory has been misunderstood.

In analysing the genesis of capitalist production, I said:

> At the heart of the capitalist system is a complete separation of . . . . the producer from the means of production . . . *the expropriation of the agricultural producer* is the basis of the whole process. Only in England has it been accomplished in a radical manner. . . . *But all the other countries of Western Europe* are following the same course. (*Capital*, French edition, p. 315.)[21]

The 'historical inevitability' of this course is therefore *expressly* restricted to *the countries of Western Europe*. The reason for this restriction is indicated in Ch. XXXII: '*Private property*, founded upon personal labour . . . is supplanted by *capitalist private property*, which rests on exploitation of the labour of others, on wage-labour.' (*loc. cit.*, p. 340).[22]

In the Western case, then, *one form of private property is transformed into another form of private property*. In the case of the Russian peasants, however, *their communal property* would have to be *transformed into private property*.

The analysis in *Capital* therefore provides no reasons either for or against the vitality of the Russian commune. But the special study I have made of it, including a search for original source-material, has convinced me that the commune is the fulcrum for social regeneration in Russia. But in order that it might function as such, the harmful influences assailing it on all sides must first be eliminated, and it must then be assured the normal conditions for spontaneous development.

I have the honour, dear Citizen, to remain
Yours sincerely,
Karl Marx

Editor's Notes

1. To avoid confusion the designation of drafts as 'first', 'second', etc. follows the usage of the original publication of 1924 (and since repeated by all the other publications to date). We actually present

them in a different order, that in which they were most probably written, i.e. 'second', 'first', 'third' and 'fourth'. For the discussion on which that re-ordering is based, see S. Hinada, 'On the meaning in our time of the drafts of Marx's letter to Vera Zasulich (1881)', Tokyo, 1975. Also, see the article by H. Wada in Part I above (pp. 64–5).

The division into text and page footnotes follows that of the original 1924 publication. The square brackets in the text indicate passages deleted by Marx. An arrowed bracket indicates shorter passages deleted first within sections which were then deleted in total.

2. Translated directly from Marx's own quotations which follow the French edition of *Capital*, Volume 1 (published in 1872). The equivalent passage in the broadly available Penguin edition of *Capital* (which follows, however, the 4th German edition of 1890 and which differs from the text Marx had preferred) can be found in Karl Marx, *Capital*, Harmondsworth, 1976, Volume 1, p. 876.
3. *Ibid.*
4. *Ibid.*, p. 927.
5. *Artel* (Russian): a team working jointly, usually under an elected leader and sharing out its net proceeds. A pre-industrial work-association, a co-operative run along traditional lines, often used by the Russian rural craftsmen and by the peasant-workers' gangs operating outside their villages, e.g. a group of seasonal construction workers, coming from the same place, under a contract to build a house in the provincial town. The term '*artel* relationship' is used broadly to refer to all types of traditional co-operation in production, ownership and landholding, inclusive of the peasant land commune (*obshchina*).
6. See Note 1 above.
7. Cf. Marx, *op. cit.*, pp. 874–5.
8. *Ibid.*
9. *Ibid.*, p. 928.
10. Marx is here referring to L. Morgan, *Ancient Society*, London, 1887, p. 552.
11. See Note 5 above.
12. Marx referred here to the city-states of Russia, of which the Great Novgorod in the North West was the most prominent by its riches and by an elaborate self-government.
13. *Volost* (Russian): in the period in question, a territorial subdivision of specifically peasant rural administration, incorporating a number of peasant communes. A *volost* was run by peasant elders and local magistrates closely controlled by the state officialdom. Only the peasants came under its jurisdiction.
14. See Note 5 above.
15. A Russian measure of land area = 1.09 ha = 2.7 acres.
16. See Note 7 above.
17. Cf. Marx, *op. cit.*, p. 928.
18. An additional footnote was introduced here by D. Ryazanov, attempting to decipher a single deleted passage, but failing to establish any consistent sentences within it.

19. Marx refers to the Executive Committee of the People's Will organisation. For an interpretation which doubts that this approach to Marx by the Executive Committee was actually made, see the article by Wada, p. 68, this volume. B. Nikolaevskii has suggested that the 'first' and 'second' drafts presented were actually unrelated to Marx's letter to Zasulich and formed part of preparations for a separate pamphlet concerning the Russian peasant commune at the request of the Executive Committee of People's Will (B. Nikolaevskii, 'Legenda ob 'utaenmom pis'me' Marksa', *Sotsialisticheskii Vestnik*, 1957, vol. 37, no. 5 (705), p. 96), but the evidence available seems to negate that view.
20. *Ibid.*
21. See Note 7 above.
22. *Ibid.*

David Ryazanov: The discovery of the drafts (1924)[1]

Already in 1911, when I was involved in arranging the Lafargue collection of Marx's papers, I came across a number of octavo-size letters written in his small handwriting. They were full of deletions, and contained various insertions and addenda also mostly crossed out. As soon as I had completed the initial classification, I realized that I was dealing with a draft, or rather several drafts, of the reply to Zasulich's letter of 16 February 1881. One of the drafts bore the date 8 March 1881, and it was reasonable to assume that this had been the basis for the final reply.

I then wrote to Plekhanov, only to be told that no reply to Zasulich's letter was in existence. Using various third persons, I asked the same question of Zasulich herself, but the result was no more favourable. I am not sure whether I also addressed myself to Axelrod. Probably I did, and probably I received the same negative answer.

And yet I remembered that during my stay in Switzerland in 1883, I had heard stories, sometimes of a quite fantastic nature, about an exchange of letters between the Emancipation of Labour (*Osvobozhdenie Truda*) group and Marx concerning the Russian peasant commune. There had even been thoroughly implausible anecdotes about a clash between Plekhanov and Marx in which the former had opposed, and the latter defended, commune property.

In the obituary of Marx published in the 1889 *People's Will Yearbook* (*Kalendar Narodnoi Voli*), the author recalled 'how readily Marx decided, in the last year of his life, to write a special pamphlet for Russia at the invitation of the St. Petersburg Committee (as he mentioned in a letter to Zasulich), dealing with a question of such burning interest for Russian socialists: namely, the possible development of our peasant commune'.[2]

The early drafts, however, involved a reply to Vera Zasulich's letter of 16 February 1881; while the *Yearbook* referred to 'the last year' of Marx's life. The categorically negative answers from Plekhanov and Zasulich forced me to conclude, wrongly as it turned out, that the letter from Marx mentioned in the *Yearbook* might have been written on another occasion.[(a)]

When I was in Berlin in the summer of 1923, B. Nikolaevskii informed me that a letter by Marx had been found in Axelrod's archive.[(b)] A comparison of this letter to Zasulich with the various drafts showed that it exactly corresponded to the one dated 8 March 1881. All that was missing from the draft were some quotations from *Capital*, the address and Marx's signature. I could then have had my draft published, but I preferred to wait until the latest editors had brought out the letter.

This happened quite soon. In the second volume of a Russian language edition of P.B. Axelrod's archive, which appeared in Berlin under the title *Material on the History of the Revolutionary Movement*, Marx's letterr to Zasulich was published in the French original (alongside a facsimile) together with an introduction by Nikolaevskii. A German translation may be found in Nikolaevskii's article, 'Marx und das russische Problem' (*Die Gesellschaft*, Year 1, no. 4, July 1924, pp. 359–66).

The editor stated that he still did not know 'the true reasons why this letter from Marx fell into oblivion, dealing as it did with a question of such burning interest to Russian revolutionary circles'.[3] The letter was 'so thoroughly forgotten that P.B. Axelrod, for example, who spent the winter of 1880–81 in Romania (the period covering the letter's arrival), could not recall the slightest thing about a letter from V.E. Zasulich or a conversation that he undoubtedly instigated, nor any other point of relevance.'[4(c)]

We have seen that Plekhanov and the addressee, V. Zasulich, forgot the letter just as thoroughly. It must be said that, precisely in

(a) (Russian text) I had to delay for various reasons my initial plan to publish the drafts despite this failure [to establish what happened to the letter. TS]. I intended to do so last year as announced in my booklet concerning the Marx Engels Institute but some unexpected circumstances led to yet another delay in the publication.

(b) (Russian text) I was permitted to photograph it [Marx's letter. TS] on the condition that I shall have it published only after it is issued in print in Berlin by the 'Russian Revolutionary Archives' [the major historical journal of the Mensheviks in exile in the 1920s. TS].

(c) (Russian text). Apparently the real reasons for the lack of publication of Marx's letter concerning questions which were so vital within Russian revolutionary circles were unknown to the letter's contemporary publishers.

view of the exceptional interest which the letter must have aroused, such forgetfulness has a very strange quality. For specialized psychologists, it is probably one of the most interesting examples of the remarkable inadequacy with which our memory functions.

Without doubt, Marx must have been strongly impressed by the Zasulich letter: by its uncommon naivety, straightforwardness and theoretical helplessness; by the way in which it placed the whole question of the peasant commune on a socio-ethical basis; and by the torment, apparent on every line, which the fate of the peasant commune caused Zasulich and her comrades (the contents must surely have been known to Plekhanov and Deich[5]). All this explains why Marx hastened to send an immediate reply.

As may be seen from the drafts printed below, he originally intended to reply in detail. Nikolaevskii is therefore clearly wrong in thinking that Marx's dissatisfaction with the Black Repartition group (*Chernyi Peredel*) held him back from giving a frank and detailed reply. His own position on the Black Repartitionists would not have influenced him even if he had known that Zasulich belonged to this party. Neither L. Hartmann nor N. Morozov, who kept Marx informed about the split in the Land and Liberty organization, could have had a disparaging word to communicate about Zasulich. Thus I stick to the view already expressed in my lectures on Marx and Engels: namely, that it was only Marx's undermined capacity for work (signs of which may be found in the drafts) which prevented him from replying in as much detail as he had originally intended.[6] Another restraining factor, to which he alludes in the letter, may have been his promise to the Executive Committee of People's Will. At the very least, this letter was a way of putting off the Black Repartitionists[(d)] – above all, for the period in which Zasulich's letter was sent, between the first and second numbers of the *Black Repartition* journal. Marx categorically stated that 'the peasant commune is the fulcrum for social regeneration in Russia', but that 'the harmful influences assailing it on all sides must first be eliminated, and it must then be assured the normal conditions for spontaneous development'. Above all else, then, absolutism must be overthrown. His reply was in any case more definite than the one he gave in the foreword to the Russian edition of the *Communist Manifesto*, where the only necessary condition for

(d) (Russian text) 'Anyway, this letter is ambivalent in so far as the Black Repartition is concerned.'

the conversion of the peasant commune into a starting-point of communist development is that the Russian revolution should take place at the same time as a workers' revolution in the West.

Bernstein is closer to the mark when he says[7] that Marx and Engels 'occasionally refrained from expressing their scepticism, so as not to disappoint too much the Russian revolutionaries, who, as they knew, attached great significance to the question of commune property.' In the drafts published below, this scepticism is quite clearly articulated.

We should note that Engels had a few years earlier replied to Tkachev, who, for all his Jacobinism, showed no less hope in the peasant commune than the supporters of People's Will and of the Black Repartition.

> It is apparent that communal property is long past its heyday in Russia, and to all appearances is moving towards its dissolution. The possibility cannot be denied, however, that this social form will be led to a higher one – so long as it survives until the conditions are ripe for such a change and it proves capable of developing in such a way that the peasants no longer divide up the land, but till it in common.[c] In this case, Russian peasants may proceed to the higher form, without having to go through the intermediate stage of parcellized bourgeois property. But this can only happen if, before communal ownership is completely destroyed, a victorious proletarian revolution in Western Europe provides the Russian peasant with the conditions requisite for such a transition, particularly the material conditions which he requires in order to accomplish the revolution of his whole system of agriculture. It is thus a sheer bounce for Mr. Tkachev to say that the Russian peasants, though 'property-owners', are 'nearer to socialism' than the propertyless workers of Western Europe. Quite the contrary. If anything can still save Russian communal ownership and enable it to change into a new and truly viable form, it is a proletarian revolution in Western Europe.[8]

The qualified conclusion of Marx and Engels was taken up by Plekhanov in *Socialism and Political Struggle* and by V. Zasulich in

(c) (Russian text) 'Peasants cultivate the land no longer separately but in common.'

her preface to the Russian translation of *Socialism: Utopian and Scientific.*

Less than two years after her letter to Marx, Vera Zasulich reached the conclusion that the disintegration of the peasant commune was becoming an unstoppable process. In the above-mentioned preface she wrote as follows:

> This process, which points to the disintegration of the peasant commune, is every year becoming more evident to the students of peasant life. The *kulak*, forcing his way into every description of peasant life, appears as the most tangible sign and the strongest, incontestable factor. He undermines all the foundations of social being; turns to his account all the elements of customs and norms acquired during the *mir*'s[9] centuries-long praxis and which ensured that the affairs of the *mir* would be justly conducted; draws advantage from such institutions as the agrarian banks which were to be directed precisely against the *kulak*; and would even, if circumstances allowed, profit from the expansion of peasant land holdings. He can be destroyed only if the possibility of unequal land-ownership is itself eliminated. Hence there is no way of escaping the progressive dissolution of communal property, the accumulation of capital, and the extension of large-scale industry. Russia's immediate future belongs to the growth of capitalism – but only its immediate future. For capitalism will hardly outlive the final dissolution of the peasant commune. Russia's whole economic development is too closely bound up with the development of Western Europe, and there the days of capitalism are already numbered. Socialist revolution in the West would also spell the end of capitalism in the East, and then what is left of communal property may prove to be of great service to Russia.[10]

We have seen that the first Russian Marxists themselves drew all the necessary logical conclusions from Marx's and Engels's qualified judgment. This view was reflected in the first programme of the Emancipation of Labour group, and in Plekhanov's book *Our Differences.* It was only later – above all in Plekhanov's work after 1890 – that the position on the peasant communes was sharply altered, and a sceptical approach to the possibilities of the peasant commune changed into a sharply negative attitude.

We do not intend to make a lengthy analysis of Marx's own viewpoint. In spite of the fact that we are dealing only with drafts, they are of such great interest for the study of Marx's and also Engels's view on the development of communal property that we put off dealing with them until the publication of other unpublished works by Marx and Engels on East Indian and Germanic landed property. We need hardly mention the significance of the following drafts as a means of acquainting us with Marx's methods of work.

In spite of the many repetitions, I decided for this very reason to give all four of Marx's drafts in full, as well as all the deleted passages in so far as they could be deciphered, and in so far as they exhibit even a slight variation from one another and from the unerased text. Two of the drafts, the first and second, are extremely jumbled; some pages were at first sight so chaotic that it seemed impossible to unravel them. There are numerous deletions, within which unerased words can sometimes be made out only with considerable difficulty; inserted lines which run into one another; chaotically written additions; further inserted material; repetitions, often word for word, within the same draft – this whole lack of outward form made it necessary for me to edit the raw material in such a way as to group together parts with a common theme (where Marx himself did not indicate any order). In addition, I have placed a few of these in footnotes.

Although the drafts display such outward confusion, it was not especially difficult to prepare the texts once they had been deciphered. For the study of the unfinished construction is itself plainly visible in the first, and outwardly most confused, of the drafts, where Marx's train of thought is carried to the end. Passing from an interrogation about the future of the Russian rural commune (I) to a consideration of the supposedly historical inevitability of its ruination (II), the draft goes on to describe the commune's specific historical environment (III) and its present, highly intricate crisis (IV) before it reaches the final conclusion: the necessity of revolution (V).

In deciphering Marx's manuscript, I was helped by N. Bukharin in Vienna in 1913. This work was completed by E. Smirnov and E. Czóbel.[f]

(f) (Russian text). The translation reproduces exactly the order of Marx's manuscript. The same is true of the unfinished phrases of the text.

Editor's Notes

1. For biographical details concerning Ryazanov see the article by Sanders, The Russian Scene, (p. 176). At the time when the Introduction was written, Ryzanov was Director of the Marx-Engels-Lenin Institute in Moscow, i.e. the *ex officio* chief spokesman of Marxist studies in the USSR.

   The Introduction was published more or less simultaneously in German and in Russian, respectively, *Marx-Engels Archiv*, Volume 1, Frankfurt, 1924, and *Arkhiv K. Marksa i F. Engel'sa*, Volume 1, Moscow, 1924. It was translated from the German in a somewhat longer version by Patrick Camillar. When the Russian text added to or departed from the German one a page footnote was introduced to indicate it.
2. For considerable doubts concerning that story see the article by Wada (p. 68).
3. For biographical details concerning Nikolaevskii see p. 176.
4. P.B. Axelrod was a leading Marxist writer and activist, co-founder of the Black Repartition, then of the Emancipation of Labour Group and eventually of the ISKRA and RSDWP and leading spokesman of the Menshevik wing of it.
5. L.G. Deutsch, a leading revolutionary activist since the 1870s, was co-founder of the Black Repartition, the Emancipation of Labour Group and the RSDWP.
6. The Russian text used a somewhat stronger expression to describe the limitations of Marx's capacity to work, namely *nadorvannaya*, ie. 'torn'.
7. In *Minuvshie Gody*, no. 11, St. Petersburg, 1908, p. 17.
8. K. Marx and F. Engels, *Selected Works*, Moscow, 1973, vol. 2, p. 395.
9. A synonym of Russian peasant commune or communal assembly. See p. 125, fn. 5.
10. For biographical details see p. 178.

Karl Marx: A letter to the Editorial Board of Otechestvennye Zapiski[1]

Dear Sir,

The author of the article 'Karl Marx on trial before Mr. Zhukovski' is obviously a clever man, and if, in my account of primitive accumulation, he had found a single passage to support his conclusions, he would have quoted it. For want of such a passage, he is forced to seize upon an incidental text – a kind of polemic against a Russian 'man of letters' appended to the first German edition of *Capital*.[2] My reproach against this writer had been that he discovered the Russian commune not in Russia but in the book by Haxthausen, a Prussian government councillor; and that, in his hands, the Russian commune merely served as an argument to show that old, rotten Europe must be regenerated through the victory of pan-Slavism. My assessment of this writer may be right and it may be wrong, but it cannot in any event supply the key to my views on the efforts by the Russian people to find for their motherland a road of development different from the one along which Western Europe has proceeded and still proceeds ('*russkikh lyudei naiti dlya svoego otechestva put' razvitiya, otlichnyi ot togo, kotorym shla i idet zapadnaya Evropa*'), etc.[3]

In the afterword to the second German edition of *Capital* – which the author of the article on Mr. Zhukovski knows, because he quotes it – I speak of a 'great Russian scholar and critic' with the high regard he deserves.[4] In an outstanding series of articles, he discussed whether Russia, as its liberal economists would have it, must begin by destroying the rural commune in order to pass on to the capitalist regime, or whether, on the contrary, it may develop its own historical foundations and thus, without experiencing all the tortures of this regime, nevertheless appropriate all its fruits. He, himself, pronounces for the second solution.[5] And my respected critic would have had at least as much reason to infer from my regard for this 'great Russian scholar and critic' that I shared his views on this matter, as to conclude from my polemic against the pan-Slavist 'man of letters' that I rejected them.

Finally, as I do not like to leave 'anything to guesswork', I shall be direct and to the point. In order to reach an informed judgment on Russia's economic development, I learnt Russian and then for many years studied official and other publications relating to the question. I have come to the conclusion that if Russia continues along the path it has followed since 1861, it will lose the finest chance ever offered by history to a people and undergo all the fateful vicissitudes of the capitalist regime.

II

The chapter on primitive accumulation claims no more than to trace the path by which, in Western Europe, the capitalist economic order emerged from the womb of the feudal economic order. It therefore presents the historical movement which, by divorcing the producers from their means of production, converted the former into wage-labourers (proletarians in the modern sense of the word) and the owners of the latter into capitalists. In this history 'all revolutions are epoch-making that serve as a lever for the advance of the emergent capitalist class, above all those which, by stripping great masses of people of their traditional means of production and existence, suddenly hurl them on to the labour-market. But the basis of this whole development is the expropriation of the agricultural producers. Only in England has it so far been accomplished in a radical manner . . . . but all the countries of Western Europe are following the same course' etc. (*Capital*, French edition, p. 315). At the end of the chapter, the historical tendency of production is said to consist in the fact that it 'begets its own negation with the inexorability presiding over the metamorphoses of nature'; that it has itself created the elements of a new economic order, giving the greatest impetus both to the productive forces of social labour and to the all-round development of each individual producer; that capitalist property, effectively already resting upon a collective mode of production, cannot but be transformed into social property. I furnish no proof at this point, for the good reason that this statement merely summarizes in brief the long expositions given previously in the chapters on capitalist production.

Now, what application to Russia could my critic make of this historical sketch? Only this: if Russia is tending to become a capitalist nation like the nations of Western Europe – and in the last few years she has been at great pains to achieve this – she will not succeed without first transforming a large part of her peasants into proletarians; subsequently, once brought into the fold of the capitalist regime, she will pass under its pitiless laws like other profane peoples. That is all. But it is too little for my critic. He absolutely insists on transforming my historical sketch of the genesis of capitalism in Western Europe into a historico-philosophical theory of the general course fatally imposed on all peoples, whatever the historical circumstances in which they find themselves placed, in order to arrive ultimately at this economic formation which assures the greatest expansion of the productive forces of social labour, as well as the most complete development of man. But I beg his pardon. That is to do me both too much honour and too much discredit. Let us take an example.

At various points in *Capital* I allude to the fate that befell the plebeians of ancient Rome. They were originally free peasants, each tilling his own plot on his own behalf. In the course of Roman history they were expropriated. The same movement that divorced them from their means of production and subsistence involved the formation not only of large landed property but also of big money capitals. Thus one fine morning there were, on the one side, free men stripped of everything but their labour-power, and on the other, ready to exploit their labour, owners of all the acquired wealth. What happened? The Roman proletarians became, not wage-labourers, but an idle mob more abject than those who used to be called 'poor whites' in the southern United States; and what opened up alongside them was not a capitalist but a slave mode of production. Thus events of striking similarity, taking place in different historical contexts, led to totally disparate results. By studying each of these developments separately, and then comparing them, one may easily discover the key to this phenomenon. But success will never come with the master-key of a general historico-philosophical theory, whose supreme virtue consists in being supra-historical.

Editor's Notes

1. For the context and for the controversy concerning the exact date when the letter was written, see the article by Wada (pp. 56–60). The translation was made by Patrick Camiller from the French original as published in K. Marx and F. Engels, *Ausgewählte Briefe*, Berlin, 1953, pp. 365–8.
2. The article was written by N. Mikhailovskii. The 'man of letters' referred to was A. Herzen; his name was left out to avoid interference by the Russian censorship. For biographical deatils, see pp. 174–5. See also Wada, *op. cit.*
3. Quoted in Russian by Marx from the article by Mikhailovskii he debates.
4. A reference to N. Chernyshevskii, once again put indirectly to avoid interference by the Russian censorship. For biographical details, see pp. 181-2. See also Wada, *op. cit. op. cit.*
5. See extracts from Chernyshevskii in Part III, pp. 00–00.

Karl Marx and Friedrich Engels: Preface to the Second Russian edition of the Manifesto of the Communist Party[1]

The first Russian edition of the *Manifesto of the Communist Party*, translated by Bakunin, was published early in the 1860s by the *Kolokol* press.[2] At the time, the West could see no more than a literary curiosity in this, the *Russian* edition of the *Manifesto*. Such a view would be impossible today.

The limited compass of the proletarian movement in December 1847 is most clearly shown by the final section of the *Manifesto*: 'Position of the communists in relation to the various opposition parties in various countries'. Missing here are precisely Russia and the United States. It was the time when Russia constituted the last great reserve of wholesale European reaction; and when the United States was absorbing Europe's surplus proletarian forces through immigration. Both countries supplied Europe with raw materials, as well as being market-outlets for its industrial goods. Thus, in one way or another, both countries were then pillars of the existing European order.

How completely different things are today! It was precisely European immigration which fitted North America for huge-scale agricultural production, whose competition is shaking European landed property, both big and small, to its very foundations. It also enabled the United States to exploit its colossal industrial resources, with an energy and on a scale which must shortly break the industrial monopoly hitherto enjoyed by Western Europe and particularly England. Both these circumstances react in a revolutionary way upon America itself. The farmers' small and medium-size landholdings, which underpin the whole political system, are gradually succumbing to the competition of giant farms; while a massive proletariat and a fabulous concentration of capitals are developing for the first time in the industrial regions.

Now for Russia! During the 1848–49 revolution, not only European princes but also European bourgeois discovered Russian intervention as their only deliverance from the just-awakening proletariat. The Tsar was proclaimed chief of European reaction. Today he is in Gatchina,[3] a prisoner-of-war of the revolution, and Russia forms the vanguard of revolutionary action in Europe.

The *Communist Manifesto* set out to announce the inevitably approaching dissolution of modern bourgeois property. In Russia, however, we find that the fast-blossoming capitalist swindle and newly-developing bourgeois landed property stand face to face with peasant communal ownership of the greater part of the land. This poses the question: Can the Russian *obshchina*,[4] a form, albeit heavily eroded, of the primitive communal ownership of the land, pass directly into the higher, communist form of communal ownership? Or must it first go through the same process of dissolution which marks the West's historical development?

Today there is only one possible answer. If the Russian revolution becomes the signal for proletarian revolution in the West, so that the two complement each other, then Russia's peasant communal land-ownership may serve as the point of departure for a communist development.

Karl Marx F. Engels[5]

London, 21 January 1882

Editor's Notes

1. Written at the request of P. Lavrov (see p. 174)., It was first published in Russian in the issue no. 8-9 of *Narodnaya Volya*, the People's Will clandestine journal dated 5 February 1882. First German publication in *Der Sozialdemokrat*, no. 16 (April 1882). The text has been translated by Patrick Camiller from the German original in K. Marx and F. Engels, *Werke*, Berlin, 1962, vol. 19, pp. 295–6.
2. *Kolokol* (*The Bell*), a paper of the Russian radical opposition published abroad 1857-1869 by A. Herzen (see p. 174).
3. A palace near St. Petersburg adopted for a time as the residence of Alexander III out of fear of further attacks by the People's Will.
4. I.e. Russian peasant commune, written in Russian, transliterated into Latin script by the authors.
5. The signature kept as in the original, i.e. Engels using his initial only.

Karl Marx: Confessions[1]

Your favourite virtue – Simplicity
Your favourite virtue in man – Strength
Your favourite virtue in women – Weakness
Your own chief characteristic – Singleness of Purpose
Your idea of happiness – To fight
Your idea of misery – Submission
The vice you excuse most – Gullibility
The vice you detest most – Servility
Your pet aversion – Martin Tupper[a]
Favourite occupation – Bookworming
Poet – Shakespeare, Aeschylus, Goethe
Prose writer – Diderot
Hero – Spartacus, Kepler
Heroine – Gretchen
Flower – Daphne
Colour – Red
Name – Laura, Jenny
Dish – Fish
Favourite maxim – *Nihil humanum a me alienum puto.*[b]
Favourite motto – *De omnibus dubitandum.*[c]

(a) Victorian poet of fame, since forgotten, who was best known to his generation for trivial dialectic moralising in blank verse.
(b) Nothing human is alien to me.
(c) Doubt everything. (Adopted as the motto of our publication.)

Editor's Note

1. In an autobiographical aside within Marx's biography, we are told by David Ryazanov that while surveying Marx's papers in the summer of

1910 at the house of Laura Lafargue, he expressed his sorrow at the fact that there is so little 'subjective' material within the documents he was working upon. Laura Lafargue then suddenly remembered that both she and her sister Jenny had asked their father, Karl Marx, to answer a set of questions as part of the game of 'Confessions', which was popular at the time. She then proceeded to look for that paper, managed to locate it and handed over its copy to Ryazanov. Ryazanov has suggested that it was probably written in the early 1860s, but a similar fragment since discovered, written by Engels probably at the same time, was dated April 1868 by its publishers (K. Marks i F. Engels's *Sochineniya*, Moskov, 1960, vol. 16, p. 581). Ryazanov's comment on Marx's 'Confessions' was that while 'the framework is one of jest . . . a good deal of the content is earnest after all.' He has proceeded to substantiate that view in a whole section of his biographical sketch of Marx.

D. Ryazanoff, *Karl Marx: Man, Thinker and Revolutionist*, London, 1927, pp. 268-82 (Marx's text and Ryazanov's comment quoted appear on page 269).

Marx after Capital*: a biographical note (1867-1883)*

Derek Sayer

This biographical note takes the extremely unliterary form of a bald chronological summary of Marx's life from 1867, the year Volume I of *Capital* was published, until his death. It does not detail all known facts about Marx's life during this period, but concentrates on his political activities and intellectual work. Within this there is a further concentration on matters most relevant to the themes of this book, notably Marx's relations with Russia and Russian revolutionaries. However, most of Marx's speeches and all but the most ephemeral of his writings during these years are cited, with the important exception of his correspondence, which is only skimmed. This note also attempts, albeit schematically, to document Marx's day-to-day engagement with the issues, parties and people of the socialist and popular movements of the time. The starting-point, 1867, is somewhat arbitrary, and no imputation of any radical break in his thought in that year is intended. I list major sources used at the end. Where there were discrepancies the responsibility for judgment (and therefore error) was mine.

1867

The German Socialist leaders Bebel and Liebknecht elected to Reichstag. Bismarck elected Chancellor of the German Bund. The Irish Fenian revolutionaries, the 'Manchester Martyrs', executed.

January Marx in great financial difficulty and ill with carbuncles and insomnia. Work on *Capital* I. Speech on Poland, in which he argues that the 1861 Emancipation merely facilitated governmental centralisation in Russia: 'It did not free them [the serfs] from Asiatic barbarism, for civilisation is a process of centuries' (22nd). *February* Marx sends denial to *Zeitung für Norddeutschland* of that paper's report of a proposed continental tour by him to agitate on behalf of a Polish insurrection (18th). Talk to German Workers Educational Association on wage labour and capital, and social conditions in Germany: the German proletariat 'will be forced by its geographical situation to declare war on oriental barbarism, for it is from Asia that the whole reaction against the West has come' (28th). Around this time helps Eccarius on 'A working man's refutation of J.S. Mill'. *March* Included in General Council (GC) deputation to procure financial aid for striking Paris metal workers from London Trade Unions (5th). *April* Finishes MS of *Capital* and takes it to Hamburg for printing (10th), staying in Germany with Kugelmann until mid-May. *May* Seeks French translator for *Capital*. Tells Meissner, his publisher, that Books 2 and 3 of *Capital* will be ready by autumn and Book 4 by the winter. Returns to London, with proofs of Volume I (19th). Visit to Engels in Manchester (*c*. 21st, to 2nd June). *June* On Kugelmann's suggestion writes 'didactic' Appendix on 'Form of value' for *Capital* (17th-22nd), 'not only for philistines, but also for the young people, eager for knowledge' (22nd). *July* Edits, with Lafargue, GC address inviting affiliates to participate in Lausanne Congress of International (IWA) in September. Chosen for GC delegation to annual conference of London Trade Unions (16th). Speech at GC refuting press claims that Trade Unions were holding back the development of the iron industry (23rd, published 27th). Preface to *Capital* (25th). *August* Speech at GC on forthcoming peace congress in Geneva attacks Russia (13th). Corrected proofs of *Capital* go to Meissner (16th). Starts work on Volume 2, particularly on turnover of fixed capital (*c*. 24th). Sends editor of *Courier Français* criticism of his paper's position on Russia (27th). Instructs Borkheim for his anti-Russian speech at the Geneva Peace Congress (*c*. 29th). *September Capital* published in first edition of 1000 copies (*c*. 2nd). Marx sends *Courier Français* news item on government admissions of mass poverty in Prussia (4th). Second IWA Congress at Lausanne, which Marx does not attend. *October* Advises Liebknecht on tactics in the North German Reichstag. Studies Irish question (October/November). Engels publishes first of several reviews of *Capital* (30th). *November* Carbuncles and insomnia disrupt work (November/December). GC debates Fenian trial; address by Marx adopted (19th/20th). Prepares, but does not deliver, speech on the Irish question for GC meeting of 26th. Borkheim gives Marx a written résumé of Serno-Solovyevitch's Russian pamphlet *Our Domestic Affairs* and information about Chernyshevskii. Marx contacts Elie Reclus regarding a French translation of *Capital* (30th). Marx sends *Zukunft* article attacking von Hofstetten's plagiarism of *Capital* in a recent speech (6th). Talk on Ireland to German Workers Educational Association (16th). Work on *Capital* from late December until end of April 1868, studying statistical material, Bluebooks and literature on agriculture by Morton, Frass and von Thünen. Other reading for 1867 included Rogers's *History of Agriculture and Prices in England* (January), Poppe's *History of Mathematics*, Lange's *The View of J.S. Mill on the Social Question*, and works by Courrier and Arndt.

1868

Spanish revolution. Persecution of IWA members in France (which continues until 1870).

January Continuing carbuncles and severe headaches for much of year. *February* Reads and excerpts Dühring (February/March). *March* 'The Russians won't miss any chance of provocation. They will be done for if they don't succeed in plunging Germany and France into war' (to Engels, 6th). Reads and finds 'extraordinarily interesting' works by Maurer. *April* Resumes work on Volume 3 of *Capital*; very detailed letters on this to Engels (22nd and 30th). *May* Work on Book 2, rereading Smith, Turgot and Tooke (turnover of capital). GC denounces Charleroi massacre of striking miners by Belgian government at Marx's suggestion (12th). Talk on wages to German Workers Educational Association (20th). Visit to Manchester (29th, to *c.* 15th June). *June* Sends information to Wilhelm Eichoff for forthcoming pamphlet on IWA (*c.* 26th). *July* Marx asks Meyer in New York for material on landed property and agriculture in the US for *Capital* (4th). On Marx's proposal GC repudiates Felix Pyat's call for assassination of Napoleon III (7th). Unpublished article 'My plagiarism and F. Bastiat' (*c.* 11th). Resolution at GC denouncing British government withdrawal of title 'Polish refugees' in list of its pensioners as manifestation of 'subserviency to Russia' (14th). Remarks at GC on machinery (28th, and 11th August). *August* GC adopts resolutions by Marx on machinery (11th) and shortening the working day (25th) for the Brussels Congress. Edits 'Proclamation of the German workers in London' for the IWA Congress (11th). Marx's message on forthcoming ADAV [Lassallean German socialists] Congress published in *Sozial-Demokrat* (28th). *September* Marx draws up report of GC to Brussels IWA Congress (adopted 1st). Briefs Lessner and Eccarius for this congress. On Marx's advice the following is appended to the congress resolution opposing war between France and Germany: 'all European wars, and notably that between France and Germany, must be considered today as civil wars, benefitting Russia at most whose social status is not yet at the heights of modern civilisation' (10th); his resolutions on machinery and the working day also carried. Plans, with Engels, a popularly written summary of *Capital* (16th). Writes to Liebknecht on tactics against the Lassalleans whilst refusing to intervene publicly. *October* Danielson writes to Marx (received 4th) suggesting a Russian translation of *Capital*, the idea originally being Lopatin's (see p. 175), this volume). Marx sends Danielson autobiographical details and bibliography of his works (7th). Writes address of GC in support of Odger's parliamentary candidacy (adopted 13th). Attends conference of Trade Unions to discuss new trade union laws as GC representative (14th). Empowered by GC to disown London French branch of the IWA, which is under Pyat's influence (20th). Reading on problems of ground rent, with particular attention to the agrarian commune among Slavs, especially in Russia, with Borkheim translating for him the most important Russian sources (October/November). Investigation of Bluebooks and other material on property relations and tenant rights in Ireland. *November* Letters to Charles Collet (published as article in *Diplomatic Review* 2nd December) on the 1884 Bank Act which 'delivers England . . . *to the mercy of the Muscovite government*' (9th). Edits English translation of IWA Brussels Congress resolutions. Conflict with German Workers Educational Association because of its Lassalleanism (23rd). Engels settles Marx's debts and guarantees him an annual income of £350. *December* Appointed IWA archivist (1st). Reads Tenot on Napoleon's *coup d'état*. GC rejects Bakuninist Alliance's application for membership of IWA (15th) and passes and circulates Marx's resolution on the Alliance (22nd).

1869

SDAP, the Social-democratic Workers Party, founded by Bebel and Liebknecht at Eisenach, Germany.

January Marx excerpts *Money Market Review* and *Economist* for 1868. Illness prevents work on Books 2 and 3 of *Capital* until mid-February. Marx proposes support for striking Rouen cotton workers at GC (5th). Preparation of second edition of *Eighteenth Brumaire*. *February* Marx proposes financial aid for striking Basle weavers and dyers at GC (2nd). Resumes work on *Capital*, studying questions of credit and bank circulation (Foster, Feller, Odermann) (*c*. 13th until August). Puts problems of landed property, credit and general education on next IWA Congress agenda (16th). The Belgian socialist De Paepe informs Marx that he is unable to find a publisher for the planned French edition of *Eighteenth Brumaire* (16th). Marx translates Engels's report for GC on coal miners' guilds in Silesia (adopted 23rd) into German for publication. *March* Again in bad health (March/April). Reads literature on 1848 revolutions in France (Castille, Vermorel). Studies organic chemistry as a 'Sunday amusement'. Drafts GC circular accepting dissolved sections of Alliance into IWA providing their programme conforms to its statutes (9th). *April* Liver complaint hinders work (*c*. 12th till early May). Report to GC on Social-democratic Deputies in N. German Reichstag (13th). *May* Reads on child labour in agriculture in England for *Capital*. Draws up addresses for GC on massacre of Belgian miners (approved 4th) and to the Union of American Workers (approved 11th) opposing possible war between Britain and the USA. Helps Borkheim place a series of articles on Russian politics in *Diplomatic Review*. Visit to Manchester (25 May to 14 June). *June* Meets geologist J. R. Dakyns; they agree on positivists: 'the only positive thing about them is their arrogance.' Preface to second edition of *Eighteenth Brumaire* (23rd). Attends conference of Trade Unions in support of draft laws extending trade union rights (23rd). *July* Engels leaves commerce (1st). Marx's correspondence comes under police surveillance (*c*. July/August). Declines Liebknecht's invitation to the Eisenach Congress (*c*. 2nd), but advises him on the new party and urges its affiliation to the IWA. Sends De Paepe, at latter's request, detailed critique of Proudhonian doctrine on landed property (*c*. start July). Remarks on property and property rights at GC (6th). Visits Lafargues in Paris under pseudonym J. Williams (6th to 12th). An abscess hinders work (18th to 30th). Attacks Bakuninists on abolition of right of inheritance in GC (20th). Criticises Becker's suggestion of breaking down IWA into national organisations (to Bebel, 27th). On Bakunin: 'it is high time . . . we raised the question of whether a Panslavist has any right at all to be a member of an international working men's association' (to Engels, 30th). *August* GC adopts Marx's resolution for Basle Congress on laws of inheritance (3rd). Eisenach Conference (7th to 9th). At GC Marx advocates free, compulsory but *not* state-controlled education: 'neither in the elementary schools nor in higher education should one teach subjects which could have a party or class interpretation'. (10th and 17th). *September* Basle Congress of IWA (6th to 11th); Marx writes GC report but does not attend. Trip to continent with daughter Jenny; meets Kugelmann, Stumpf and Dietzgen (early September to 11th October). Speech to Lassallean Trade Unionists in Hanover discusses trade unions and warns against personality cults (30th). *October* Visited by the German socialists Bracke, bonhorst and Spier (3rd); discussions with Meissner (8th to 9th). Visit from Engels on Marx's return to London (12th to *c.* 18th). Marx sends Lafargue comments on Keller's French translation of the second chapter of *Capital* I (18th). Receives Flerovskii's (see p. 172, this volume) *The Situation of the Working Class in Russia* from Danielson and begins to learn Russian soon after. Work on ground rent for Book 3 (reading includes Carey's *Principles of Social Science* and Johnston's *Notes on North America*; October/November). Further reading on Ireland (Young, Wakefield, Davies, Curran, E. and A. O'Connor, Cobbett's *Political Register*, Prendergast; mid-October to December). Participates in Hyde Park demonstration to free the imprisoned Fenians (24th). Edits Eccarius's address of Land and Labour League (October/November). *November* Reads, in Russian, Herzen's *Prisons and Exiles* (*c.* November to 9th January). Heated debates in GC on issue of amnesty for Fenian prisoners (16th, 23rd and 30th). Letters to Kugelmann (29th) and Engels (10th December) on Irish question. *December* Paper on nationalisation of land (3rd). GC discusses Bakunin's attacks on the GC, and authorises Marx to draft message on behalf of GC to the Federal Council of Romance Switzerland (14th). Letter to De Paepe on the Alliance, for formal presentation to the Belgian IWA Federal Committee (*c.* 17th). Marx edits report on Basle Congress prepared by Eccarius (end December). In either 1868 or 1869 he excerpted or noted works by Macleod, Patterson, Laing, Cherbuliez, Lange, Labor, Sandelin, and Foster; Lyell's *Principles of Geology*, Goschen's *Theory of Changes*,

Hausener's *Comparative Statistics of Europe*, Alison's *Principles of Population*, Stadler's *Ireland*; a report of a conference of December 1868 on Jevons; numerous tables and statistics from *The Economist*.

1870

Outbreak of Franco-Prussian war. SDAP leaders in Germany tried for high treason. Russia repudiates Treaty of Paris. Capture and fall of Napoleon III of France.

January Marx in ill health, housebound after mid-January for a month. Writes circular for GC to Federal Council of Romance Switzerland on Bakunin's activities (*c.* 1st to 8th). Studies Russian 'as if it were a matter of life and death' (Jenny Marx to Engels, 17th). Work on landed property for *Capital*; requests detailed bibliography on landed property and agriculture in Belgium from De Paepe (24th). *February* Begins study of Flerovskii: 'At all events, it is the most important book that has appeared since your *Condition of the Working Class*' (to Engels, 10th); 'a terrible social revolution is imminent' (to Engels, 12th); 'the misery of the Russian peasantry has the same cause as the misery of the French peasantry under Louis XIV: taxes to the State and the *obrok* paid to the great landowners; far from creating poverty, common ownership has, on the contrary, diminished it' (to Kugelmann, 17th; cf. to Lafargues, 5th March). Reads and approves Engels's Foreword to second edition of his *Peasant War in Germany*. Article 'The English government and the imprisoned Fenians' (21st), for the Brussels *Internationale*. Assists daughter Jenny with articles on Irish question for *La Marseillaise* under signature J. Williams (February 27th to 19th April). *March* Work on Book 2 of *Capital* (*c.* 10th to 23rd, completing first somewhat ready for press draft). GC on Marx's proposal admits Positivist Proletarians of Paris to IWA as 'proletarians' pure and simple (15th). Sets out views on Irish question to Piggott, editor of the *Irishman* (19th). Invited to represent anti-Bakuninist Russian members of IWA in Geneva grouped around *Narodnoe Delo* (N. Utin, A.D. Trusov, Dmitrieva-Tomanovskaya, Korvin-Krukovskaya, V.I. Bartenev) on GC. Accepts. Writes the GC response stressing need to support Polish revolution and praising Flerovskii and Chernyshevskii (24th). Carbuncles and cough (22nd to *c.* 10th April). Writes to Brunswick SDAP

Committee on Bakunin (28th). Sometime this spring, reads Volume 3 of the Geneva edition of Chernyshevskii's works and (August) orders Volume 4 from Geneva. Asks Lafargue to 'keep an eye on' Bakuninists in Paris (end March/start April). *April* Continued reading on Ireland, especially on tenant right (1870 government reports). Letters to Lafargue on sectarianism (18th), and 'this damned Muscovite' Bakunin: 'proclamation of the *abolition of inheritance* would not be a serious act, but a foolish menace, rallying the whole peasantry and the whole small middle class around the reaction' (19th). Marx moves GC dissolves all ties with the *Bee-Hive* (26th), because of its preaching 'harmony with the capitalists', and writes GC declaration of this. Marx receives copies of the first Russian translation of the *Manifesto* (translated by Bakunin, published Geneva 1869). *May* GC adopts Marx's proclamation denouncing police persecution of IWA activists in France (3rd). Marx advises Liebknecht to take public stand against Bakunin in *Volksstaat* (*c.* 4th). Marx moves acceptance of SDAP invitation to hold next IWA Congress at Mainz (17th). Receives material from Sorge on situation of workers in the US (*c.* 23rd). Visit to Manchester (23 May to 23rd June). *June* Marx and Engels write to committee of SDAP, warning against possible Lassallean disruption of forthcoming IWA Congress at Mainz (14th). Marx moves resolution at GC supporting Swiss Federal Committee against Bakuninists in Romance Switzerland (28th). *July* Ill with liver complaint. Marx's address on lock-out of building trades in Geneva adopted by GC (5th). G. Lopatin visits Marx and gives news from Russia, i.e. of Nechayev's activities and Chernyshevskii's and Flerovskii's exile (3rd and 4th). Agenda for Mainz IWA Congress, drawn up by Marx, approved by GC (12th), and sent to committee of the SDAP (14th). Marx writes and sends confidential communiqué for GC to IWA sections on whether the GC seat should stay in London (14th). Writes 1st GC/IWA Address on the Franco-Prussian War (written 19th to 23rd, approved 26th). Writes to Liebknecht approving his and Bebel's Reichstag protest on the war (29th). Signs Eugen Oswald's protest of London French and Germans on the war, after some alterations at his request (31st). *August* GC adopts Marx's proposal to postpone the IWA Congress because of the war (2nd). From now until December Marx handles virtually all GC international correspondence. Stay in Ramsgate because of ill health (rheumatism and insomnia). Short visits to doctor in London and Engels in Manchester. Marx and Engels write to committee of SDAP urging opposition to annexation of Alsace-Lorraine and underlining risks of Franco-Russian alliance against Germany and future war should this occur (end August). *September* Receives telegram from Longuet announcing proclamation of republic in France (5th). Meets Serraillier and discusses French situation (6th). Writes second GC/IWA address on the Franco-Prussian war (adopted 9th). Works hard for international recognition for French Republic (September/December). Sends notices to newspapers on arrest in Germany of the committee members of the SDAP (14th). Asks Dupont, via Engels, to protest against the chauvinist manifesto of the Marseilles IWA section (16th) and Beesly to publicise second address on the war in *Fortnightly Review* (16th). Engels moves to London (20th); hereafter he and Marx meet almost daily. At GC Marx urges pressure on the English government to abrogate the 1856 Treaty of Paris, which he sees as strengthening Russia's position (27th). *October* A. Slepzov, editor of the St. Petersburg journal *Znanie*, invites Marx to contribute. Engels elected to GC on Marx's proposal (4th). Marx reports failure of Bakunin's coup in Lyon to GC (11th). On Marx's proposal GC condemns the Bakuninist-dominated Belgian Federal Council's failure to publish the second address on the war and other official IWA documents (18th). *November* Regular reports to GC on IWA in Europe and US (November/December). Marx testifies before Lord Mayor of London, for defence in SDAP leaders' treason trial, that SDAP had never sought to become a branch of the IWA (17th). *December* Sends Sorge, in US, IWA publications. Receives news from Lopatin of his plan to arrange Chernyshevskii's escape from exile. Regular contact with Tomanovskaya, sent by the Geneva Russian section, with whom he discusses the prospects for the agrarian commune in Russia (December 1870 to February 1871). Reads Chernyshevskii on communal property in Russia (end December/start January).

Between 1865 and 1870 (exact dates are uncertain) Marx had drafted four MSS of *Capital* 2. Engels gives details in his Preface (1885). MS I, of 150 folio pp. is the first separate but fragmentary draft of Volume 2 as now arranged (1865 or 1867). MS II (1870) is 'the only somewhat complete elaboration of book 2'. MS III elaborates specific points (on Volume 2, Part 1, Smith on fixed and circulating capital, rate of surplus-value and rate of profit); MS IV is a version of volume 2, Part 1 and Part 2, Chapter 1 'ready for press'.

1871

German Reich proclaimed with Bismarck as Chancellor (18th January). Bebel elected to Reichstag, standing as a socialist. Germany demands cession of Alsace-Lorraine and 5 billion franc indemnity. In France Gambetta resigns, replaced by Thiers. Revolution in Paris and Paris Commune proclaimed (18th March). Commune bloodily suppressed (week following 22nd May). Trial of eighty-seven alleged co-conspirators of Nechayev in Russia for murder of student Ivanov.

January Marx and Engels organise financial help for families of imprisoned German Social Democrats. Marx receives letter from Tomanovskaya on agrarian policies of tsarist government and material on effects of the 1861 reform on the *obshchina* (7th). Letter to *Daily News* attacking Bismarck for imprisoning Bebel and Liebknecht: 'France . . . fights at this moment not only for her own independence, but for the liberty of Germany and Europe'. (16th). Marx asks Harney for information on public land in US (*c.* mid-January). Attacks Russia and England's pro-Russia policies at GC (31st, 14th February, 7th and 14th March). *February* Reports on persecutions of IWA members in Germany and Austria to GC (14th). Meets Serraillier, fresh from Paris (19th). *March* Marx sends Frau Liebknecht information for Liebknecht's defence (3rd). Reports to GC on IWA in the USA and is asked to reply to New York (7th). On receipt of news of Commune argues in GC for sympathy demonstrations (21st); in the ensuing months Marx writes several hundred letters supporting the Commune. Writes denial for GC of reports that French Federal Council had expelled German members (adopted 21st). First of many denials (*Volksstaat*, 29th; *The Times*, 22nd; *De Werker*, 31st; *The Times*, 4th April; *Morning Advertiser*, 13 July; *La Verité*, 30th August) of reports on IWA involvement in the Commune. Again meets Serraillier before latter's second trip to Paris (28th). Proposes GC address to people of Paris and is delegated to write it (28th; eventually not issued). Asked by Frankel in name of Commune Workers Commission for advice on social reforms (30th). From 18th March onwards collects press cuttings and other material on the Commune. *April* Meetings with Fox Bourne, editor of *The Examiner*, resulting in favourable coverage for the Commune (April/May). Marx criticises Commune in private correspondence (to Liebknecht, 6th, to Kugelmann, 12th) for undue 'good nature', but praises it for attempting to smash the state. Informs Liebknecht, for publication in *Volksstaat*, of Commune's discovery that Karl Vogt was a Bonapartist spy (*c.* 10th). Passes information and advice to the Commune through a German businessman (mid/late April). Advises Liebknecht to print extracts from *Capital* in *Volksstaat* (13th). Starts work on first draft of GC address *The Civil War in France* (*c.* 18th), on GC instructions. *May* Marx's daughters Jenny and Eleanor arrested while visiting Lafargues in Bordeaux (start May). Marx meets P. Lavrov (see p. 174, this volume), sent by Commune to GC (start May). Has more news of Commune from Tomanovskaya (1st). Marx ill (*c.* 2nd to 22nd). Writes piece on Vogt for *Volksstaat* (4th). Starts on second draft of *The Civil War* about 18th, and final text mid-May. Speaks at GC on significance of Commune (23rd). *The Civil War in France* read to GC, adopted as address (30th) and printed as a pamphlet (13th June). Marx continued systematically to collect material on the trials and executions of Communards for some months. *June* Work on behalf of Commune refugees, obtaining them work, money and passports (for rest of year). Denial of *Pall Mall Gazette* report of his arrest in Holland (8th). Declaration to press (with Engels) attacking the French minister Jules Favre's circular against IWA (11th). Thanks Danielson for material on property relations in Russia including Chernyshevskii's 'On landed property', and informs him of state of work on *Capital* (13th). Danielson asks Marx to send him all IWA publications (20th). Attacked in GC by the English trade unionists Odger and Lucraft over *The Civil War* (20th and 27th), whose authorship he publicly admits to. Reply to attacks in *Daily News* on *The Civil War* (26th). Second edition of *The Civil War* agreed by GC (27th). Open letter to *Pall Mall Gazette* on Jules Favre (30th). *July* Interview with New York *World* (3rd, published 18th) on the IWA and the Commune. Denies Vienna *Neuen Freien Presse* report of a meeting with Herzen (4th). Defends J.P. MacDonnel's record as Irish leader and supports his election to GC (4th). Writes GC address to US sections on anti-Commune behaviour of American ambassador in Paris (11th).

Issues denial of Paris police forgeries of letters allegedly written by him (*c*. 11th). Meeting with Lavrov and other Commune refugees (16th). Interview with New York *Herald* (20th), whose report he disowns when he sees the published version (17th August). Studies Russian material on the Nechayev trial (late July). GC decides on third edition of *The Civil War* (25th). Writes to Utin in Geneva informing him of GC decision of 25th to call closed IWA Conference in London (27th). *August* Sends material to A. Hubert for help in forthcoming trial of Communards (10th to 16th). Marx proposes agenda of forthcoming IWA Conference be restricted to questions of organisation and policy (15th). Visit to Brighton, in precarious health (*c*. 16th to 29th). Letters to *Public Opinion* (19th) and *Evening Standard* (4th September) on calumnies against IWA in Prussian government organ *Nationalzeitung* (19th). GC delegates Marx to write appeal to American workers to support Commune refugees (22nd, sent to Sorge 5th September). Letter to *The Sun* (US) on arrest of Marx's daughters (25th). *September* Preparations for IWA closed London conference, which takes place from 17th to 22nd; Marx prepares GC report (delivered orally); supports and helps draft Vaillant's resolution on working-class political action, in the process speaking of the limitations of trade unions as well as attacking political abstentionism; supports proposal for all-female sections in the IWA; speaks to commission on the Alliance, condemning all secret societies as authoritarian and 'inconsistent with the development of the proletarian movement'. Speech on seventh anniversary of IWA (25th). Letters from Marx and Engels to SDAP leaders call for closer links with IWA (end September to mid-November). *October* Marx and Engels prepare definitive text of London conference resolutions and new translations of IWA Statutes and Rules. Marx re-elected Corresponding Secretary for Russia (3rd). Marx delegated to write GC disclaimer of Nechayev (7th, published 1st November). Challenges statutes of new *émigré* 'French section of 1871' at GC (17th and 7th November). *November* Marx ill from overwork: unable to attend GC. Letter to Danielson with alterations and proof corrections to Russian edition of *Capital* (9th). Bakuninist congress at Sonvilliers (12th). Marx urges Liebknecht, on pain of a breach, to take a clear anti-Bakuninist position in *Volksstaat* (first half of November). Letter to Bolte in New York on decisions of London conference and splits in the American IWA (23rd). Discussion with Meissner on second edition of *Capital* (*c*. 30th). Marx asks Borkheim for information on Bakunin (*c*. 30th). *December* Reworking of Chapter 1 of *Capital* for second German edition. Correspondence with G. Luciani on labour movement in Italy. Letter to *Eastern Post* attacking Charles Bradlaugh's slanders of the IWA (20th).

1872

Emperors of Germany, Austria and Russia meet to find means of isolating France. Bismarck begins *Kulturkampf* against the Catholic party of the centre.

January Work on second edition of *Capital*; first twenty-four printer's sheets to Meissner (*c*. 20th). Contacts Roy regarding a French translation (mid-January). Conflict in GC over British Federal Council Statutes (2nd, 9th, and 16th). Marx writes reply to Sonvilliers circular (*c*. 3rd). Begins work with Engels on the anti-Bakuninist pamphlet *Alleged Splits in the International*. Further letters to *Eastern Post* on Bradlaugh (16th to 27th). *February* Contracts with Lachâtre for French edition of *Capital* in installments, which he considerably restructures and in which he makes many changes from the German edition. Reports to GC Swiss authorities' search of Utin's house, at Russian government behest (13th), and writes GC proclamation on this (10th). *March* Gives report to GC on split in the North American Federation and drafts resolution requiring US sections to have a membership of at least two-thirds wage-earners (5th and 12th). Work on French edition of *Capital* (March to May). Helps Dupont draft document on nationalisation of land for Manchester section of IWA (start March to start May). *Alleged Splits* adopted by GC (5th), published (Geneva) in June and distributed privately to all IWA sections. Letter to *La Liberté* refuting allegations in Lefrançais's book on the Commune (12th). Marx draws up resolutions for London meeting celebrating the first anniversary of the Commune (13th to 18th). Frequent meetings with the Irish leader J.P. MacDonnel (second half March to start May). Preface to French edition of *Capital* (18th). Russian edition of *Capital* I (27th), 3000 copies, 900 sold in six weeks and most by end of year. *April* Marx deeply involved in GC conflict over split in American Federation (April/May). Letter from Danielson on Chernyshevskii and Lopatin (received start

April). Helps with GC protest at police terrorisation of Irish members of IWA (adopted 9th). Sends Meissner corrections of second edition of *Capital* up to Sheet 42 (*c.* 10th), with a blurb. Writes GC declaration against the MPs Cochrane's, Eastwick's, and Fawcett's slanders of the IWA (adopted 16th). Work on French translation of *The Civil War in France* (end April/May, published Brussels, June). *May* Continues to correct proofs of second German edition of *Capital*, and works on French edition. Letter to *Volksstaat* denying Brentano's allegations of misquotation in Marx's 1864 IWA Inaugural Address (23rd). Plans to withdraw from IWA after September to work on *Capital*. Negotiations to hold next IWA Congress in Holland. Marx thanks Danielson for sending him Russian edition of *Capital* and asks him for information on Bakunin's influence in Russia and his relations with Nechayev (28th). *June* Continues work on French edition of *Capital*, simultaneously with preparations for IWA Congress (June to August). Marx opposes Belgian, English and Swiss IWA members who refuse to apply 1871 London conference motions on working-class political action. Bakuninist Jura Federation replies to *Alleged Splits* (10th). Marx proposes Hague for next IWA congress and argues need for organisational questions, especially for GC powers, to be the major item on the agenda (11th). Preface to second edition of the *Manifesto* with Engels (24th, published Leipzig, July). Marx speaks at GC on need to widen its powers (25th). Sends Meissner last corrected proofs of second edition of *Capital* (*c.* end June). *July* Discussions with Nobre-Franca on possible Portuguese edition of *Capital*; Marx also requests information on landed property in Portugal (July/August). First installment of second German edition of *Capital* published (*c.* 16th). Marx writes the proclamation 'To the striking miners in Ruhrtal' (21st). At GC supports Vaillant's proposal to insert the London conference resolution on working-class political action into the IWA Statutes (23rd), and suggests additional proposal that each IWA section be composed of not less than three-quarters wage earners. Second letter to *Volksstaat* on Brentano (28th). *August* Marx and Engels write letters to Spanish IWA sections on Alliance activities in Spain (8th). Marx receives MS of Chernyshevskii's *Unaddressed Letters* (see pp. 190–203, this volume) and extensive Russian reviews of *Capital* from Danielson (15th). He receives information on the Nechayev trial from Utin, and incorporates it into his report on the Alliance for the Hague

Congress. Between now and 12th December he translates the whole of Chernyshevskii's first letter into German and makes copious excerpts from the rest. *September* Hague Congress of IWA. Marx delivers GC report (written end August) and speaks on the Alliance to special IWA commission. Congress agrees to incorporate London conference resolution on working-class political action into IWA Statutes (Vaillant's proposal, drafted by Marx), to strengthen GC powers (Marx's proposal), to move GC headquarters to New York (Engels's proposal, supported by Marx), and to expel Bakunin and others (Marx's proposal) (5th to 7th); in preliminary debates on delegates' mandates Marx accuses English trade union leaders of having sold themselves to the bourgeoisie (3rd and 4th). Speech at Amsterdam on the significance of the Hague Congress (8th). Publication of first installment of French edition of *Capital* (17th); Marx sends copies to various of his correspondents, including Danielson (end September to mid-October). Marx and Engels write up Hague resolutions and correspond on the congress with Sorge in New York and others (September/October). *October* Correspondence with Bignami over possible Italian translation of *Capital*. *November* Work on French translation of *Capital*, with Longuet's assistance. Marx and Engels attack *Volksstaat*'s 'accommodation' of Lassalleans. *December* Marx asks Danielson for information on Chernyshevskii, following the failure of Lopatin's plan to help him escape (and Lopatin's own consequent arrest), with a view to a publication on Chernyshevskii (12th). Same letter announces Marx's plan to deal with Russian forms of landed property in *Capital* III. Conflict with the English reformist trade unionist John Hales at IWA and split in the British Federal Council: Marx prepares address on behalf of the minority (20th to 23rd) and he and Engels write an open letter on the split to the *International Herald* (21st). Tries, with Urquhart's help, to secure Lopatin's release through diplomatic channels in Constantinople (December/January). During 1872 Marx studies extensively Russian agrarian materials.

1873

An alliance of Emperors of Germany, Austria and Russia (the *Dreikaiserbund*) concluded. Revolution in Spain. Economic crisis hits Europe.

January Marx discusses possible publication of collected works with Meissner. Letter to *The Times* disowns description 'autocrat of the proletarian movement' (2nd). Between November 1872 and now writes article o.. Political indifferentism' for *Almanacco Republicana*. Writes British Federal Council circular on Hales (published 25th). Afterword to second German edition of *Capital* I (dated 24th). Work on materials sent by Danielson on agricultural conditions in Russia and the peasant question since the 1861 Emancipation (books by Golovachev, Skrebitskii, Saltykov-Shchedrin, Ziber and the Chicherin/Beliayev debate on the agrarian commune) (January to March). *February* Further criticisms of *Volksstaat*'s position on the Lassalleans and its neutrality on the British IWA split (February/March). *March* Letter to Danielson discusses the Chicherin/Beliayev controversy: 'every historical analogy speaks against Chicherin. How could it be that in Russia this institution [the *obshchina*] was introduced purely as a fiscal measure, and an appurtenance of serfdom, whereas everywhere else it arises spontaneously, and constitutes a necessary stage in the evolution of a free people' (22nd). Marx and Engels take part in London second anniversary celebration of Commune, which issues an address containing extracts from Marx's *The Civil War in France* (24th). Work, with Lafargue, on French translation of *Capital*. *April* Further reading on Russia, including Chernyshevskii and A. Severtzev's review of Chernyshevskii's work. Danielson sends requested biographical details on Chernyshevskii. Marx sends Meissner last corrected proofs of second edition of *Capital* (5th). Preparation, with Engels, of the pamphlet *The Alliance of Social Democracy and the IWA* (April to July). *May* At Marx's request Danielson sends an extensive critical review of literature on the Russian peasant commune – the *obshchina* (22nd). Marx in worsening health: goes to Manchester to consult Dr Gumpert, who orders him to work no more than four hours a day. Notwithstanding this Marx continues work on the French edition of *Capital* (May to July). Marx discusses with his friend Samuel Moore the possibility of mathematically determining 'the principal laws of crisis'. *June* Second edition of *Capital* I published in book form in Hamburg. Letter from Engels to Bebel, in name of Marx and self, on relations with Lassalleans (20th). Continued work on agricultural conditions and communal landownership in Russia (Beliayev, Nevolin, Kalatshov, Sergeevich, Skaldin) (June/July). *July* Marx contributes to conclusion of Engels/Lafargue pamphlet *The Alliance of Social Democracy and the IWA* (dated 21st). *August* Marx sends Danielson last part of second German edition of *Capital* (12th). Danielson advises Marx that it would be inopportune for him publicly to support Chernyshevskii at this stage (end August). *September* Marx, Engels and supporters boycott IWA Geneva Congress. Marx again very ill. Sends copies of second edition of *Capital* to Darwin and Herbert Spencer (25th to 30th). Asks Sorge for information on the economic crisis in the USA (27th). *November* Marx and Engels meet Utin in London several times. Doctor forbids all activity; visit to Harrogate for cure (24th to 15th December). Engels meets Lopatin, who has escaped from Siberia, in London and reports on the meeting in detail to Marx (25th to 28th).

1874

In Germany nine socialists (six Eisenachers, three Lassalleans) elected to Reichstag. Gladstone falls, Disraeli becomes prime minister in Britain.

January Work on physiology of plants and chemistry of fertilisers, and landed property, for Volume 3 of *Capital*, and study of Bluebooks on the recent history of English economic policy (January to May). Marx's health again deteriorates (February to April). *March* Visits from Lopatin and Lavrov, Lopatin passes Marx articles by Ziber. Extensive reading of Russian books, including Bakunin's *Statism and Anarchy*, on which Marx makes extensive notes (dating uncertain: between January 1874 and start of 1875). *April* Three-week stay in Ramsgate (returning 5th May) to cure insomnia and headaches; doctors advise complete rest and trip to Karlsbad. *May* Resumes work, interrupted by illness, on French edition of *Capital* I (May to July). *July* Rest in Ryde (15th to 30th). Marx and Engels warn German Party leaders against Dühring's growing influence. *August* Marx ill with liver complaint, frequently unable to work. Letter to Sorge foresees European war (4th). Correspondence with La Cécilia over possible Italian edition of *Capital* (end August to October). Visit with Eleanor to Karlsbad (19th August to 21st September), returning via Dresden, Leipzig (meeting Liebknecht and Blos), Berlin and Hamburg. *September*

Seventh IWA Congress in Brussels, for Engels (to Sorge, 12th and 17th) 'the death of the International'. *October Volksstaat* reprints (October 1874 to January 1875) Marx's *Revelations on the Trial of the Cologne Communists*. Marx and Engels informed of unification negotiations between Eisenachers and Lassalleans (*c.* 20th to 30th). At the end of 1874 Marx reads Chernyshevskii's *Cavaignac* and rereads his *Unaddressed Letters*.

1875

Eisenachers and Lassalleans unite at Gotha Congress to form the Social Democratic Workers Party of Germany, the SDAPD.

January Afterword to *Revelations on the Trial of the Cologne Communists* (8th). Speech commemorating Polish insurrection of 1863–4 (23rd). Marx finishes work on French translation of *Capital* I. Urges Engels to reply to Tkachev's 'Open letter to Mr. F. Engels' (end 1874 or start 1875). *February* Marx reads Russian *émigré* publications sent by Lavrov and praises Lopatin's article on religious sects as a form of protest against tsarist autocracy (start February). Plans to make extracts from an article in Lavrov's Russian journal *Vpered* for *Volksstaat* (11th). *March* Letter from Engels (in name of himself and Marx) to Bebel criticising Gotha Programme draft (18th to 28th). *April* Afterword to French edition of *Capital* (28th). *May* Reads Haxthausen's *Die ländliche Verfassung Russlands* (see Wada, this volume). *Critique of the Gotha Programme* (5th) (not published until 1891, and then in abridged form). Maintains close contact with Lavrov until end of year. *August* Supervises second edition of Johann Most's popular abridgment of *Capital*. Visit to Karlsbad (15th August to 11th September) where he frequently meets the Russian scholar Maxim Kovalevskii (see p. 174). Engels reports Marx in much improved health on his return (to Bracke, 11th October). *October* Letter to Lavrov discusses the Bakuninist pamphlet *A Few Words from a Socialist Revolutionary Group*: 'This schoolboy exercise doesn't deserve a reply' (8th). *November* Marx continues reading and collection of materials relating to the agrarian conditions in Russia (Samarin, Dmitriev, Kavelin, Koshelev, official documents of the tax commission [of which Danielson had sent ten volumes]) (November 1875 to February 1876). Last part of French edition of *Capital* published;

Marx sends copies to friends, including Lopatin, Danielson, Lavrov and Kovalevskii. *December* Declines invitation from Lavrov to speak to a Polish meeting on health grounds, but reaffirms that 'the liberation of Poland is one of the conditions for the liberation of the working class in Europe' (3rd). Some time this year (between May and August?) Marx drew up a detailed mathematical MS *The Relation of the Rate of Surplus-value to the Rate of Profit* (his title) and compiled an index (not published) for the French edition of *Capital*. His reading notes for this year additionally include works on the Russian economy by Parlyaevskii and Engelhardt; and *History of Commerce and Banking* by Roth and Hüllmann.

1876

First French labour congress held in Paris. Land and Liberty organisation formed in St. Petersburg (see p. 10). Serbo-Turkish war declared.

February Speech at commemorative celebration of German Workers Educational Association (7th) treats history of Communist League. Fragment for *Capital* III on 'differential rent'. Studies of vegetable, animal and human physiology – Schleiden, Ranke, Hermann and others (until mid-May). *April* Marx requests Sorge in New York to send him US library catalogues for American literature on agriculture, landed property and credit, and Engels's and his own New York *Tribune* articles, of which he has no copies, from the socialist Weydemeyer's estate (4th). *May* Requests literature from Frankel on landed property in Hungary (*c.* 24th). Marx and Engels agree to oppose Dühring's growing influence in the German Party and Engels begins to work on *Anti-Dühring*. Marx begins extensive study of forms of communal property, especially among Slavs (Maurer, Hanssen, Demelic, Utiesenovic, Cardenas) (end May) [sources vary here: possibly December for all except Maurer]. *July* Bakunin dies (1st); Marx and Engels express opposition to the unqualified complimentary obituaries in *Vpered* and *Volksstaat*. *August* Trip to Karlsbad with Eleanor (15th August to 25th September). Receives Lavrov's *The State Element in Future Society* in Karlsbad, where he meets the historian of Jews, Heinrich Grätz, with whom he discusses tsarism. Returns via Prague, Kreuznach, and Liège (meeting Utin). *September* Writes to Bracke on the importance of Lissagaray's *History of the Commune*, offering to review and correct a German translation himself (23rd). *October* Letter to Liebknecht discusses German and British relations with Russia and urges *Volksstaat* to take up the issue (7th). Marx advises Barry on latter's leading articles on foreign policy in the *Morning Advertiser* (mid-October). Informs Lavrov, for publication in *Vpered*, of plans of Golovachov and others to set up a conservative English language paper in London on Russian affairs (21st). Work on *Capital* III (end October). *November* Marx sends Charles D. Collet information on Gladstone's Russian policy for use in articles in the *Diplomatic Review*. Ill with rheumatism and bronchitis (*c.* 16th to 30th). Marx asks Hirsch in Paris to send him reports on the French workers' movement (25th). *December* Kovalevskii a regular visitor to Marx household. Marx edits first section of Isolde Kurz's translation of Lissagaray (end December). This year Marx also read Cremazy on French and Hindu law, Carlyle's *Oliver Cromwell's Letters and Speeches*, Yates's *The Natural History of the Raw Material of Commerce*; and Kostomarov's *Historical Monographs*, taking detailed extracts on Stenka Razin's mutiny [sources again vary; possibly end 1879 to start 1880].

1877

Russia declares war on Turkey and occupies Rumania. Governmental crisis in France. Reichstag elections in Germany give Social Democrats twelve seats.

January Marx closely follows Russo-Turkish conflict, supporting Turkey and predicting revolution in Russia as the eventual outcome. He is jubilant about Social Democrat successes in the Reichstag elections. Studies official documents relating to Britain's Eastern policy and Slade's *Turkey and the Crimean War.* Conducts press campaign against Gladstone's pro-Russian policy through Maltman Barry, the articles appearing anonymously in *Whitehall Review*, *Morning News* and *Vanity Fair* (January to March). Work on Kurz's translation of Lissagaray (January to March). *February* Frequent contact with Lavrov (February to April) and several meetings with Utin's wife (February/March). Writes first part of his chapter 'From the critical history' for *Anti-Dühring* (sent to Engels 5th March). *March* At Marx's suggestion Engels writes piece on the Italian labour movement, attacking Anarchist influence (6th to 14th). Marx asks Lavrov (16th) for information on police and judiciary persecutions in Russia and himself gives information on Russian government persecution of Polish unitarian priests to the Irish MP Keyes O'Cleary for parliamentary debates. Danielson asks Marx for piece on Russian landed property for *Otechestvennye Zapiski* (22nd). Marx fixes work for Lavrov on *Fortnightly Review* through Beesly (22nd). Begins seventy-page redraft of parts of *Capital* II. *April* Correspondence with Bracke urging German socialist press to devote more attention to the Eastern question, about which 'the working class is too little concerned ' (21st). Further work on Lissagaray's book (*c.* 10th to 30th). *May* Receives his and Engels's New York *Tribune* articles from Sorge (*c.* 12th). Insomnia and high cerebral blood pressure. *July* Frequent meetings with the German communist Karl Hirsch, visiting from France, and discussions of French politics and the situation in the German Party (23rd to 29th). Letter to Engels discusses strikes in the US: these 'may well be the starting-point for a genuine workers party in the US' (25th). Reads Mehring on German social democracy, Kneiss on money and the Russian economist and statistician I.I. Kaufmann (July/August). *August* Completes his chapter for *Anti-Dühring* (sent to Engels 8th, along with an annotated copy of Quesnay's *Tableau Economique*). Assembles, reads and excerpts writings by Robert Owen for (Engels's) chapter on socialism in *Anti-Dühring*. Visit with wife and daughter Eleanor to Neuenahr and Black Forest, returning around 27th September. *September* Letter to Sorge discusses Russia: 'all strata of Russian society are in decay, economically, morally and intellectually. This time the revolution is starting in the East, where the hitherto unshattered bastion and reserve army of the counterrevolution are situated' (27th). After return from Germany recommences study of Owen. *October* Letters to Sorge (19th) and Bracke (23rd) deplore theoretical decline in German Party since the Unity Congress. Marx sends Sorge list of changes to *Capital* I for a proposed English translation, and requests information on the conditions of miners in Pennsylvania (19th). Begins fair copy (three sides) of Chapter 1 of *Capital* II (26th). *November* Letter to Blos about the translation of Lissagaray, rejects 'personality cult': 'when Engels and I first entered the secret society of the communists, we did so on condition that everything would be excluded from the statutes that might encourage trust in authority' (10th). Begins redraft of Chapter 1 of *Capital* II for press (seventeen sides). Letter to *Otechestvennye Zapiski* [possibly 1878: see article by Wada, pp. 56–60]. Reading for this year also included Moses Hess's posthumous *Dynamische Stofflehre*, Adams on Anglo-Saxon law, and much material on Russia, especially on agrarian conditions since the Emancipation (including Vasil'chakov, Neruchchev, Sokolovskii).

1878

Anti-socialist law in Germany. In Russia Vera Zasulich attempts to assassinate St. Petersburg prefect Trepov. The Turks eventually defeated by Russia.

February Letters to Liebknecht (4th and 11th), discussing Russo-Turkish war and its European implications: Liebknecht publishes extracts from these in his pamphlet *The Eastern Question or Will Europe Turn Cossack?* (March). *March* Notebook of over 300 pages on I.I. Kaufmann's *Theory and Practice of Banking* (end March to May). Marx also notes Kaufmann's *Nachalo* article on the *obshchina*. Letter to *The Labour Standard* (New York) on Russia (31st). *April* Meetings with Liebknecht, on a visit from Germany (15th to 20th). *May* Meeting with Kovalevskii (12th). Summaries of statistical material, received from the US, for Volumes II and III of *Capital* (21st to end of month). Studies of agricultural chemistry and geology – Jukes (a notebook of over 300 pages), Hlubeck, Koppe, Johnstone (end May to June). *June* Letters to *Daily News* (12th), and *Frankfurter Zeitung* (27th) denouncing Bismarck's anti-socialist measures. *July* Article on 'Mr. George Howell's history of the IWA' (written early July, published in *The Secular Chronicle* 4th August). Engels's *Anti-Dühring* published in book form in Leipzig. Marx writes seven folio pages (dated 2nd) – the second and last attempt to prepare *Capital* II for press – then interrupts work on *Capital* until October. Supplies John Stuart-Glennie with material on socialism for his proposed new journal (July/August). *August* Supplies Maltman Barry with information on German socialism for lectures and articles. *September* Stay in Malvernbury where Jenny Marx is taking a cure (4th to 14th). Drafts report for *Daily News* (unfinished) on Reichstag debates on anti-socialist law (24th); this discusses peaceful and violent roads to socialism. *October*

Supplies M. Kaufmann with information for his book *Utopias* (*c.* 13th). Work for *Capital* on the history of banking and monetary circulation (books by Rota, Ciccone, Hüllman, Cossa, Mann, Walker and others) (October/November). Marx and Engels advise Liebknecht to circumvent the anti-socialist law by publishing a Party paper in Switzerland for illegal distribution in Germany (end October). *November* Marx learns from Kovalevskii of discussions of *Capital* in the Russian press (early November). Marx gets Liebknecht position of correspondent for *Whitehall Review*, via Barry. Starts to excerpt Avenal's *Lundis révolutionaires* (12th). Letters to Danielson discuss economic development in the USA since the Civil War, Volume II of *Capital* (which Marx hopes to have ready by end of 1879) (15th), the industrial crisis in England, and the need for changes in any second Russian edition of *Capital* I (28th). Further work for *Capital*: Hanssen and Jacobi on the history of agriculture, and 1870 Report of the US Commission of the General Land Office; reading on French history (second half November to first half December). Engels receives detailed information from Lopatin, returned from an illegal trip into Russia, on Populist activities (*c.* 26th). Marx reads studies of Leibniz (Caspari and DuBois-Reymond) and Descartes's posthumously published writings on mathematics and physics (November/December). *December* Interview with *Chicago Tribune* (18th, published 5th January 1879), discusses amongst other things the workers' movement in the US. Continued reading on financial and banking questions (Bonnet, Diest-Daber, Rey, Brissot de Warwille, Gassiot). Marx also continued to read on the *obshchina* this year (Sokolovskii, Kaufman) and began systematically studying algebra and mathematics. The latter researches continued until 1882: Marx kept separate notebooks for his mathematical studies and at some point wrote an outline MS on the history of differential calculus. In 1878 he also read Dakyns's *The Antiquity of Man* and Ingram's *The Present Position and Prospect of Political Economy*.

1879

Germany and Austria sign Vienna Alliance. Second congress of French Labour Party at Marseilles. Land League founded in Ireland. As a result of split of the Land and Liberty organisation, People's Will and Black Repartition founded in Russia.

This year Marx's health worsened, as did that of his wife Jenny. *February* Marx reads a summary prepared by Danielson on the Russian financial situation over the previous fifteen years. *March* Marx annotates Kovalevskii's *Slovo* article on the draft Bulgarian constitution. *April* Letter to Danielson discusses the labour movements in the US and Britain, and the structure of US and Russian economic development (10th). *June* Marx excerpts Meyer's *Politische Gründer*. Marx and Engels help plan illegal socialist journal in Germany (*Sozialdemokrat*); Marx supports Hirsch for editor (June/July). *July* Letter to Carlo Cafiero on his résumé of *Capital* sees as the major omission 'the proof that the necessary *material conditions* for the emancipation of the proletariat are generated spontaneously by the process of capitalist production' (29th). *August* Receives detailed information from Danielson on the financial situation and the condition of agriculture in Russia. Engels writes to Bebel in his and Marx's name dissociating themselves from the *Sozialdemokrat* because of growing influence in the party of petty-bourgeois elements (led by Höchberg) (4th). Holiday in Jersey and Ramsgate (*c.* 8th August to *c.* 17th September). Marx reads Carlton's *Traits and Stories of the Irish peasantry*. Receives official reports from the labour bureaux of Massachusetts, Ohio and Pennsylvania, through Sorge (*c.* 25th). *September* Circular letter written by Engels in his and Marx's name to German party leaders on affairs in the party, threatening a public break if the elements around Höchberg gain control (17th/18th). Marx extensively excerpts and annotates Kovalevskii's *Rural Communal Ownership*; from now until October 1880 he reads extensively and comparatively on the rural communes. *October* Some time between now and October 1880 he compiles chronological notes on Indian history from 664–1858 AD, paying particular attention to the colonial period. *December* Reading on ancient history, especially Roman law (Reitemeier, Lange, Ihering, Friedländer, Bücher) (December/January). Between now and the end of 1880 he writes marginal notes on Wagner's *Textbook of Political Economy*. In 1879 Marx's reading also included the fiscal material from Danielson, Karayev's *Peasantry and the Peasant Question in France in the Last Quarter of the 18th Century*, Guesde's *Collectivism and Revolution*, and Redgrave's *The Factory and Workshop Act*. He also compiled a copious bibliography on matriarchal law.

1880

People's Will influence on the increase in Russia. It makes unsuccessful attempt on life of tsar. Anti-socialist law renewed in Germany. Government change in France and amnesty for Communards.

March Lev Hartmann of People's Will in regular contact with Marx (until July 1881). Marx writes introductory comments to reprint in *Egalité* of parts of *The Poverty of Philosophy* (end March). *April Workers' Questionnaire* written by Marx for the French socialists. *May* Helps Jules Guesde draw up programme of French socialist working men's party, himself dictating the theoretical preamble (start of month). Writes Preface to Engels *Socialism: Utopian and Scientific* (4th/5th, published end May in Paris). Edits MS of Lafargue's manifesto for the French party (after 21st). *June* Authorises the Dutch socialist Domela Nieuwenhuis to publish a popular summary of *Capital* in Dutch (27th). *August* Ordered by doctors to stop work for a time; family (including Longuet and Lafargue) holiday in Ramsgate (mid-August to 13th September). There Marx meets the American journalist John Swinton and discusses the international situation, 'speaking hopefully of Russia'. *September* Marx declines, on grounds of health, to write an article himself on Russian economic development since 1861, but urges Danielson to publish his *Sketches* and authorises him to use anything relevant from his (Marx's) letters for this (12th). Correspondence with Robert Banner on a possible workers' party in Scotland (September to December). Marx studies the programme of People's Will (see Part III, this volume). Visited by Liebknecht, in London to discuss party problems (end September). Notes and annotates Annenkov's memoirs in *Vestnik Evropy* (*c.* September to November). *October* Frequent contact with the English socialist Hyndman, with whom Marx discusses possibility of a workers' party in England (October 1880 to *c.* May 1881). Renewed reading for *Capital*: study of Bluebooks, especially on Californian economic development (October 1880 to March 1881). *November* Writes to Swinton seeking aid for victims of Bismarck's anti-socialist law (4th). Letter to Sorge discusses German and French socialism, and the Russian revolutionary movement; Marx praises People's Will, and criticises the Black Repartition Geneva group as latter-day Bakuninists; he also asks Sorge to send material on Californian economic development (5th). People's Will writes to Marx praising his work and asking him to help them gain support in Europe and the USA (6th). Marx, Engels, Lessner and Lafargue address a letter to a Geneva meeting to commemorate the Polish insurrection of 1830 (27th). *December* Morozov of People's Will pays Marx two visits to tell him of the struggle in Russia. Bebel, Bernstein and Singer visit Marx and Engels in London to discuss the German Social Democrat party questions (*c.* 9th to 16th). Marx reads the Russian satirist Saltykov-Shchedrin, paying particular attention to his expression of class struggle between large landowners and peasants since 1861. Marx's 'Ethnological notebooks' – notes and comments on works on precapitalist societies and colonial societies, including Morgan's *Ancient Society* and books by Phear, Maine, Money, Dawkins and Sohm – were probably begun this month, the work continuing until about June 1881. Marx also worked intermittently on *Capital* during 1880, drafting a new variant of Part 3 of Volume II. Other reading included works on the Irish land question, American and Indian agriculture, Australian economic development, Loria on ground rent, the tsarist government statistics for 1877-9, and Letourneau's *La Sociologie d'après l'Ethnographie.*

1881

In England Hyndman establishes Democratic Federation. German Social Democrats win twelve Reichstag seats. In St. Petersburg People's Will assassinate Alexander II. Trials and executions of its leaders.

January Marx suggests to English working-class leaders (Hyndman and others) and sympathetic MPs (Cowen, Butler-Johnstone, etc.) tactics for their co-operation. (January to March). Extensive reading on Russian socio-economic development, including Chernyshevskii (whose *Unaddressed Letters* Marx reread, making a summary of its contents), Danielson, Skrebitskii, Golovachov, Yanson and Skaldin (January to June). Letter to Longuet on a proposed abridgment of *Capital* and translation of the 1859 *Critique*, which also provides information for a proposed *Justice* article on Bradlaugh, 'one of the most clamorous supporters of

Gladstone's demagogic Russophile campaign against Disraeli' (4th). Marx meets Russian economists Ziber and Kablukov (*c.* 4th). Indicates changes needed for second edition of Nieuwenhuis's popular summary of *Capital* (mid-January to February). *February* Catarrh and insomnia; night work forbidden (February to June). Receives letter from Zasulich (18th); writes four drafts of a detailed reply on the nature of the *obshchina* and its place in a Russian revolution, but in the end sends brief reply (8th March). Letter to Danielson discusses railways and the public debt in England and the USA, colonial exploitation in India, and Danielson's *Sketches* (19th). Letter to Nieuwenhuis discusses socialist revolution, with particular reference to the Paris Commune (22nd). *March* Letter to chairman of the Slavonic Meeting (Hartmann of People's Will) in celebration of tenth anniversary of the Commune praises assassination of Alexander II (with Engels, 21st). Marx and Engels write to *Daily News* defending the arrested socialist Johann Most from press slanders (31st). Contact with the Russian revolutionary Chaikovskii. Marx reads Allisov's *Alexander II osvoboditel'* and Dragomanov's *Tiranoubiistvo v Rosii* arguing for personal terrorist action in Russia (March/April). *April* Marx closely follows the People's Will trial in St. Petersburg, commenting 'they are sterling people through and through', whose '*modus operandi* is a specifically Russian and historically inevitable method about which there is no more reason to moralise – for or against – than there is about the earthquake in Chios' (to Jenny Longuet, 11th); the same letter unfavourably contrasts the Black Repartition group as 'mere doctrinaires, confused anarchist socialists' without influence in Russia, relates Marx's first – none too flattering – impression of Kautsky, and discusses Gladstone's Irish land act. Marx reads Henry George's *Progress and Poverty*, which he sees as 'simply an attempt, trimmed with socialism, to save capitalist rule' (April to May; letter to Sorge, 20th June). *June* Breaks with Hyndman over latter's plagiarisation of *Capital*. Reading on monopolies, large-scale industry and child labour in the USA (articles by Lloyd, House, Grohmann, Cliffe-Leslie, Barrow and Brown). Visit to Eastbourne with his sick wife (end June to *c.* 20th July). *July* Visit with wife to Longuets at Argenteuil (26th to 16th August): here Marx reads on landed property, handicrafts, guilds, finance, and the peasantry before the French revolution (Fleury), following this with work on the situation and history of colonial peoples (including Manis's

Java; August/September). *August* Meeting in Paris with Lavrov and Hirsch (between 3rd and 8th). Visits from Jaclard and Lissagaray, with whom Marx discusses the situation in the French workers party (8th/9th). After return to London Marx compiles a list of 'Russian books on my bookshelf' – nearly 200 titles. Reads Hook on the Chinese empire. *October* Marx gravely ill with pleurisy and bronchitis (13th, to early December) whilst his wife is bedridden with cancer of the liver. Meissner asks Marx to prepare a third edition of *Capital* (22nd). *December* Death of Marx's wife Jenny (2nd), Marx forbidden by doctors to attend funeral. Goes to Ventnor to convalesce (29th). Around this time he began to compose a gigantic chronology of world history, covering events from the first century BC to the mid-seventeenth century and concentrating in particular on the origin of the modern nation state, the development of capitalism and the struggles of the bourgeoisie for political power, and the importance of the Reformation in that context (see p. 17). The MS amounts to 1,700 printed pages; Marx's main sources were Schlosser, Botta, Cobbett, Hume, Machiavelli, Karamzin, De Segur and R.H. Green. It was also around now that he drafted his MS 'Remarks on the 1861 reform and Russia's post-reform development'. Some time in 1881 he read Gumplowicz's *Rechtsstaat und Sozialismus.*

1882

The Emancipation of Labour group, led by Plekhanov, founded in Geneva. The People's Will activities and trials proceed in Russia. Britain occupies Egypt.

January Marx returns to London (16th). At Lavrov's request writes Preface to Russian edition of the *Manifesto* (with Engels, 21st; first published in Russian *Narodnaya Volya*, 5th February). *February* On medical advice leaves London for Algiers, staying en route at Argenteuil (9th to 16th) and meeting the socialists Guesde, Deville and Mesa in Paris. In Algiers his health worsens, while 'my mind is to a large extent absorbed by the memory of my wife.' Discussions in Algiers on Arab landed property and French colonialism with the civil judge Albert Fermé. *May* Leaves Algiers (2nd) for Monte Carlo, where his pleurisy is finally cured. *June* Again at Argenteuil (6th, until 22nd August); frequent meetings with Lafargue. Reads two new pamphlets by Loria and studies chemistry (June 1882 to January 1883). *August* Meets Guesde, Lafargue and Deville in Paris (2nd). Goes to Lausanne (23rd) and then Vevey (27th, until 25th September) with daughter Laura. *September* Reads and makes numerous notes on the study of the Russian countryside by Engelhardt (September/October). On way back from Vevey stays again at Argenteuil (28th until start October). Passes through Paris, commenting to Engels: 'the "Marxists" and the "anti-Marxists" at their respective conferences . . . have done everything possible to spoil my stay in France.' *October* After only three weeks in London moves to Ventnor (30th). Asks Bernstein, through Engels, for copy of Swiss factory law for third edition of *Capital*. Around this time reads Mulhall, Blunt, Keay and Peter the Hermit on Egypt, noting the growing role of joint stock companies in colonial exploitation, and Lubbock's *Origin of Civilisation*. A new bronchial infection keeps Marx indoors. *November* Reading on differential calculus and applications of electricity (Hospitalier). Correspondence with Engels (11th, 22nd) on the French workers party. *December* Asks Engels to arrange publication in *Sozialdemokrat* of material on conditions in Prussian state mines, to resist Wagener's 'state socialism' (8th). Letter to Laura Lafargue on his growing influence in Russia: 'nowhere is my success more delightful; it gives me that satisfaction that I damage a power, which, besides England, is the true bulwark of the old society' (14th). Praises Engels's MS on the Mark (18th). Marx reads intensively on Russia through the year (besides Engelhardt, Semevskii, Issaev, Mineiko, Vorontzov, Skrebitskii), he also read in 1882 Brousse's *Le Marxisme dans Internationale*.

1883

January Letter to his daughter Eleanor on the 'shameless Christian-hypocritical conquest' of Egypt. Eleanor brings Marx news of his daughter Jenny's death (11th): later she wrote: 'I have lived many a sad hour, but none so sad as that.' Marx returns to London (12th), where he developed laryngitis and bronchitis, and in February a tumour on the lung. *March* On 14th March, at 2.45 in the afternoon, Marx died peacefully in his study. He was 64. He was buried at Highgate cemetery in London on 17th March. Engels delivered the main graveside speech, comparing Marx with

Darwin in discovering the fundamental law of human history. Longuet read messages from French and Spanish socialists and from Lavrov (see p. 174) parting 'on behalf of all the Russian socialists' from 'the most outstanding contemporary socialist'. Liebknecht spoke for the German Party, celebrating Marx as the man who gave to the proletariat and its party 'social science . . . which kills capitalism'. From Russia, contributions for wreaths were received from student organisations in St. Petersburg, Moscow and Odessa.

A note on sources

There is no space here to list all sources used. I found the following most helpful: the chronologies and editorial notes to the relevant volumes of the Marx-Engels, *Werke* (Berlin, Dietz-Verlag); *Karl Marx: Chronik seines Lebens in Einzeldaten* (Moscow, 1934); M. Rubel and M. Manale, *Marx without Myth* (Oxford, Blackwell, 1975); M. Rubel, *Marx: Life and Works* (London, Macmillan, 1980); *Karl Marx: A Biography* (Moscow, Progress, 1973); *Archiv K. Marksa i F. Engel'sa* (Moscow, 1924 onwards); and the following editions and anthologies of Marx or Marx and Engels, all from Progress, Moscow unless otherwise indicated: *Documents of the First International* (5 volumes, 1962); *The Hague Congress of the First International* (1976–8, 2 volumes); *Ireland and the Irish Question* (1978); *On the Paris Commune* (1971); *Selected Correspondence* (edns of 1934, ed. D. Torr, London, Lawrence & Wishart, 1956 and 1975); *Letters to Kugelmann* (London, Martin Lawrence, n.d.); *Letters to Americans* (New York, International, 1969); *Writings on the Paris Commune* (New York, Monthly Review Press, 1971); *The First International and After* (Harmondsworth, Penguin, 1974), *Capital* vols 1-3, *Ethnological Notebooks* (ed. L. Krader, Assen, Van Gorcum, 1972); and L. Krader, *The Asiatic Mode of Production* (which contains a MS by Marx on Kovalevskii) (Assen, Van Gorcum, 1975). A fuller version of this chronology is available in *Working Paper* no. 4, Department of Sociology, University of Glasgow.

The Russian scene: a biographical note

Jonathan Sanders

Bakunin, Mikhail Alexandrovich (1814–1876) Russian revolutionary and anarchist leader in Europe; Marx's chief opponent in the first International. From a noble family; educated in St. Petersburg at the artillery school. Went abroad in 1840, arrested and extradited to Russia for participation in the Dresden revolution. Consequently spent six years in prisons before being exiled to Siberia from where he escaped abroad in 1861. Bakunin's writings, especially the tract *State and Anarchy* (1873), greatly influenced many Russians. His exhortations to agitate among the people significantly contributed to the 'to the people' movement of the mid-1870s.

Barannikov, Aleksander Ivanovich (1858–1883) Populist revolutionary. From a noble family, left army officers' school to 'go to the people' under an assumed name. Member of Land and Liberty, worked as blacksmith at one of its settlements. Member of the Executive Committee of the People's Will since its creation. Arrested in 1881, sentenced to life imprisonment with penal labour. Died in Petropavlovsk prison in 1883.

Bervi (Flerovskii), Vasilii Vasil'evich (1829–1918) Populist theorist and activist. Son of a professor at Kazan University from which he graduated in 1849. A state official, dismissed and confined to a psychiatric hospital for denouncing the insufficiencies of the peasant emancipation of 1862 (he explained its shortcomings in a letter to Marx in 1871). Observations made in provincial exile formed the basis for his 1869 book, *The Situation of the Working Class in Russia*. Including peasants in his definition of the working class, Bervi emphasized the possibilities of socialist advance through communes and industrial co-operatives. Arrested for his *Alphabet of Social Science* and participation in secret circles, Bervi spent most of the 1870s and 1880s in confinement.

Chernyshevskii, Nikolai Gavrilovich (1828–1899) Major Populist theorist, writer and journalist. Son of a priest, educated at theological seminary and St. Petersburg University. Member of the Petrashevskii radical circle. Published in 1855 his influential Master's Essay, *The Aesthetic Relationship of Art and Reality*, calling for art to become the forum for posing moral and political questions in Russia. Editor of *The Contemporary* (*Sovremennik*) – the main radical journal of Russia. Wrote extensively about history, economics, sociology, aesthetics, etc. Arrested in 1862. While in prison wrote a didactic novel, *What is to be Done?* in which positive heroes, new men and women, exemplified Chernyshevskii's socialist views about life in co-operative communities. His ascetic goal-oriented heroes and heroines became models for several generations of Russian revolutionaries. Chernyshevskii spent the remainder of his life under arrest, mostly in Siberian prisons and exile.

Danielson (Nikolai-on), Nikolai Frantsevich (1844–1918) Populist economist, first translator of *Capital* into Russian. Born in Revel (Talin), attended St. Petersburg University. Arrested in 1870 for involvement in the 'Nechaev affair'. In the 1870s and 1880s reputed to be the foremost exponent of Marxism in Russia. Carried on long correspondence with Marx who urged Danielson to write his *Outlines of Our Post-Reform Economy* (an article in 1880, a book in 1893). Danielson believed that the socialization of labour could be accomplished without passing through the capitalist stage of development if the state would carry out the unification of agriculture and industry. Plekhanov singled out Danielson for attack in *Our Disagreements* (1884), as did Lenin later in *The Development of Capitalism in Russia* (1899).

Deich, Lev Grigorevich (1855–1941) Revolutionary activist. From a merchant family. Joined Land and Liberty and in 1877 attempted to organize a peasant insurrection. Member of Black Repartition, co-founder of Emancipation of Labour. Extradited from Germany, spent thirteen years in Russian prisons. Joined the RSDWP Menshevik wing. In 1917 member of Plekhanov's Edinstvo group.
Gartman, Lev Nikolaevich (Leo Hartman) (1850–1913) Populist revolutionary. Son of a German colonist family, graduated from an Arkhangel'sk gymnasium and then moved to St. Petersburg where he became involved in the radical youth movements. An active

member of Land and Liberty, he participated in the 'to the people' movement. Subsequently joined the People's Will. After playing a key role in the ill-fated attempt to blow up the tsar's train (1879), Gartman fled to Western Europe and appointed official representative of the People's Will. In close contact with Marx. Co-edited *Russian Socialist-Revolutionary Library* which published the second Russian translation of *The Communist Manifesto*.

Herzen (Gertsen), Aleksandr Ivanovich (1812-1870) Major Populist theorist, radical journalist and memoirist. Illegitimate son of a wealthy noble. Admirer of Decembrists, attended Moscow University. Left Russia in 1846, never to return. Participated in the 1848 revolution in France. Disillusioned by this and by the moral decay of Western Europe, Herzen suggested that Russia might skip the bourgeois stage of development and move directly to socialism, putting to use its specific social organizations, especially the peasant commune. In London published the journals *The Polar Star* (1855-62) and *The Bell* (*Kolokol*) (1857-67), smuggled into Russia where their emancipationist advocacy was influential.

Kibal'chich, Nikolai Ivanovich (1853-1881) Populist revolutionary and scientist. From a priest's family, educated as an engineer and a medical doctor. Chief 'technician' of the People's Will party and the bomb-maker for the final attack on Tsar Alexander II. Arrested and while awaiting execution Kibal'chich worked on plans for jet propulsion of flying machines. Publicly executed in 1881.

Kovalevskii, Maksim Maksimovich (1851-1916) Historian, sociologist and ethnographer of law, later a liberal politician. Kovalevskii graduated from Kharkov University and studied at the major universities of Western Europe. A professor at Moscow University 1878-87, Kovaleskii was dismissed for oppositional views and spent most of the period 1888-1905 abroad. Well acquainted with Marx, visited him in London and maintained correspondence with him. Author of works on the social structure of medieval Europe as well as of comparative studies of traditional communal agriculture (extensively reviewed in Marx's notes).

Lavrov, Petr Lavrovich (1823-1900) Major Populist theorist and writer. Son of a landowner. Educated at the St. Petersburg artillery school, later mathematics professor there. His *Historical Letter* (1870), calling on the critically thinking minority to repay their debt to the common people, influenced the 'to the people' movement of the 1870s and the 'settling among the people' tendency of the 1880s. Member of the Land and Liberty organization. Escaped abroad where he edited *Forward!* (1873–7) and co-edited the *Messenger of the People's Will*. Developed much of the Populist 'subjective sociology'. Offered major theoretical argument against Bakunin's anarchism. Joined the first International. Participated in the Paris Commune. Met with Marx in 1871, establishing a lasting relationship. Founding member of the second International in 1889.

Lopatin, German Aleksandrovich (1845–1918) One of the most active Russian revolutionaries of the 1870s and 1880s. Son of a bureaucrat; graduate of St. Petersburg University. Active in organizations which aimed to spread Populist ideas in the 1860s and 1870s. In London established close personal relations with Marx. Began first translation of *Capital* into Russian. Member of the General Council of the first International where he aided Marx in his confrontation with Bakunin. Arrested in 1879 trying to organize Chernyshevskii's escape from Siberia. After the mass arrests of 1881 and 1882 joined and tried to revive the People's Will organization. Member of its newly constituted leadership. Arrested in 1884, Lopatin was tried in the 1887 'trial of 21' and sentenced to death; his sentence commuted to life imprisonment.

Mikhailov, Aleksandr Dmitrievich (1855-1885) Populist revolutionary from a noble family, expelled from the St. Petersburg Technological Institute in 1875 for student disturbances. Played a leading role in the Land and Liberty organization. Theorist of strong and centralized revolutionary organization. Considered the finest politician and conspiratorial organizer of the 1870s. Member of the Executive Committee of the People's Will since its creation. Arrested in 1880. Death sentence commuted to life imprisonment with heavy labour. Died in the Petropavlovsk prison.

Mikhailovskii, Nikolai Konstantinovich (1842-1904) A major sociologist, writer and journalist of the non-revolutionary wing within the Populist movement. From a noble family, Mikhailovskii graduated from the St. Petersburg Institute of Mining Engineers.

Editor of *Notes of the Fatherland* (*Otechestvennye Zapiski*). Since the early 1890s editor of the highly influential *Russian Wealth*. (*Russkoe Bogatstvo*). Sympathized and helped with the People's Will.

Morozov, Nikolai Aleksandrovich (1854–1946) Populist revolutionary. Illegitimate son of a noble landowner and an enserfed peasant woman. Morozov participated in the radical youth movements of the 1870s and went abroad where he helped produce the newspapers of Bakunin and Lavrov. Member of the first International. Returning to Russia he joined Land and Liberty and then the People's Will. In 1880 Morozov travelled to London where he briefed Marx on the activities and views of the Russian revolutionary Populists. Upon his return to Russia in 1881 he was arrested and imprisoned in the Schlisselburg Prison until the 1905 amnesty. In prison he devoted himself to science.

Nikolaevskii, Boris Ivanovich (1887-1966) Activist, historian and archivist of the Russian revolutionary movement. From a family of clerics. Expelled from high school for revolutionary activities. A Bolshevik in 1905, a Menshevik afterwards, and after his exile from the Soviet Union in 1922 a pillar of the Menshevik movements abroad. Author of 'The Letter of an Old Bolshevik'. Editor of *Socialist Courier* (*Sotsialisticheskii Vestnik*). In the 1920s acted as D. Ryazanov's (see below) representative in Europe collecting manuscripts for the Marx-Engels-Lenin Institute in Moscow. Saved extensive archives of Marx and Engels from the Nazis. Moved to United States in 1940. Curator of his own collection of Russian revolutionary materials at the Hoover Institute until his death.

Plekhanov, Georgi Valentinovich (1856–1918) Major Marxist theorist, 'Father of Russian Marxism'. From a noble family. Expelled from St. Petersburg Mining Institute in 1876 for revolutionary activity. Co-author of programme of Land and Liberty and after its split founder of the Black Repartition group. Afterwards converted to Marxism and helped to found the Emancipation of Labour (1883). In *Our Differences* (1885) Plekhanov attacked the basic notions of Russian Populism. Co-founder of the second International, of 'Iskra' and of the RSDWP. Eventually joined its Menshevik wing. A war-supporter (*oboronets*) in 1914–17. Returned to Russia after the February 1917 revolution, leader of the Edinstvo group which supported the Provisional Government and opposed both the Zimmerwaldists, left-wing Mensheviks of Martov, and the Bolsheviks.

Ryazanov (Gol'denbakh), David Borisovich (1870–1938) Marxist scholar and archivist. Joined the Social-Democratic movement in Odessa in the 1890s. Emigrated in 1900 and formed the *Bor'ba* group. Remained a 'non-fractional' member of the Social-Democratic Party until 1906 when he joined the Mensheviks. Internationalist and Zimmerwaldist during the First World War, he was a member of the Mezhraiontsy faction in Petrograd, which joined the Bolshevik Party in August 1917. Delegate to most of the party congresses. Often the *enfante terrible*, he frequently disagreed in public with Lenin and Stalin. (Famous for interrupting a speech by Stalin with the remark, 'Stop it Koba, don't make a fool of yourself. Everybody knows that theory is not exactly your field.') Played a leading role in the Socialist Academy, first director of the Marx-Engels-Lenin Institute. Stripped of offices in 1931. Exiled in 1937. Died under unknown circumstances.

Tikhomirov, Lev Aleksandrovich (1852-1923). Populist revolutionary, later a renegade. Studied at Moscow University. Arrested in 1873 for revolutionary propaganda among workers. Member of Land and Liberty and later of the Executive Committee of People's Will. Left Russia in 1882, edited (together with Lavrov) the *Messenger of the People's Will*. Later made his peace with the government, returned and came to edit the violently monarchist *Moskovskie Vedomosti*.

Tkachev, Petr Nikitich (1844–1885) Revolutionary activist, proponent of Jacobinism. From noble family, expelled from St. Petersburg University in 1861 for his role in student disturbances. Opposing Lavrov, Tkachev argued that a conspiratorial seizure of political power by a disciplined elite was necessary to realize socialism in Russia. Delaying such action, he believed, would obviate the possibility of skipping the capitalist stage of development by allowing Russia's incipient capitalism to grow. In the 1880s he gradually lost his grip on reality, and was confined to a French psychiatric hospital where he died.

Ulianov, Alekansandr Il'ich (1866-1887) Populist revolutionary, leading participant in the last attempt to re-establish the People's Will party. Son of a government official enobled for service. Elder brother of Lenin. Attended St. Petersburg University, where he became instrumental in organizing the mainly student Revolutionary Faction of the People's Will. Arrested in 1887 for plotting to assassinate Tsar Alexander III. Executed the same year.

Utin, Nikolai Isaakovich (1841-1883) Political activist. Son of a rich merchant family. Expelled from university and arrested for participation in the 1861 'student disturbances'. Member of Land and Liberty. Abroad co-edited *People's Course* (*Narodnor Delo*) and *Egalité*. From 1867 Secretary of the Russian section of the International, based in Switzerland.

Zasulich, Vera Ivanovna (1849-1919) Revolutionary activist. From a noble family, trained as a schoolteacher. In 1878 she shot the St. Petersburg governor Trepov for flogging a prisoner. In a great political trial she was acquitted. She joined Plekhanov in the Black Repartition and in exile in Geneva. Subsequently with Axelrod, Plekhanov and Deich she founded the Emancipation of Labour Group. Co-founder of the *Iskra*, the RSDWP, later a Menshevik. In 1917 a member of the Social-Democratic Edinstvo group lead by Plekhanov.

Zhelyabov, Andrei Ivanovich (1851-1881) Populist revolutionary. Son of household serfs from southern Russia. Active in student movement at Odessa University from which he was expelled in 1872 for organizing demonstrations. Independently spread Populist propaganda among Odessa workers and students. After being imprisoned for oppositional activities Zhelyabov gave up peaceful propaganda and devoted himself to 'fighting with deeds'. Member of the Executive Committee of the People's Will, he was particularly active among the workers of St. Petersburg. (See Programme of the Workers Organization, pp. 231-7). Co-planned the 1881 regicide, but was arrested days before it was accomplished. Publicly executed in 1881.

Part III
The Russian Revolutionary Tradition 1850 to 1890

Views concerning the impact of Russian revolutionary populism of the 1850s to the 1880s on the attitudes of Marx (and of Lenin) run the whole gamut from total denial to assumptions equating Marx with Chernyshevskii (and Lenin with the Slavophiles). The complex way such cross-influences work, the continuities and changes in the work of major social theorists and political leaders, make simple yes/no answers useless in such a dispute. The translations which follow should help the readers to work it out for themselves, but to do so, all of it must be read on its own terms, i.e. in the context of the Russian society of the 1850s to 1880s and the revolutionary challenge rooted in its social, political and intellectual experience.

Part Three begins with two writings by Chernyshevskii which claimed the particular attention of Marx. The impact of the first of those items on Marx's own thought can be clearly seen by direct comparison with Part Two above. The ironically oblique form of the *Unaddressed Letters* (written for a heavily 'censored' journal) clearly did not preclude their understanding by the generation to which they belonged. The whole sequence of articles was banned and their author sentenced for high treason shortly afterwards, never to become a free man again. On 'the other side of the barricade', it was passed for decades from hand to hand within the Russian revolutionary circles, while outside Russia, Marx was involved in attempts to have it published and even translated its 'first letter' in full.

The documents of People's Will begin with a letter from their Executive Committee to Marx and the organisation's Programme, which Marx read with particular attention. An article by Kibalchich which follows offers a particularly illuminating insight into the theoretical position adopted by People's Will as it moved away from the early 'ruralism' of the populists within the Land and Liberty organisation. The Tactical Programme of the Party ('the preparatory work') extends and specifies the tactical considerations and the class analysis accepted by the organisation. This was further developed in the specific programmes offered by People's Will to the different sections of the revolutionary camp they attempted to construct, i.e. urban workers, army officers, etc. Finally, the two last letters should make clear the issues which concerned the militants of the People's Will on trial for their lives, the type of men and women they were and the impact their trials had on their own generation.

The last article is devoted to Marxism and vernacular revolutionary traditions. It brings the volume to conclusion by suggesting some relations between its Parts I, II and III, as well as ways all of these mesh with the concerns of our own generation.

Nikolai Chernyshevskii: Selected writings

Nikolai Chernyshevskii (1828–1889) was a representative, a symbol and a spiritual leader of the radical wing of the first generation of Russians who were 'Western' by education, yet neither nobles nor foreigners by birth (the *raznochintsy*). His character and fate were as significant to his social role as were his views and his writings. Chernyshevskii was born of a long line of ecclesiastics in the city of Saratov, a major centre of Russian provincial dissent. He spoke of himself, rightly, as 'self-taught', acquiring none the less extensive knowledge of European history, philosophy and economics as well as of the conditions of Russia. Doggedly opposing the pressures of the authorities and censorship, Chernyshevskii came to exercise considerable impact during the 1853–62 period, as the editor and major writer of *Sovremennik* (*The Contemporary*), the most radical journal published in Russia. After refusing a pointed suggestion by the governor of St. Petersburg to emigrate to the West, Chernyshevskii was arrested in 1862 and spent two years of preliminary detention in the Peter and Paul fortress, while his judges struggled with the regrettable lack of evidence of actual law-breaking. Undeterred, they finally sentenced him to penal labour in Siberia, to which a 'civic execution' depriving him of all his legal rights was added for good measure. He was never subsequently a free man.

The impact of Chernyshevskii on further generations of Russian radical intelligentsia did not come to an end with his arrest. His didactic novel, *What is to be done?*, written in the Peter and Paul fortress, has even further extended his impact on the views and the self-image of the Russian left. A number of attempts were made by Russian revolutionaries to 'spring' Chernyshevskii from his Siberian imprisonment, one of them by Lopatin who was befriended by Marx and who provided a living link between Marx, Chernyshevskii and the People's Will (see p. 175). Later, in the 1880s, the People's Will had agreed to a cease fire for the duration of the coronation of Alexander III in exchange for Chernyshevskii being transferred from exile in Siberia to easier conditions of house arrest in European Russia. By the time he came back to Europe in 1883 he was very ill, never to recover. Neither his death and the fact that many of his writings were banned by censorship, nor the considerable changes on the political map of Russia in the 1890s, made Chernyshevskii's influence disappear. Young Lenin was still to choose for his own first book a title directly repeating that of Chernyshevskii's novel which he had read and admired, together with the whole of his own generation, i.e. *What is to be Done?*

Chernyshevskii never read Marx. The texts which follow are known to have been read and reread by Marx, who translated in full the first part of the *Unaddressed Letters* and took steps to help with their publication in Western Europe.

The text which follows was translated by Quintin Hoare from the contemporary full edition of Chernyshevskii's writings. It contains extracts from two items:

A. The *Critique of Philosophical Prejudices Against Communal Ownership* (1859) (this page);

B. The *Unaddressed Letters* (1862) (page 190) – a series of five articles aimed at Tsar Alexander II and representing their author's response to the actual results of the emancipation of serfs, 1861, as enacted by the government. They were prepared for the 1862 (No. 2) issue of the *Sovremennik* and banned by censorship.

A Critique of Philosophical Prejudices against Communal Ownership

Before the question of the rural commune (*obshchina*) acquired practical importance, with the beginning of work on the transformation of village relations, the Russian *obshchina* constituted an object of mystical pride for exclusive worshippers of the Russian national character, who imagined that nothing resembling our communal system existed among other peoples and that it must, therefore, be regarded as an innate peculiarity of the Russian or Slav race, of exactly the same kind as, for instance, cheekbones broader than in other Europeans, or a language which calls men *muzh* and not *mensch*, *homo* or *l'homme*, and which has seven cases, not six as in Latin or five as in Greek. By now, educated and impartial people have shown that a communal land system, in the form which now exists in our country, exists among many other people who have not yet emerged from relations close to the patriarchal way of life, and did exist among all the rest when they were close to that way of life. It turned out that communal ownership of land had existed among the Germans, among the French, among the forebears of the English, among the forebears of the Italians, in short among all European peoples; but then in the course of subsequent historical evolution it gradually fell out of use, giving way to private land ownership. The conclusion from this is clear. It is no use our considering communal ownership as a peculiar, innate feature of our national character; we should regard it rather as a general human property, belonging to a certain period in the life of every people. Also, there is certainly no point in our taking pride in the fact that this remnant of primitive antiquity has been preserved, just as in general no one should take particular pride in anything antique whatsoever, since preservation of the antique only testifies to the slow and sluggish nature of historical development. Preservation of the *obshchina* in relation to land, while among other peoples it has disappeared in this sense, proves only that we have lived far less than these peoples. Thus this fact is quite useless for the purpose of crowing over other nations.

Such a view is absolutely correct; from it, however, Russian and foreign economists of the old school have taken it into their heads to draw the following conclusion: 'Private landed property is a later form that has supplanted apparently communal ownership, which with the historical development of social relations has proved unable to stand up to it; hence, like other nations, we must abandon it if we want to go forward along the path of development.'

This conclusion serves as one of the most fundamental and general bases for rejecting communal ownership. One could hardly find a single adversary of communal ownership who would not repeat with all the others: 'Communal ownership is a primitive form of land relations, while private landed property is a second stage; how should one then not prefer the higher form to the lower?' There is only one strange thing here, for us. Many of the adversaries of communal ownership are followers of the new German philosophy: some boast of being Schellingists, others strongly support the Hegelian school. So what puzzles us about these same people is how they have failed to notice that, by stressing the primitive nature of communal ownership, they were bringing out precisely that aspect of it which must extremely powerfully predispose in favour of communal ownership all those who are familiar with the discoveries of German philosophy regarding the continuity of forms in the process of world development. . . .

For our part, we are not disciples of Hegel, still less disciples of Schelling. But I cannot but acknowledge that both these systems have rendered great services to science, by discovering the general forms through which the development process moves. The basic result of these discoveries is expressed by the following axiom: 'In its form, the higher stage of development resembles the source from which it proceeds.' This notion contains within itself the fundamental essence of Schelling's system. It was revealed even more precisely and in greater detail by Hegel, whose whole system consists in the enactment of this basic principle through all the phenomena of world life, from its most general conditions to the minutest details of each particular sphere of existence. For readers familiar with German philosophy, our subsequent amplification of this law will not represent anything new; it must serve only to highlight the inconsistency of people who have failed to notice that they are providing weapons against themselves when they so forcibly stress how primitive a form communal ownership is. . . .

* * *

The perusal of articles against communal ownership has convinced us that dislike of this form of land relations is based not so much on facts or ideas specifically related to the object in question, as on general philosophical and moral views about life. We consider that prejudices concerning the particular question which interests us can only be destroyed through the exposition of sound ideas, in opposition to the backward philosophemes or philosophical and moral oversights upon which their prejudices are based. . . .

* * *

Leaving aside the political system, whose history could also serve as a striking confirmation of our argument regarding the general predominance of this norm of development, we shall cite as examples only two further social institutions.

In the beginning, society knows no separate estate of judges; justice and punishment in the primitive tribe are meted out by all the independent members of the tribe at a general meeting (village assembly). Gradually judicial power is hived off from the citizens and made the monopoly of a specific estate; the public character of legal proceedings vanishes, and a trial procedure that is very well-known to us is established – it existed in France and Germany too. But now society develops further: instead of judges, delivery of the verdict is entrusted to jurors – in other words, ordinary members of society who have no learned training in juridical technique – and the original form of the court returns. (1. Society passed judgment; 2. jurists appointed by government authority pass judgment; 3. jurors, i.e. simply representatives of society, pass judgment.)

Like justice, the military function too in primitive society is a property of all members of the tribe, without any specialization. The form of military power is at first everywhere identical: irregulars who take up arms on the outbreak of war and revert to peaceful pursuits in time of peace. There is no specific military estate. Gradually one forms, and attains, a high degree of individuality with long terms of service or with mercenary recruitment. We can still remember a time when a soldier in our country became a soldier for his entire life, and no one apart from these soldiers knew the military craft or took part in wars. But then terms of service begin to grow shorter, and the system of indefinite furlough becomes more and more widespread. Finally (in Prussia), it reaches a point where absolutely every citizen becomes a soldier for a certain time (two or three years), and soldiering no longer belongs to a specific estate, but is merely a certain period in the life of every man in each estate. Here its specificity has been maintained only in a periodic-service stipulation. In North America and Switzerland there is no longer even that: exactly as in the primitive tribe, in peacetime the army does not exist while in time of war all citizens take up arms. So once again there are three phases, with the highest, in form, representing a complete return of the most primitive: 1. absence of regular troops, militia in time of war; 2. regular troops, no one except those specifically wearing uniform is called up or can take part in war; 3. a nationwide militia returns once more, and there is no regular army in peacetime. . . .

The norm we have described, which no one in the least familiar with contemporary thinking about the general laws of the world can doubt, will inevitably lead to land relations being formed as follows:

- Primitive state (beginning of development). Communal ownership of land. It exists because human labour does not have durable, valuable connections with a certain plot of land. Nomads have no agriculture, they do not carry out any work on the land. Agriculture, too, is at first not combined with the outlay of almost any capital strictly upon the land.
- Second stage (intensification of development). Agriculture requires outlays of capital and labour strictly upon the land. The land is improved by a whole number of different methods and works, of which manuring represents the most general and universal necessity. The man who lays out capital on the land must now inalienably own it; as a result, the land passes into private ownership. This form achieves its aims, because landownership is not an object of speculation but a source of regular income.

These are the two systems about which the adversaries of communal ownership speak. But only two, you see: where is the third? Is the course of development really exhausted by these two?

Industrial-commercial activity intensifies and produces a colossal growth of speculation. Speculation, after enveloping all other departments of the national economy, turns to the fundamental and most extensive branch: agriculture. That is why individual landed property loses its former character. Formerly, the owner of the land was the person who worked it and laid out his capital to improve it (the system of small proprietors cultivating their plots with their own hands; also the system of tenancy and hereditary share-cropping, with or without servile dependence). But now a new system appears: contract farming. Under this, when rent goes up as a consequence of the improvements the farmer has introduced, it falls into the hands of another person who has either not participated at all or only participated to a quite insignificant extent with his capital in improving the land, but who nevertheless profits from any return that the improvements may yield. Thus private ownership of land ceases to be a method of recompensing outlay of capital on the improvement of land. At the same time, cultivation of the land begins to require capital inputs that exceed the means of the vast majority of cultivators, while the farm economy requires dimensions which far exceed the capacities of an individual family and which – in terms of the extent of economic plots – also exclude (under private ownership) the vast majority of cultivators from sharing in the benefits afforded by the operation of that economy, thus turning this majority into hired workers. With these changes, the reasons which existed in former times for the advantage of private property in land over communal ownership are being destroyed. Communal ownership is becoming the sole means to give the vast majority of cultivators a share in the returns which the land comes to yield as a result of improvements effected in working it. Thus communal ownership is necessary not only for the well-being of the agricultural class, but also for the progress of agriculture itself. It appears the only full and rational way of combining the farmer's gain with improvement of the land and productive methods with conscientious execution of work. And without this combination, fully successful production is impossible.

Anyone familiar with the basic ideas of the modern world-view is irresistibly led to this most powerful conviction, precisely by that very characteristic of primitiveness which the adversaries of communal ownership adduce as its decisive disadvantage for them. Precisely this characteristic compels one to regard it as the form which relations on the land must assume, if a high level of development is to be achieved; precisely this characteristic indicates that communal ownership represents a higher form of man's relations with the land.

Whether at the present time our civilization has actually reached that high level whose features must include communal ownership is a question which can no longer be resolved through logical inductions or deductions from general world laws, but only through analysis of the facts. . . .

* * *

History, like a granny, is terribly fond of its younger grandchildren. *Tarde venientibus* she gives not *ossa* but *medullam ossium*,[(a)] in breaking which Western Europe has hurt its fingers so painfully.

But we have been carried away in a dithyramb, we have been addressing the reader and forgetting that we must speak to the

(a) To the latecomers, she gives not bones but the marrow from the bones.

adversaries of communal ownership, in other words concern ourselves with the ABC. We shall now return to elementary concepts.

We were concerned with the question of whether a given social phenomenon has to pass through all the logical moments in the real life of every society, or whether under favourable circumstances it can leap from the first or second stage of development directly to the fifth or sixth, omitting the ones in the middle, as happens with the phenomena of individual life and in the processes of physical nature. . . .

Two whole printer's sheets have brought us to two conclusions which, for any reader at all familiar with the ideas of modern science, could have been adequately conveyed in six lines:

1. the higher stage of development coincides in form with its source;
2. under the influence of the high development which a certain phenomenon of social life has attained among the most advanced peoples, this phenomenon can develop very swiftly among other peoples, and rise from a lower level straight to a higher one, passing over the intermediate logical moments.

What a meagre outcome of arguments occupying two whole printer's sheets! Any reader with a modicum of education and sharpness of wit will say that it would have been enough simply to state these basic truths, which are obvious to the point of banality, like such facts as that the Danube flows into the Black Sea, the Volga into the Caspian, that Spitzbergen has a cold climate, the island of Sumatra a hot one and so on. To demonstrate such things in a book intended for literate people is indecent.

Quite so. To demonstrate and explain such truths is indecent. Yet what are you to do when conclusions drawn from these truths are rejected, or when people complacently repeat to you a hundred times, as if it were an unanswerable objection, some fantastic idea which can only be clung to through forgetfulness or ignorance of some elementary truth?

For example, you say: 'Communal ownership of land must be retained in Russia.' With a bold air of triumph they object, 'But communal ownership is a primitive form, while private property in land appeared later and is therefore a higher form of land relations.'

Have pity on yourselves, Messrs. objectors, have pity on your learned reputations: you see precisely because, *precisely because*, precisely because communal ownership is a primitive form, one must consider that it is impossible for a higher stage of development of land relations to manage without this form. . . .

Just as that poor toiler the parochial teacher keeps up his strength with the thought of his wearisome occupation's high and great significance, so we too have fortified ourselves by recalling the weighty significance that the truisms we have been busy expounding have for clarifying our whole view of the world. . . .

Our first truism – do not judge it lightly: the eternal alternation of forms, the eternal rejection of the form engendered by a certain content or aspiration as a result of the strengthening of that same aspiration or a further development of that same content – whosoever has understood this great eternal, universal law and schooled himself to apply it to every phenomenon, oh! how calmly he invokes prospects which throw others into confusion! Repeating after the poet:

> I have let things take their chance,
> And the whole world belongs to me. . . .[b]

he has no regrets for anything which has had its day, and says: 'Whatever will be, will be, but in the end our day will come all the same'.

The second principle is almost more striking even than the first. For anyone who has grasped this principle, how entertaining is all talk about the inevitability of this or that evil, about how for a thousand years we must necessarily drink the bitter cup which others drank: but, you see, it has been drained by others, so why should we drink it? Their experience has instructed us, and their good offices assist us to prepare a new beverage, tastier and healthier. All that others have attained is a ready-made legacy to us. Not we laboured to invent the railways, but we use them.

Not we have fought against the mediaeval system, but when it falls in other countries it will not hold out in ours. You see, we too live in Europe and that is enough – all good achieved for itself by any advanced people is thereby already three-quarters prepared for us as well. All that is necessary is to find out what has been done

(b) From J.W. Goethe, *Vanitas*

and how, all that is needed is to understand the advantage, and then everything will be easy.

The hand of time lies heavy on us,
Labour exhausts us.
Fortune is all-powerful, life fragile –
But that which has once been gripped by life,
It is not in the power of the Fates to remove from us.[(c)]

(c) From N. Nekrasov, *Novyi god*

Unaddressed Letters[1]

I

First Letter

Saint Petersburg,
5 February

Dear Sir,

You are displeased with us. Let that be as you choose: no one can command their feelings, and we are not seeking your approval. Our aim is a different one, which you probably have as well: to be of service to the Russian people. Consequently, you must not expect real gratitude from us, nor must we from you, for our respective labours. A judge of them does exist, outside your numerically restricted circle, and outside even our circle which, though far more numerous than yours, still represents only a negligible fraction of the tens of millions of people whose welfare we and you would like to promote. If this judge knew all the facts of the case and could deliver an assessment of your labour and ours, any explanations between you and us would be superfluous.

Regrettably, this is not the case. You, he knows by name; yet being completely alien to your mental universe and your milieu, he certainly does not know your thoughts or the motives which guide your actions. Us, he does not know even by name. You must agree, dear sir, that the situation is a false one. To work for people who do not understand those who are working for them is both very awkward for those doing the working and unhelpful to the success of the work itself. You think some deed will be beneficial, then see it remain unaccomplished due to lack of sympathy among the very people on whose behalf it has been undertaken. You have experienced this with every one of your fine deeds. We too have very often had the same experience. It grieves and ultimately enrages those to whom it happens. One becomes suspicious and short-tempered. One does not have the courage to explain one's failure by its real cause – the lack of any community of ideas between yourself and the people for whom you are working. To acknowledge this cause would be too painful, since it would destroy any hope of success for the whole mode of activity one is pursuing. One does not want to acknowledge this real cause, but strives to find trivial explanations for failure in unimportant, incidental circumstances, since it is easier to change these than it is to transform one's mode of activity. Thus you heap the blame for your failures upon us, while some of our people put the blame for their failures on you. How fine it would be, if these people of ours or you were right to explain their and your respective failures in this way. Then the problem could easily be resolved by eliminating the external obstacle to the success of the enterprise. Sadly, however, none of our activity against you or of yours against us can lead to anything beneficial. The people remains apathetic: so what result could all your trouble or our effort on its behalf produce, even if you or we were to remain alone on the field of operations?

You tell the people: you must proceed like this. We tell it: you must proceed like that. But in the people's midst, almost everyone is slumbering. And those few who have awoken answer: appeals have long been dispensed to the people for it to proceed in one way or another, and on many occasions it has endeavoured to accept these appeals, but they have brought no advantage. They called on the people to save Moscow from the Poles – the people came, saved the city and was left in a condition worse than before, worse than it would have been under the Poles.[2] Then they said: save the Ukraine; the people did so, but neither they nor the Ukraine were any better off for that.[3] The people was told: get yourself a connection with Europe: so it conquered the Swedes and, with the Baltic harbours, won itself only military levies and the confirmation of serfdom. Subsequently, after fresh appeals, it many times defeated the Turks, took Lithuania, destroyed Poland – but once again received no benefit for itself. They mobilized it against Napoleon: it won supremacy in Europe for its sovereign, but was itself still left in its former condition. It has garnered just the same benefit from all the appeals made since. Why ever should it now be carried away by new appeals of any kind? It does not expect to gain any more from these than from the previous ones.

Are you or we to blame for this popular mistrust? The present complexion of the people's views has been created by a long course of events which occurred before you and us. Let us strive to comprehend this.

The truth is equally bitter for you and for us. The people does not consider that anything really useful to it has resulted from anyone's concern about it. We all, separating ourselves from the people under some name or other – under the name of the authorities, or under the name of this or that privilged stratum; we all, assuming we have some particular interests distinct from the objects of popular aspiration – whether interests of diplomatic and military power, or interests of controlling internal affairs, or interests of our personal wealth, or interests of enlightenment; we all feel vaguely what kind of outcome flows from this complexion of the people's view. When people come to think: 'I cannot expect any help in my affairs from anyone else at all', they will certainly and speedily draw the conclusion that they must get down to running their affairs themselves. All individuals and social strata separate from the people tremble, at this anticipated outcome. Not you alone, but we too would like to avoid it. For the idea has also been disseminated among us that our interests too would suffer from it, even the one we like to present as the sole object of our aspirations, because it is absolutely pure and unselfish – the interest in enlightenment. We think: the people is ignorant, full of crude prejudices and blind hatred for all who have renounced its savage ways. It makes no distinction among people wearing alien clothes: it would start treating all of them in the same way. It will not spare our science, our poetry or our arts. It will begin to destroy all our civilization.

That is why we too are against the people's anticipated attempt to shrug off any kind of tutelage and set about organizing its own affairs. We are so blinded by fear for ourselves and our interests that we do not even want to discuss what course of events would be more beneficial for the people itself, and aversion to an outcome which horrifies us makes us ready to forget everything: our love for freedom and our love for the people alike.

Under the sway of this feeling I am turning to you, dear sir, with an exposition of my thoughts regarding the means whereby an outcome equally dangerous for you and for us may be averted.

When I do this, I understand what I am doing.

I am betraying the people.

I am betraying because – guided by personal apprehensions for a thing more valuable to me than to the people, namely enlightenment – I am no longer thinking about whether a concern to resolve the complications of the Russian nation's position through your efforts and ours is useful to the people, or whether on the contrary the people would not gain more by conducting its national affairs independently of us than by a continuation of our efforts on its behalf. In this case, for my own ends I am repressing my inmost conviction that nobody's external concern can bring people the same benefits as can independent action upon their own affairs. Yes, I am betraying my conviction and my people: that is base. But we have been forced to commit so many base acts that one extra means nothing to us.

But I have a premonition that it will be quite superfluous and the pitiful aim for which I am betraying the people will remain unachieved. No one has the power to alter the course of events. Some would like to, but do not have the means; and others have the means, but perhaps not the desire.

For what reason am I becoming a traitor to the people, when I am well aware that I shall not help either you or myself? Is it not better to remain silent? Yes, it would be better; but the despicable writer's habit of relying upon the power of words is befuddling me. I am not capable of sticking to the vantage-point of common prudence, from which I can very clearly see that all explanations are vain. No sooner do I attain it than I am led astray by a habitual writer's thought: 'Oh, if it were only possible to explain the matter, it would be settled!' Therefore, I have kept silent for more than two years only because I did not have any possibility of 'beating the air with words', and as you see I am resuming this futile labour at the very first moment – or so it has seemed to me – that it is possible for me to do so.[4]

Why has this seemed to me to be the case? Whatever journal or newspaper I glance into, everywhere I find signs of the fact that a need has apparently been felt for our explanations. Very probably these signs are deceptive. But the predilection for striving to achieve good results through explanations is so strong in writers, that I am carried away by it.

This enthusiasm is inexcusable after so many experiences. But I try to close my eyes to its pitiful comicality, by repeating to myself facts which are really such, dear sir, that you might really wish for an explanation. Here are some of them. The former landlords' serfs, now termed 'temporarily-bound',[5] do not receive statutory deeds; the prescribed extension of obligatory labour has proved impossible; the prescribed voluntary agreements between landowners and the 'temporarily-bound' peasants living on their lands have proved impossible; being placed in an untenable position by the impracticability of the proposed solution, the landlords are grumbling and putting forward demands which they did not dare speak about only a year ago; in the State, a general penury has appeared and is intensifying; the exchange-rate is falling, which is equivalent to a rise in the value of the coinage in comparison with paper money or, which comes to the same thing, to a fall in the value of the paper rouble. These facts alone from the Russian people's life are already sufficient, and I have no need to touch either on many other significant facts about it,[6] or on other no less important phenomena appertaining to the relations of the Russian people with the life of other peoples now forming part of a single whole with it.[7]

Please believe, dear sir, in the sincerity of the feelings which have induced your most humble servant to enter upon these explanations, as I have the honour, etc.

II

Second Letter (extracts)

6 February

The source of those difficulties in the internal life of the Russian people to which I referred at the end of my first letter is reckoned by many people – and not in your milieu alone but in ours also – to be the so-called peasant question. I have no need to prove to you, dear sir, that you were not wrong to devote your initial attention to it.[8] But I venture to conclude from certain things you have said that it will not be superfluous to elucidate for you why it has acquired such significance in your eyes. Often a person does not perceive the relationship of external motivations to his own actions, and because of this lack of awareness he can err too regarding the character of his actions: some fact of his life may seem to him to have sprung from his own will, when it has been produced by external circumstances not depending upon him.

The need to concern itself with the peasant question was imposed on Russia by the course of our last war. A rumour went round among the people that the French emperor was demanding the abolition of serfdom, and had agreed to sign a peace only when a secret clause was introduced into the treaty, ordaining that freedom be given to the serfs. I do not know, dear sir, if this story, which was accepted as true by all our people, came to your knowledge; but if it did reach you, then of course you knew even better than I how unfounded such a strange notion is. It would be idle though, to attribute it only to the ignorance and gullibility of the common people; these qualities meant only that an instinctive presentiment of the inescapable connection of events found expression among the people in a crude form whose absurdity is obvious not only to you, dear sir, but also to anyone who has any notion of international relations. But that presentiment, which expressed itself in a form so ludicrous to us, was correct: it told the people that the Crimean War had made emancipation of the peasants a necessity. The connection between these two facts is the following: the military failures revealed to all layers of society the bankruptcy of the whole order of things under which it had lived before the war. I have no need to enumerate to you, dear sir, those mighty forces which should seemingly have ensured the triumph of Russian arms; you know better than I the immensity of the means which Russia then had available. The number of our soldiers was immeasurable; their bravery beyond doubt. With confidence in our monetary system and credit institutions then unshakeable, or dare I say blindly unconcerned, and with our system of fixing taxes, there could seemingly be no lack of monetary resources. Therefore, Russian society was by no means exceeding the bounds of what was possible when, at the outset of the war, it expected that we would take Constantinople and destroy the Turkish Empire. When the war took a quite different course, it was impossible to ascribe this disappointment to anything except deficiencies in the machinery which had disposed our forces. The necessity of changing the unsatisfactory system was revealed. Its most prominent feature was considered at the time to be serfdom. Of course, the latter was only one particular application of the principles on which the entire old order was constructed; but the inner connections between this particular fact and the general principles were, at that time, not yet understood by the majority in our society. Therefore, the general principles of the old order were left in peace and all of society's reforming vigour was directed against the most tangible of its external applications.

I must mention to you, dear sir, that this mood of public opinion suffered from the most unfortunate inconsistency. Serfdom, of course, contained within itself the possibility of many abuses, and you are very well aware of cases of cruelty, greed or cynical violence resulting from serfdom. But numerous as these were, one has to agree with what the former advocates of serfdom said, namely that all such scandalous infringements of the law were an exception to the general rule; and that the vast majority of landowners were people who were by no means evil, and who were not violating rights over the peasants which they had been given by law, or by custom firmly established under the influence of the law. The legal essence of serfdom was hard upon the serfs and harmful to the State. Yet it was in conformity with the whole nature of our system, hence, the latter *per se* could have no power to abolish it. But meanwhile, society was proposing to abolish serfdom by the power of the old order.

This mistake, so evident now to all, shows that the reason which had compelled society to set about its attempt to abolish serfdom was not strong enough to stimulate clear ideas about the bases of its former life. But you really know better than I, dear sir, that the Crimean War, with all its failures and with all its rigours, did not inflict too heavy a blow on Russia. The enemy barely touched our frontiers in two outlying provinces, far from the Russian heartland; one might even say that his touch was only perceptible in one province, the Black Sea region – since the mooring of an allied fleet before St. Petersburg, the bombardment of Svesborg and minor landings on the Finnish coast could not be considered serious attacks and caused us more grounds for mockery than for well-founded anxiety. But what on earth are the Crimea, Taganrog and Kerch for the inhabitants of Great Russia? Just far-off colonies, about which the native Russian has never much bothered his head. And besides, thanks to the character of the terrain and to his own ignorance, and perhaps in part also through deliberate policy on the part of the French emperor, the enemy did not penetrate more than a few versts from the coast in this region either. Even his victories over us were not definitive routs of our military forces. Our armies fell back, but they did not run away; they grew weak, but they were not annihilated and still maintained the solidity and power which had inspired the enemy's respect. And neither could our own respect for the old order vanish: it too merely wavered momentarily, but did not fall.

Such was the depth of the impression that had turned our thoughts to reforms: it was shallow and superficial. The Anglo-French (as we then called the allies) tore a little rent in our clothing, and at first we thought it only needed repairing; but once we started to darn, we gradually noticed how dilapidated the material was, wherever we chanced to touch it; and as you can now see, dear sir, all of society is beginning to declare that we must clothe ourselves anew from head to toe: it wants no repairs. To speak more plainly, once our society had committed itself to the abolition of serfdom, it set itself a most serious task. It did so with unthinking, carefree lack of foresight, in the belief that it was possible to dispatch this task through insignificant alterations of our former internal treaties, as trivial as were the alterations in the former diplomatic treaties which had proved sufficient to conclude the Paris Peace. But the internal matter did not turn out the same as the external one. In connection with it, our society began willy-nilly to learn seriousness. Society had to do a lot of thinking, and you can now see, dear sir, how widely the work of regeneration – to which initially such narrow limits were set – is developing. . . .

In actual fact, what was the state of affairs at the beginning of the peasant reform (*delo*)? There were four main elements to it: the régime, which until then had had a bureaucratic character; educated people from all classes, who found the abolition of serfdom necessary; the landowners, who were so afraid for their financial interests that they wanted to postpone the whole matter; and lastly the serfs, who were oppressed by their present status. Aside from these four elements, there was the remaining half of the population:

the State peasants, the petty bourgeois, the merchants, the clergy, and that majority of landless officials which obtained no great benefits from the bureaucratic order. Certain people – the most educated – from all these classes, and also from the landowners themselves, constituted a single party, which we called earlier the 'party of educated people' and which in recent years has begun to call itself our own liberal party. But here we are speaking not about these particular people, who have risen to a greater or lesser extent above their own class outlooks and who have been concerned to a greater or lesser extent about social matters; we are speaking here about that mass – of all classes apart from the serfs and the nobility – which knew nothing beyond its class or personal interests. About this we are saying that it stood aside when the serf question began to boil up. Having no interest in preserving serfdom, it was ready – from natural human feeling – to be in sympathy with its abolition. But because of its inexperience in social matters, it still did not realize that it would be compelled by its own interests to take part in this. . . .

III

Third Letter (extract)

13 February

Serfdom was created and diffused by the régime; the régime's normal rule was to lean on the nobility, which did not emerge here of its own accord or in struggle with the régime, as in many other countries, but instead under the patronage of the régime, which gave it privileges willingly. Why then, out of the privileges it had itself established, did the régime set about abolishing the very one which the nobility prized most highly? The answer has already been provided in my second letter. The unsuccessful policy which subjected the country to an ill-starred war gave power to the so-called liberal party, which demanded the abolition of serfdom. Thus the régime took upon itself the implementation of someone else's programme, based upon principles not in accordance with the régime's own character.

As a result of this contradiction between the essence of the enterprise undertaken and the qualities of the element which set about executing it, the enterprise was bound to be executed unsatisfactorily. The source of the inevitable unsatisfactoriness was the usual arbitrary way of conducting the matter. The régime did not perceive that it was tackling a matter not of its own devising, and wished to remain fully mistress of its conduct. But this way of conducting the matter meant that it had to be carried through under the influence of the régime's two basic habits. The first of these consisted in the bureaucratic character of its actions, the second in its bias in favour of the nobility. . . .

We have seen how, at the beginning of the serf question, the bulk of the other classes not directly affected by it remained indifferent. But it was impossible for this mass to maintain its indifference, when it saw the *dénouement* for which the bureaucratic solution of the question had paved the way. The serfs had not believed that the freedom promised them would be limited to those formal changes to which the bureaucratic solution had limited it. So there were clashes everywhere between the serfs and the régime, as the latter strove to carry through its solution. Scenes occurred which could not be contemplated with equanimity.[9] Sympathy for the serfs gripped massive sections of the other classes. And meanwhile the serfs, despite all reprimands and pacification measures, remained convinced that they should expect another, genuine freedom. This mood will inevitably produce new clashes, if their hope is not fulfilled. Thus the country has suffered unrest and fears it anew. And the time of unrest was hard for everybody. Hence, the idea that the solution to the peasant question must be altered in order to deflect unrest began to gain wide support among the other classes. Once forced by circumstances to think about social matters, all classes naturally passed on from the particular question which had steered their thoughts in that direction to the general state of affairs – and, of course, they had no trouble working out whether this accorded with their own interests. They at once perceived that certain features of the present order were equally disadvantageous to all classes, and united in a desire to change those features.

You well know, dear sir, what general changes all the classes not directly affected by the particular question of serfdom began to seek. They all felt the weight of the arbitrary administration, the unsatisfactory judicial system and the complex formalism of the laws. The nobility suffered from these deficiencies in just the same way as the other classes did. Hence, a way of finding support it needed presented itself of its own accord. Nobility (has by now) become the spokesman of the aspiration for reforms needed by all classes.[10]

IV

Fourth Letter (extracts)

13 February

Tell me, dear sir, would a dinner turn out well if the chef began unconditionally to accept all your or my opinions on how to cook soup or roast a joint of beef? After all, you or I do have certain ideas on this matter. But we do not so much as express our opinion concerning the chef who has been given the job of preparing dinner for us. And we are quite right not to express our opinion here. But under a bureaucratic system, the matter would proceed as follows. The chef would not be guided by his knowledge and experience, but would strive to ascertain what we think about the arrangement of the kitchen stove, about the shape of the saucepans and burners, about how long the dishes should be kept on the fire, and so on and so forth. . . .

This is exactly how it turned out in the Drafting Committees too.[11]

I am going to speak seriously. Under a bureaucratic system, the intelligence, knowledge and experience of the people given responsibility for some matter are quite useless. These people function like machines without any opinion of their own; they conduct the matter by casual hints, and conjectures about what the opinion of this, that or the other individual having absolutely no direct involvement in the matter might be with regard to it. We can all see what the result of that is, in this same example of the Drafting Committees. . . .

V

Fifth Letter (extracts)

16 February

I wanted to get a rough idea of what change is being actually effected by the Statutes in the existing allotment of land, and in the obligations being served or paid by the peasants to the landowners. . . . before beginning the study I adopted the two following rules:

1. After making a list of the administrative districts (*uezdy*) in the same order in which they are arranged in the 'Annexes to the Proceedings of the Drafting Commissions', I began to discard those *uezdy* in which the sum total of registered land estates contains less than ten thousand serf 'souls', leaving on my list only *uezdy* with more than that number. The aim of this procedure is clear: I wanted only to study *uezdy* presenting a sufficiently broad basis for conclusions about the effect of the change produced by the Statutes. Thus I was left with 175 *uezdy*, in each of which landed estates with over ten thousand serfs, in total, were registered.
2. Of these, I decided to take every tenth one, in other words the first *uezd*, the eleventh *uezd*, the twenty-first *uezd* and so on. . . .

For all 18 *uezds* chosen thereby, the total number of serfs who paid quit-rent in money (*obrok*) as entered in the 'Annexes to the Proceedings of the Drafting Commissions' is 125,324 souls. Their former allotment is shown as amounting to 419,406½ desyatinas. The total annual quit-rent which they paid to the landowners under serfdom was 842,728 roubles, 50 kopeks. Thus, under the old servile system, there was taken from the peasants on average per each desyatina of the allotment: 2 roubles, 9 kopeks. Under the regulations laid down by the new Statutes, of the former allotment 101,767¾ desyatinas had to revert to the landowner. The peasants were left with 317,638¾ desyatinas. For these, quit-rent of 731,346 roubles was established. That is to say, according to the new regulations, the peasants had to pay 2 roubles, 30½ kopeks for each desyatina of land of their allotment. In other words, under the new Statutes, the emancipated peasants must pay the landowner 1 rouble, 10 kopeks for every rouble which they paid him under the old servile order.

Did you, dear sir, expect such a result?

I dare not presume upon your attention any longer. But if I dared to suppose that the information I am supplying would be accepted by you with the same exclusive concern for the value of truth which inspired me to acquire the information, I would consider it a pleasure to expound in the fullest detail the question of the fate of the quit-rent (*obrok*) holdings under the new Statute; then I would go on to the question of the estates which are under corvée; lastly, I would present you with information about the real significance of those aspects of the new system which only affect such and such estates. But I have already expended enough time in uninvited conversation with you, dear sir, and I cannot expend any more without knowing whether it will be entirely wasted. In any case, you can now judge what the nature of my further conversation with you would be; consequently, you can judge for yourself whether you need it.

I am aware, dear sir, that I have broken the rules of propriety in thrusting myself with my explanations upon a man who had in no way asked me for them; so it will be no surprise to you if I do not adhere to those rules at the conclusion of my correspondence either, and do not sign in the customary way 'always at your service' or 'your most humble servant', but sign simply –

N. Chernyshevsky

Editor's Notes

1. The *Unaddressed Letters* were written in 1862 and directed at the tsar Alexander II whose name was, of course, not to be mentioned. While presenting Chernyshevskii's major criticism of the 1861 rural reforms (the emancipation of the 'private' serfs) it was written in parts on behalf of the whole dissenting intelligentsia ('our circle'), with the author disassociating himself at times from the position of his own social environment. Despite its indirect, purposefully oblique and ironic form, the main point of the letter was not missed by the censorship, which banned the publication of the whole series. They were published initially abroad, in 1874, i.e. nearly a decade after their author was sent to Siberia.
2. Reference to the 'Time of Troubles' 1598–1613 when for a time a Polish army occupied Moscow to be expelled from it by a national movement led by Prince Pozharskii and by Minin, a commoner from a

provincial city.

3. Reference to the struggle between Moscow and Poland over the control of the Ukraine during the seventeenth century.
4. During the 1859–62 period, Chernyshevskii did not express in writing any views concerning the emancipation of serfs. The *Unaddressed Letters* are his first reaction to those laws and to the actual form the reform took.
5. A legal term defining peasants placed in the transitory position between 'private' serfdom, i.e. belonging to members of nobility, and the emancipation from serfdom, at that stage still under obligation to perform some of their past duties to their ex-owners. For the best study available in English of the emancipation from serfdom, see G.T. Robinson, *Rural Russia Under the Old Regime*, New York, 1949.
6. Reference to the 'peasant disorders' which peaked sharply during the period in which the emancipation of serfs was considered.
7. Reference to the non-Russian provinces of the Russian Empire, especially to Poland where revolutionary tension was then building up towards the revolt of 1863.
8. Reference to the well-known and often quoted statement by the tsar Alexander II at his meeting with the representative of nobility in the Moscow province in 1856: 'We must proceed to change the laws of serfdom and it will be better to have them changed from above rather than from below'.
9. See above, footnote 6.
10. Chernyshevskii refers to the rapid crystallisation of liberal opposition of nobles within the newly created regional authorities (*zemstva*) which was to play a considerable role between the 1860s and the 1905 revolution. Probably, a specific reference to the nobility in the province of Tver' which petitioned to extend the reforms enacted by the government in 1861.
11. I.e. the committees charged with preparation of the legislation concerning the emancipation from serfdom.

The People's Will: Basic documents and writings

The Social Revolutionary Party of the People's Will (*Sotsialno-revolyutsionnaya partiya Narodnoi Voli*), to give it its full name, was created by the majority within the Land and Liberty (*Zemly i vol'ya*) organization after it split in 1879. The minority had simultaneously established a rival Black Repartition (*Chernyi peredel*) organization.[1] The split occurred following the adoption by a majority of a new strategy of 'political' action, i.e. of direct armed challenge to the tsarist State, aimed to overthrow it as a necessary prelude to the social transformation of Russian society. The minority held to the earlier Populist views by which action devoted to the raising of consciousness of peasants was to remain the main viable strategy. The Black Repartition had failed to make significant impact, most of its leaders emigrated and by 1883 embraced Marxism, adopting the new name of The Emancipation of Labour Group (*Grupa osvobozhdeniya truda*) – the first organization of the Russian Marxists.

On the other hand, the People's Will and its following of active sympathisers had shown remarkable elan, organizational capacity and ability to regenerate despite massive arrests and executions by the authorities. At its height, it offered a serious challenge to the regime it fought. The organization was led by the Executive Committee – both a national leadership and the core organization for armed attack on tsardom's leading figures, a way of action adopted as a major plank of the organization's tactics.[2] Separate branches were established to act within different regions and in different milieux: workers, the army, intelligentsia, youth. After several attempts, the Executive Committee succeeded in 1881 in killing the tsar, Alexander II. It lost by the end of 1881 most of its members in waves of arrests and the executions which followed. Its task was taken over by a Moscow Center, then by the Military Organization, with the structure of People's Will re-established, again and again to go into action and to be decimated by new arrests. The struggle continued with new and younger 'generations' of activists and leaders coming forth. Only by 1887 was the organization finally destroyed by police action.

A number of articles in this volume have presented and described the extent of interaction between Marx and the People's Will. In considering the basic documents and writings of the People's Will Executive Committee, which follow, two major points should be kept in mind. First, to do justice to the text, the contemporary reader must overcome the tendency to read it through the glasses of our own generation and in particular to treat the People's Will activists as crypto-Marxists who did not quite make it the whole way, or else as emotional romantics, not quite understood (or else condescended to) by Marx and Engels. They were not Marxists, they were highly effective revolutionaries and they have worked out an alternative revolutionary analysis directed to the conditions of Russia in their time. Marx understood this and treated them with the utmost respect for what they were. Second, the revolutionary reputation of the People's Will as well as the ideological needs of further generations have made for the tendency to treat them in dismissive admiration as no more than a band of bomb-throwers of courage and determination (as 'fanatics' to their foes). Such a view sorely underestimates the analytical brilliance and shrewd tactical insight of the People's Will leaders into their own social and political environment. It was silenced only by prisons and gallows, the main argument the tsardom had to offer to those who defined themselves as 'socialists and populists' and stated that 'under our political regime, one of absolute despotism, of absolute negation of people's rights and will, social reform can come only as Revolution; that is understood by all.'[3]

The translation made by Quintin Hoare has used the texts of the clandestine journal of the People's Will and other documents of 1879-82, republished by the Russian *émigrés* in *Literatura partii narodnoi voli*, Paris, 1905. The documents concerning the People's Will party which follow are:

Editor's Notes

1 The adjective 'black' has designated in medieval Russia (among other things) peasant lands which were not divided between nobles as well as plebeian guilds or classes (described as of 'black bone'). The expression Black Repartition came later to be used to define the idea of general and equal repartition of all Russia's land by its farming population, i.e. the peasant communes and their members.
2 The often repeated view that the original Land and Liberty organization split over the issue of 'terrorist' action is quite wrong. Both wings of the organization accepted 'terror' against government leaders and police spies as necessary in some circumstances (hence the early 'terrorist' career of Vera Zasulich). The main difference which divided the group was the place of the state and of the struggle against it in their consideration of future political action, for which see the article by Kibalchich (pp. 212-18).
3 From the editorial statement of *Narodnaya Volya*, no. 3 (dated 1 January 1980).

Letter from the Executive Committee of People's Will *to Karl Marx*[1]

Citizen,

The educated and progressive classes in Russia, always attentive to the development of ideas in Europe and always ready to respond to them, received the appearance of your scientific works with delight.

In them, the best principles of Russian life are recognized in the name of science. *Capital* has become the daily reading of educated people. But in our realm of Byzantine darkness and Asiatic despotism, any progress of social ideas is regarded as a revolutionary movement. It goes without saying that your name is associated with the internal political struggle in Russia. It has stimulated some to deep esteem and ardent sympathy, others – to prosecutions. Your works have been banned, and the very fact of studying them is now regarded as a sign of political unreliability.

So far as we are concerned, most esteemed citizen, we know with what interest you follow every manifestation of the Russian revolutionaries' activity, so we are happy to be able to inform you that this activity has by now reached the highest level of intensity. The earlier revolutionary struggle tempered our fighters, and not only established the revolutionaries' theoretical programme, but at the same time also set their practical revolutionary struggle onto the right path for its realization.

The various revolutionary fractions, inevitable in so new a movement, are coming together, fusing and by their common efforts striving to unite with the aspirations and hopes of the people, which in our country are just as ancient as servitude itself.

In such circumstances, the moment of victory is drawing nearer. Our task would be significantly easier for us, if the clearly expressed sympathies of the free peoples were on our side. For this only one thing is needed – knowledge of the true state of affairs in Russia.

To this end, we are giving our comrade Lev Hartmann the task of organizing, in England and America, a flow of information concerning the present development of our social life.

We are turning to you, esteemed citizen, with a request to help him in fulfilling this mission.

Firmly resolved to break the fetters of servitude, we are convinced that the time is not far distant when our unhappy fatherland will occupy a place in Europe worthy of a free people.

We consider ourselves fortunate to have this chance of expressing to you, most esteemed citizen, the feelings of deep respect of the entire Russian social-revolutionary party.

Programme of the Executive Committee

A

In our fundamental convictions we are socialists (*sotsialisty*) and populists (*narodniki*). We are convinced that only upon a socialist basis can humanity embody freedom, equality and fraternity in its existence, and ensure general material well-being and full, all-round personal development – hence progress. We are convinced that only the *will of the people* can sanction social forms; that the people's development is only stable when it proceeds independently and freely, and when every idea that is to be translated into reality *passes first through the consciousness and will of the people.* Popular well-being and the popular will – these are our two most sacred and indissolubly linked principles.

B

1. If we examine the situation in which the people has to live and operate, we find that the (common) people (*narod*) is in a condition of absolute economic and political servitude. As a worker, it labours exclusively to 'nourish' and maintain the parasitic strata; as a citizen, it is devoid of all rights. Not only does Russian reality as a whole not accord with its will: it does not even dare express or formulate that will; it does not even have any possibility of thinking about what is good or what is bad for it; and the very notion of any kind of will of the people is seen as an offence against the existing order. Enmeshed on every side, the people is reduced to physical degeneration, stupefied, downtrodden, pauperized – enslaved in all respects.
2. On top of the people shackled in chains, we can observe enshrouding layers of exploiters, created and protected by the State. We observe that this State constitutes the mightiest capitalist power in the land; that this same State constitutes the sole political oppressor of the people; that only thanks to it can lesser predators exist. We see that this State-bourgeois excrescence maintains itself only through naked violence – through its military, police and bureaucratic organization – in precisely the same way that Genghis Khan's Mongols maintained themselves in our country. We see the total absence of popular sanction for this arbitrary, violent rule, which forcibly introduces and maintains State and economic principles and forms that have nothing in common with popular aspirations and ideals.
3. In the people itself, we see that its old traditional principles are still alive, though repressed in every way: the people's right to land; communal and local self-government; the rudiments of a federal system; freedom of conscience and speech. These principles would attain a broad development and give a quite new direction to our entire history, in a popular spirit, if the

people were only to get a chance to live and arrange matters as it wished, in accordance with its own inclinations.

C

1. We therefore hold that, as socialists and populists, we should pose as our immediate task: to free the people from the oppressive yoke of the present State; to carry out a political revolution, with the aim of transfer of power to the people. Through this revolution we shall achieve: first, that the people's development will henceforth take place independently, in accordance with its own will and inclinations; secondly, that many purely socialist principles, common to us and to the people, will be recognized and supported in our Russian life.
2. We hold that the *will of the people* would be adequately expressed and enacted, in accordance with the voters' instructions, by a Constituent Assembly, freely elected by universal suffrage. This, of course, is a far from ideal form of expression of the popular will; but it is all that is possible in practice today, so we consider it necessary to adopt precisely that.
3. Thus our aim is: to remove power from the hands of the existing régime and transfer it to a Constituent Assembly, composed as just indicated, which must review all our State and social institutions and reshape them in accordance with its electors' instructions.

D

Albeit submitting ourselves entirely to the popular will, we shall nonetheless consider it our duty, as a party, to present ourselves before the people with our own programme. We shall disseminate this up until the revolution; we shall advocate it during the electoral campaign; we shall defend it in the Constituent Assembly. This programme is as follows:

1. permanent popular representation, constituted as indicated above, and having full power on all state-wide questions;
2. extensive provincial self-government, guaranteed by election to all administrative posts, autonomy of the peasant commune (*mir*) and economic independence of the people;
3. autonomy of the *mir*, as an economic and administrative unit;

4. ownership of the land by the people;
5. a set of measures aiming to transfer all plants and/factories into the hands of the workers;
6. full freedom of conscience, of speech, of the press, of assembly, of association and of electoral agitation;
7. universal voting rights, without class or property restrictions;
8. replacement of the regular army by a territorial one.

We shall carry out this programme, in the conviction that its several points cannot be achieved in isolation from one another, but only in their aggregate would they ensure the people's political and economic freedom or healthy development.

E

In view of the aims just outlined, the party's activity is set out in the following sections:

1. Propaganda and agitational activity.

The aim of propaganda is to popularize among all layers of the population the idea of *democratic political revolution, as a means of social reform*, and also *to popularize the party's own programme.* Criticism of the existing order, exposition and explanation of the methods of revolution and social reform, constitute the essence of propaganda.

Agitation must strive to foster among the people and in society, on the widest scale possible, protests against the existing order and demands for reform in the spirit of the party – particularly the demand that a Constituent Assembly be convened. The forms of protest may be rallies, demonstrations, petitions, partisan speeches, refusal to pay taxes, etc.

2. Destructive and terrorist activity.

Terrorist activity involves annihilating the régime's most obnoxious personalities, defending the party against espionage, punishing the most notorious cases of violence and injustice on the part of government or administration, and so on. Its aim is to destroy the aura of government power; to give constant proof of the possibility of struggle against the régime; in this way to stimulate the people's revolutionary spirit and belief in the success of the cause; and finally to create forces ready for – and accustomed to – armed struggle.

3. The organization of secret societies and their unification round a single centre.

The organization of small-scale clandestine associations – for every kind of revolutionary purpose – is essential, both to implement many of the party's tasks and to train its members politically. But these small organizations, for more harmonious conduct of their struggle and especially for organizing the revolution, must at all costs group themselves around a common centre – on the basis of either full amalgamation or a federal union.

4. Acquiring an influential position and good connections in the administration, the army, the educated classes (*obshchestvo*) and the people.[a]

In order to accomplish all the party's functions successfully, a solid position in the various strata of the population is of the greatest importance. For the seizure of power (*perevorot*), the administration and army are especially important. The party must pay equally serious attention to the people. The party's main task within the people consists in preparing it to assist in the seizure of power and in laying the ground for a successful electoral struggle after the seizure of power: a struggle having as its aim the installation of genuine popular deputies. The party must recruit conscious supporters in the most prominent section of the peasantry; it must carry out preparatory work, at the most vital points and among the most receptive elements of the population, aimed at securing active assistance from the masses. In view of this, each member of the party must strive to occupy a position among the people that will enable him to defend peasant interests; to relieve peasant needs; to acquire the reputation of an honest man and well-wisher of the peasantry; to maintain the party's good name and defend its ideas and aims among the people.

5. Organization and execution of the seizure of power.

In view of the people's oppressed state and the fact that the régime can contain the general revolutionary movement for a long time

(a) The Russian terminology of the period has adopted as self evident the concepts *obshchestvo*, i.e. nominally 'society' but actually the educated classes and the public opinion as against *narod*, i.e. the people equated with manual labour and plebeian classes, i.e. within Russia, mostly peasants.

through local repressive actions, the party must itself take responsibility for initiating the actual seizure of power – rather than waiting until such time as the people is in a position to manage without it. As regards the conditions for executing the seizure of power. . . .[b]

6. Electoral agitation in connection with the summoning of a Constituent Assembly.

However, the overturn (*perevorot*) may have occurred whether as the result of an autonomous insurrection or through a conspiracy – the party's responsibility is to work for the immediate convocation of a Constituent Assembly, to which the powers of the Provisional Government established by the insurrection or conspiracy should be transferred. In its electoral agitation, the party must fight in every way against the assorted kulak candidates, fight with all its strength to get in people truly representing peasant communes.

Political Revolution and the Economic Question[2]

Never has such a difficult task fallen to the lot of a revolutionary party, as that which history has assigned to the party of social revolution in Russia. Together with our basic task – the socio-economic one – we must also take upon ourselves the job of destroying a system of political despotism: something which everywhere else in Europe was accomplished long ago, and accomplished not by socialists but by bourgeois parties. So not a single European socialist party had to sustain such an arduous struggle or make so many sacrifices as we do. Heroic efforts are needed to operate in such conditions and still hold high the banner of popular liberation. Yet for all that, even these conditions and the political situation that encompasses us contain an aspect that is advantageous for the future realization of our task. The political order, which no longer satisfies a single social class and is hated by the entire intelligentsia, must inevitably fall in the near future. But in addition, as this order reduces the people to famine and desolation, it is also digging a grave for the economic system which it supports. The process of decomposition of the existing political

(b) This part of Point 5 is not for publication (author's comment).

system has fatally coincided with a process of economic impoverishment of the people, which is progressively growing more intense as each year passes. Destruction of the contemporary political order through a victorious popular movement would inevitably also entail the collapse of the economic order that is indissolubly linked with the existing State.

We consider, therefore, that the political fight against the State is not an extraneous element in our party's socialist activity but, on the contrary, a potent means of bringing the economic (or at least agrarian) revolution nearer, and of rendering it as thoroughgoing as possible: i.e. a means of realizing part of our programme in real life.

What practical tasks such a view entails for us, under the conditions of our Russian reality, we shall state in general outline below. But first we must respond to various theoretical objections that are levelled at the political part of our programme. All these objections turn upon the question of how significant political structures are for the socio-economic development of any country.

The opinions of socialists of various hues concerning this question can all be divided into three categories. To the first category belong those who attach too much importance to political forms, ascribing to them the power to produce all kinds of economic changes in the country, simply by order of the authorities from above and by obedience of the subjects or citizens from below. In terms of their practical activity, these for the most part are Jacobins, 'étatists', striving to get power into their hands in order to decree a political and economic revolution and introduce socialist principles into the life of the people from above, without calling for the people's active participation in actual reconstruction, and even 'in some circumstances' repressing its revolutionary initiative. In our country, the organ of the Jacobin tendencies is the paper The Tocsin (*Nabat*) put out by Tkachev. To the second category belong those socialists who, on the contrary, ascribe little importance in socio-economic life to the political factor, and deny any serious influence, whether positive or negative, of political forms on economic relations: wherefore, in their practical activity, these people deem it useless and even harmful for socialists to expend any part of their energies whatsoever on political struggle. In our country, the representatives of the latter view are the faction (or more currently part of it) which has Black Repartition (*Chernyi Peredel*) as its literary organ. Finally, a synthesis of these two one-sided conceptions is represented by the view which, acknowledging the close link and interaction between political and economic factors, considers that neither can economic revolution be accomplished without certain political changes, nor on the other hand can free political institutions be established without a certain historical preparation in the economic sphere. This conception, shared by our faction and organ, we shall develop further in detail; but first we shall turn to the arguments of our antagonists.

People who do not agree with the political side of our programme often refer to Marx, who in his *Capital* showed that any country's economic relations and structures lie at the foundation of all other social structures – political, juridical and so on. From this they conclude that changes in economic relations can emerge only as a result of struggle precisely in the economic sphere, hence that no political structure or political revolution is capable of either retarding or stimulating an economic transformation. We observe that these students of Marx go further than their teacher himself, and from his essentially correct position draw absurd practical conclusions. As evidence of the fact that Marx himself does not concur with them, we shall cite the passage from his 'Civil War in France' where he defines the historical significance of the Paris Commune: 'it was . . . . the political form at last discovered under which to work out the economical emancipation of labour. . . . The Commune was therefore to serve as a lever for uprooting the economical foundations upon which rests the existence of classes, and therefore of class rule'.[3] These words occur also in the Manifesto of the General Council of the International, published immediately after the fall of the Commune; hence the thought expressed in them is shared by the entire group of representatives of European socialism.

The other authority to whom the adherents of pure economic doctrine sometimes, through a misunderstanding, refer – Lavrov – in his recently published book about the Paris Commune, offers the following advice to the militants of future revolutions: 'At the moment when the historical conjuncture permits the workers of any country, albeit temporarily, to overcome their enemies and control the course of events, the workers must carry through the economic overturn with whatever means may be expedient, and do everything they can to ensure that it is consolidated.' Moreover, it is obvious from Lavrov's entire book that neither does he exclude a political way of resolving economic problems from the range of 'expedient means'. As an example, we shall adduce his explanation of the relatively weak role played by the International at the time of the Commune: 'the International's agitation, directed to purely economic questions and not putting forward any political programme linked to its economic demands, proved ineffective at the very moment when circumstances had produced a triumphant explosion of the proletariat at one of the most important points in Europe.'[4]

One could go on to cite Louis Blanc, Lassalle, Proudhon and other outstanding socialists, who deemed it possible through such and such State measures to carry through a greater or lesser economic revolution. One could also adduce the view of the bourgeois economist and eclectic John Stuart Mill, who in his posthumous 'Chapters on Socialism' discerns in the political right of universal suffrage the seed of economic revolution in the future, when a working class grown conscious of its interests turns this political right into a weapon of social revolution. However, we shall limit ourselves simply to the views we have cited already, of the two writers to whom the adherents of exclusively economic struggle are particularly fond of referring, and shall now turn to events from European life.

At the time of the great French Revolution, the Convention expropriated the lands of the clergy and émigré nobles and, after initially making these into State property, subsequently sold the estates off to the bourgeoisie. It is true that this measure changed merely the owners, and not the actual principle of private property in land. But why did the Convention not complete the economic revolution, i.e. take all the estates and factories away from their private owners and hand them over to collective use by the people? It was, of course, not at all because a political mode of resolving an economic question is inconceivable in general, but because, at that time, history had not yet placed the social question on the agenda. Take again the 1848 Revolution in France. If the Paris proletariat had then contained within it a solid organization with a definite political and economic programme, and headed by honest and determined leaders, then the revolution which broke out with the overthrow of Louis Philippe could have led to deep changes in the economic order of France. The Paris Commune of 1871 had already taken the first steps towards resolving the economic question – by political means.

Is it possible after this to dispute that a political revolution, using the State organization as a weapon for accomplishing an economic transformation, is entirely possible? Of course, the economic transformation must previously be *prepared* by history: i.e. certain changes must first take place in the actual correlation of economic forces, but also in the ideas and habits of the mass of the people, before a successful political revolution which has seized the State organization will be able to put into practice what is acknowledged and desired by the people in economic terms.

We precisely consider that the Russian State order is specific not only as a system of sheer bureaucratic and arbitrary rule, but also in the way it lags behind and even conflicts with the economic and juridical institutions, habits and views of the mass of the people. Our State is an example of the colossal *negative* significance a political system can have if it has lost touch with the economic needs of the people. In Europe, political progress precedes socio-economic progress, and political forms – especially at a time of revolution – have been used as a means to bring the economic question to the fore and the economic transformation closer. But in our country, the constant weight of the political system holds back the economic, juridical and political reorganization which would inevitably ensue, if this system were to collapse and the people's revolutionary initiative could manifest itself freely. In actual practice, an endless series of historical and contemporary facts irrefutably demonstrate that the principles of popular life are in total contradiction with the principles on which the existing State is based. We need not dwell on this fact of the discord between State and popular concepts, since it is conceded even by many non-socialists and shared no doubt even by our 'country folk'.[5] We shall simply draw their attention to the following two important facts concerning the influence of the State upon our economic life: first, the destructive and demoralizing influence which the political system exerts on popular social institutions; secondly, the protections which the State extends to the moneyed class and the hundreds of millions which the government extracts yearly from the people's purse and hands over to our emergent bourgeois class. As a result the State, in order to maintain this entire monstrous police-kulak system, has to devour such a mass of products of popular toil that all that remains for the people to do is starve, become destitute and perish.

Apart from this, we must draw attention to the fact that there are no such independent and solidly organised classes in our country as there are in Europe. There, State power is only a political expression of the actual rule of a certain class; here, by contrast, the State has at its own discretion created or destroyed entire classes, and has carried out such experiments as it pleased on the privileged class, while repressing any feeble (for the most part individual) attempts at opposition coming from within it. Seeking to be absolutely free of all constraints, the State has repressed any political independence even of the privileged classes, and to this end has fostered disunity and disorganization among them. Such a policy has no doubt increased the centralized power of the State; at the same time, however, it must also in the future completely destroy the existing system. In reality, if State centralization is swept away by a free popular movement, what social elements will prove to be the real forces controlling the course of events? Of course, neither the privileged classes, as a result of their disunity, nor the legal parties, as a result of their disorganization, will be capable of opposing the popular movement and maintaining the old system of economic enslavement of the people. Only the people and the party of social revolution appear as the main forces on which the social and State order will depend after the revolution. So we arrive once more at the same conclusion: our party's main destructive work, both in the present and in the future, must still be directed against the State, as the principal, if not sole, effective force hostile to the realization of a better order.

One further observation for assessing the importance of the State in Russian life. Turn your attention to the causes which have provoked major or minor uprisings among the peasants. These causes have always been of a political or juridical kind and have come from above, from the sphere of the State or administration. There has been some false Tsar, pretender or mythical 'Golden Charter'; or there has been some juridical violation of the law (as understood by the people); or lastly there has been some urban revolt which has set an example to the rural population. But there has hardly been a single instance where a village or locality has rebelled without any external cause or model, simply because it was hungry. Something more is necessary: an awareness by the people that its rights have been violated, or hopes in the success of an uprising. Of course, the basic condition for almost all popular unrest is material suffering; but the actual occasion has always been some violation of the law (real or imagined) on the part of the authorities, or some insurrectionary initiative taken by an organized nucleus close in its interests to the people.

This last condition is vital, as history shows, for all great popular movements. Thus, at the time of the Pugachev Rebellion, the initial push that conjured forth all the hidden power of the uprising was provided, first, by the Schismatics[6] who had prepared and organised the movement and, secondly, by a section of the Cossacks who set an example of armed rebellion.

At the present time, however, the Schismatics have lost most of their former fighting energy, while the Cossacks constitute a privileged stratum relative to the peasantry: so neither is seemingly capable of giving the watchword for a popular insurrection. Only the social-revolutionary party, solidly entrenched in the urban and factory population and occupying many vantage-points among the peasants, can serve as the ferment that is essential to set off a movement in town and countryside. For a total overthrow of the existing system, however, a simultaneous urban and rural insurrection is indispensable. For the truth is that even the most extensive peasant movement, with the party making every effort to support and coordinate it, cannot hold its own against a centralized, lavishly armed foe, unless the latter suffers heavy blows in the centres of his material and military power – the capitals and large towns. In just the same way, even a temporary success of the insurrection in the town will not culminate in victory, if the peasantry does not back up the urban actions with a sympathetic rising in response and thus split the enemy's military forces. Furthermore, it is vital for success that at the moment of the insurrection at least some part of the army and Cossacks should pass over to the people's side. But who will take the first initiative in the uprising – the town or the countryside? In view of the greater development and mobility of the urban population, and the fact that the party's activity will probably produce greater numerical results in the town than in the countryside, we must conclude that the town not the village will give the initial signal for the insurrection. But the first success in the towns may sound the call for a revolt of millions of hungry peasants.

A. Doroshenko[a]

(a) A pseudonym of N. Kibalchich

The People and the State

(From an editorial article in *Narodnaya Volya*, year I, no. 2, dated 1 October 1879)

Here in Russia, history has created two main independent forces: the people and the State organization. Other social groups are still of only secondary significance in our country. Our nobility, for example, though the régime dragged it out into the light of day by the scruff of its neck, proved despite all its efforts to be absolutely incapable of forming a stable social group: after barely a hundred years' existence, it has now entirely effaced itself and dispersed, partly merging with the State organization, partly merging with the bourgeoisie and partly disappearing heaven knows where.[7] The bourgeoisie, fostered by all the conditions of our life and at its very birth also operating beneath the wing of the régime (*pravitelstvo*), undoubtedly has more chance of a prolonged existence; if the general conditions of Russian life do not change, it will certainly soon comprise a formidable social force, and subjugate not only the popular masses but also the State itself. But this is still a question for the future. At the present time, our bourgeoisie still merely consists of an utterly disunited horde of predators; it has not yet produced either class consciousness, a world outlook, or class solidarity. The Western bourgeois is really convinced of the sanctity of the various principles upon which his estate is based, and will lay down his life for these principles. In our country, you will nowhere meet more cynical disrespect for those same principles than precisely in the bourgeois. Our bourgeois is not a member of a social estate (*soslovie*), but just an isolated predator, intelligent and unscrupulous in his methods, who realizes in his heart of hearts that he is acting without conscience or justice. Without a doubt, this is a temporary phenomenon, springing only from the fact that our bourgeois is a newcomer to the world. Soon, very soon, he will legalize his position: another few generations, and we shall see a genuine bourgeois in our country; we shall see rapacity raised to a principle, with a theoretical basis, a stable world outlook and a class morality. All this will certainly come to pass – but only in the event that a general overturn of our State and social relations does not cut at the very roots of the bourgeoisie. But we consider that such an overturn is very possible; and if it really does occur, then our bourgeoisie will leave the stage just as the nobility did, because in essence it is created by that same State.

In part, it is created by the State quite consciously and deliberately; in part it comes about as an inevitable consequence of the conditions into which the State is driving the people, which cannot fail to bring forth from the peasants a predatory social estate of *kulaks*.[8]

From the standpoint of the whole existing system, the peasant today is nothing, worse than nothing. He is a mere draught animal; a mere sheep, existing only so that the shepherd may feed off its flesh and clothe himself in its fleece and hide. Such is the principle of our State. The people counts for nothing, so far as individual or human dignity is concerned. Its economic interests are acknowledged only insofar as this is necessary for the State. The peasant must eat, drink, clothe himself and have a roof over his head only so that he may not die of starvation: so that he can work, bring money into the exchequer, provide able-bodied recruits for war, and so on. His intellectual and moral world have a similar significance. Not much more is required of the *muzhik* than of a horse; he must have enough intelligence to walk between the shafts and not slip the traces; he is required not to be restive and to recognize his master. Everything else is superfluous and even harmful. And we can see that just as economic and moral principles have been practised upon the *muzhik* for hundreds of years, practised by a powerful (in comparison with the *muzhik* himself) and highly intelligent association permeating his entire life. From top to bottom, all State, class and social relations are formed in accordance with these principles. The results are deadly indeed.

The peasant is humiliated, as downtrodden as the State could make him. Economically, he is reduced to a condition of penury: for the sake of a crust of bread, to satisfy the most animal (yet inexorable) needs, he is compelled to wage a bitter struggle for existence. His every thought must be directed to getting a rouble wherewith to pay his taxes, meeting his numerous obligations, feeding himself and his family, and resting in preparation for fresh labour. And this day after day; yesterday, today, and tomorrow; for his entire life. No time to live for himself, for the man; no time to think, nothing to think about. Such is the situation of the individual. Such too is the situation of the *mir*. For what purpose does the *mir*, the *obshchina*, exist?[9] With what does it concern itself? Supplying recruits, collecting taxes, recovering arrears, forwarding contributions in kind – that is the life of the *mir*. And just as the peasant loses his individuality in an enforced pursuit of the rouble, so too does the *obshchina* lose its identity and become distorted, stifled by the régime in this sphere of exclusively fiscal and police obligations.

Such a situation is as if expressly designed to engender the *kulak*. In this milieu, there is no other alternative for an intelligent, energetic man who feels the need for a private life: he must either perish together with the *mir*, or become a predator himself. As a man of the *mir*, he is a beggar, a contemptible being, whom everyone orders about. As a predator, he at once rises into a special social estate which the laws do not mention, but which is recognized in practice. As a *mir*-eating *kulak*, he not only gets a chance to live pretty well in a material sense. For the first time, he becomes a man and even a citizen: the authorities and the priest alike esteem him, they will not start slapping his ugly face or mocking his human dignity; the law begins to exist for him. Can there be any choice here? We have still only taken the general picture, let us take the details. What will become of the intelligent and energetic peasant, if *mir* traditions remain unchanged? We have a candidate for the 'trouble-makers', the 'spreaders of disorder', the 'rebels'; a candidate for every kind of persecution, whipping, arrest, banishment, and worse. The humiliated, downtrodden, depersonalized *mir* is often incapable of giving even moral support in this grievous struggle; and in the majority of cases the *kulak* quite sincerely and deeply despises the *mir* for its impotence – despises it in the person both of its individual members and of the *obshchina* as a whole.

Thus the *kulak* is born. The hopeless situation drives the *muzhik* into servitude. And who is to blame for this? What else but the State's oppression: its economic oppression, which seeks to reduce the masses to a condition of material destitution and deprives them of any possibility of fighting against exploitation; and its spiritual oppression, which reduces the masses to civil and political destruction, demoralizing the people and throttling its energies. Remove this oppression, and at once you take away nine tenths of the possibility for a bourgeoisie to form.

Let us move higher up. The modern State summons a bourgeoisie to appear through the very fact of its existence; it also, in specific instances, brings it into the world quite consciously. We may recall the history of our industry. The handicrafts production of entire provinces was killed off, thanks to every kind of State protectionism for heavy industry. Branches of factory production were even created which, to this day, survive only by virtue of a protective tariff (for example, the cotton industry which destroyed popular handwoven linens). Whole principalities were created for mine-owners, and for a hundred years the Urals population was handed back into servitude, to capitalists incapable of running things even as well as the toilers themselves had done when they were left without landlords (in Pugachev's time).[10] Railway construction in our country presents a spectacle that has no like in the world: all the tracks have been built with the *muzhik*'s money, with money from the State which, for no obvious reason, has doled out hundreds of millions to various entrepreneurs. In just the same way, the *muzhik*'s gold has poured out of the government's empty pockets to sustain stock-market speculation. This paternal tenderness of the régime with respect to the bourgeoisie is something which requires no proof at all, merely to be pointed out; and our purpose in pointing it out is to emphasize the fact that in our country it is not the State that is a creation of the bourgeoisie as in Europe, but on the contrary the bourgeoisie which is created by the State.

The independent role of our State is a phenomenon of extraordinary importance, since it means that in Russia the activity of the social-revolutionary party has to assume a quite particular character.[11] Russia, generally speaking, constitutes a kind of vast manorial estate belonging to a firm entitled 'The Russian State'. Economic and political influence, economic and political oppression, here (as is to be expected) merge and reduce to a single juridical person: this very firm. In these conditions, economic and political reform are also quite inseparable from each other and merge into a single state-wide revolution. The direct source of popular misery, servitude and destitution is the State.[(c)] So as soon as we set ourselves the aim of freeing the people, providing it with land, educating it, introducing new principles into its existence or restoring the old traditional foundations of popular life to their original purity – in short, whatsoever aim we may set ourselves (provided only that it is in the interests of the masses) we must clash

(c) (author's note) Please note that we always mean by the word 'State' specifically the modern Russian State.

willy-nilly with the régime (*pravitelstvo*), which sees the people as its economic and political slave. Hence, in order to do anything for the people, it is necessary first of all to free it from the power of this régime, to break the régime itself, to do away with its seignorial power over the *muzhik*. Our activity accordingly assumes a political character. And the same thing really occurs, in practice if not in words, with every revolutionary group here, irrespective of its theoretical views; it occurs by virtue of the simple fact that the modern State is truly the greatest and most terrible enemy and destroyer of the people in all respects. Our socialist wages a political struggle as naturally as a man speaks in prose, without even having any concept of prose and poetry. Nevertheless, there is of course a great difference between understanding this fact – the significance of the modern State – and not understanding it. If we act consciously, then we shall direct all our blows against the régime and our entire strength will be put to productive, effective work. But if we strike at the régime only involuntarily, then, quite irrespectively of our wishes and intentions, first a huge proportion of our strength may be used up on vain and fanciful undertakings, and secondly the very blows we involuntarily inflict on the régime will only benefit the bourgeoisie and prepare an easier victory for it. . . .

The Tactical Programme: The Party's Preparatory Work

The task of the party's preparatory work is to develop the amount of force that is indispensable for realization of its aims.

These aims are first and foremost to create in the imminent future a State and social order under which the *will of the people* has become the sole source of the law. This is our immediate aim, and only when it has been achieved will a broad party activity become possible, with propaganda and agitation as its principal means.

But in its efforts to realize this immediate aim, the party stands for the need to smash the government system which existed until now. And it is this above all else to which the party must attend.

Destruction of the existing government system may occur, of course, in very diverse ways. It may be, for example, that the régime, on its last legs, will decide without waiting for an insurrection to embark on very extensive concessions to the people.

This would be, so to speak, a natural death of the old order, and obviously it would then be necessary to lay aside existing plans and direct all the party's forces straightforwardly into activity among the popular masses. It is also possible that, without surrendering fully, the régime will nevertheless at least grant a free constitution, in which case it will be to the party's advantage to postpone the insurrection, so that it can utilize its freedom of action to organize and consolidate itself in the best possible way. But all such considerations in no way deny the necessity *now*, at the present time, of preparing for an *insurrection*. For, in the first place, any concession by the régime, small or large, is only conceivable in the event of its being *forced* to make it; in the second place, there may very easily not be any essential concessions by the régime (indeed, it is far more likely that there will not) – but the party is obliged to carry out its tasks in these circumstances too. Hence, *the party must prepare precisely for insurrection*. After all, if this proves against all expectation to be superfluous, so much the better: the forces that have been mustered will then embark on peaceful work.

As regards the insurrection itself, in all probability it will be possible to choose a propitious moment for it, when circumstances themselves considerably facilitate the conspirators' task. Such propitious conditions may be created by a popular revolt (*bunt*), an unsuccessful war, State bankruptcy, the various complications of European politics, and so on. The party must be quick to take advantage of all such propitious junctures, but in its preparatory work it must not place all its hopes in them. The party is obliged to fulfil its tasks at all costs, which is why it must carry out its preparations in such a way that it will not prove inferior to its role even in the worst and most arduous conditions.

Such extremely unpropitious conditions arise specifically in the event that the party has to begin the insurrection alone instead of joining a popular movement, and if, into the bargain, there are no other extraordinary pieces of good fortune facilitating the first attack. We must be prepared for just such a state of affairs. The party must be strong enough to create its own propitious moment for action, launch the operation and carry it through to the end. A skilfully executed series of terrorist attacks, simultaneously wiping out ten or fifteen individual pillars of the present régime would throw the régime into panic, destroy its unity of action and at the same time arouse the popular masses: in other words, create an opportune moment for the assault. Taking advantage of this moment, previously mustered fighting forces begin the insurrection and attempt to gain control of the main government institutions. Such an attack may easily be crowned with success, if the party manages to move significant masses of workers and others to help the initial attackers. For success, it is equally vital to establish a position in the provinces that is sufficiently solid for us to be able to rouse them at the first news of the revolution, or at least to keep them neutral. Likewise, we should act in advance to secure the insurrection against the danger that the European powers may come to the régime's aid, and so on and so forth. In general, the party's preparatory work must do everything essential for the success of an insurrection initiated by the party even without any exceptional propitious conditions: i.e. in approximately the kind of situation in which Russia finds itself at the present time.

From this point of view, the main tasks of our preparatory work are as follows:

1. creation of a central combat organization, capable of launching the insurrection;
2. creation of a provincial revolutionary organization, capable of supporting the insurrection;
3. securing the support of the urban workers for the insurrection;
4. preparing the possibility of winning the Army over to our side, or paralysing its activity;
5. enlisting the sympathy and collaboration of the intelligentsia – the main source of forces for our preparatory work;
6. gaining European public opinion to our cause.

(a) The Central Organization[12]

In our Russian conditions, which do not permit open party activity, the central organization cannot be established in the form of elected representation of the party, but must be in the form of a *secret association*. This secret association, in accordance with the tasks which lie before it, must possess a combat character. It must extend to all points from which the uprising has to be launched, but this does not mean there is any need to take in the whole of Russia. On the contrary, it is more advantageous for the remaining part to be organized into autonomous groups, for it is too difficult to keep one huge association secret and protect it from the vigilance of government agents. At the same time, a tight bond between the central and other organizations is essential, so that the central organization can really be a spokesman for the aspirations of the whole party. Moreover, in view of the important role allotted to the central organization, the party must guarantee it adequate resources, by providing it with suitable people, supplying it with material means, and so on. In this connection, it would be very useful to establish regular fixed dues from all members of the party, so that the central organization would have a definite budget rather than one subject to fortuitous fluctuations. With a view to the identity of the goals and the need for unity, the central and district groups must have regularly organized relations and exchange information about presently available resources and forthcoming plans.

(b) Special and Local Organizations

Organizations of a *special* character – designed purely to make propaganda, to carry on some kind of production, to obtain resources, to pursue philanthropic ends, and so on – may arise even in the area of the centre's direct operations.[13] The connection between all such groups and the centre is maintained by individuals specially appointed for this purpose. As regards the form and aims of such groups, obviously they determine all that themselves.

Far more complicated is the question of *local* organizations, which set themselves general revolutionary aims, but limit themselves to particular geographic or ethnic spheres of activity. The enormous importance of such organizations cannot be doubted: the success of the revolutionary movement depends entirely on their development, and in their absence all the central organization's undertakings entail a risk. Only in exceptional circumstances can local groups assume the level of importance of initiating the revolution: in the majority of cases, their role consists rather in supporting a movement which has begun from the centre, and in not allowing their locality to be used to help the régime. But in this sense their intervention determines the entire outcome of the struggle. With the revolution's triumph, the importance of the local organizations increases still more. It is up to them to arouse the spirit of the masses; it is mainly up to them to influence elections to the Constituent Assembly, to formulate the peasantry's demands, and so on. In general, just as the destructive role belongs primarily to the central organization, so the constructive role belongs to the local organizations. In view of all this, the local groups must secure in advance:

(a) a position in the administration and army;
(b) influence within the peasantry;
(c) as far as possible they must get together with local liberals and constitutionalists;
(d) they must provide themselves with material resources; and
(e) thoroughly familiarize themselves with their region.

In accomplishing these aims, party members must act in a comradely fashion: supporting and succouring each other, promoting their own people to all positions of utility to the party, and taking care to maintain each other's reputation and influence.

Acquiring a position in the administration and in the army is particularly important for the initial phase of the movement. Achieving even very partial success in this respect can be of significant assistance to the cause. If, at the news of the insurrection, the local authorities take it into their heads to help the régime, not much is needed to confuse them. When a governor sees at least some of his subordinates wavering; when he hears them refer to the dangers of linking one's destiny with the tottering régime; when other party members organize demonstrations throughout society and among the people; when two or three instances of insubordination occur within the officer corps, and particularly among the heads of independent units: this is already enough for the province to remain neutral today – and consequently go over tomorrow to the revolutionaries. The armed forces are particularly important in these circumstances, and it is essential to operate assiduously within them, winning the most advanced and honest people to membership of the party and arousing a civic consciousness in the others. Above all, we must pay attention to the officer corps, as a means to influence the rank and file. So far as the peasantry is concerned, we must occupy posts where close contact with the masses is possible, so that we may earn their trust by our conduct, help them and defend their interests, relying on the collaboration of office-holding and influential party people. Though unable yet to carry out mass propaganda, we must nevertheless draw close to the best of the peasants and turn them as far as possible into conscious supporters of the party, acquainting them with its aims. In relation to the liberals, without hiding our radicalism we must point to the fact that, according to the present formulation of the party's tasks, our interests and theirs oblige us to act jointly against the régime. Our study of the province must be extremely thorough. The personalities of the people having command or influence over society, the army, the provincial assembly (*zemstvo*) or the municipal administration – their mutual relations, disputes and so on – must be accurately known. We must know who is a conscious supporter of the régime, who a mere careerist, who sympathizes with the party and is capable of supporting it. We must know the quantity of troops, their locations, and also the various depots and installations. We must observe the mood of the popular masses; know their expectations, hopes and grievances; and carefully identify popular leaders, establishing the closest possible relations with them. In short, the entire internal life of the province in question, all its available forces of any political importance, must be painstakingly studied.

It is vital that the organization of local groups be adapted to the general conditions of activity in Russia. At the centre of each local organization there must stand a closely united group, a secret association, linked on the one hand with the centre and on the other with its sub-groups. While propagating a programme of activity in conformity with the party's overall plans, the local group must nevertheless keep details of its activities, relations and resources secret, and not allow little-known individuals to worm their way into it simply by taking it into their heads to pose as like-minded people.

(c) Urban Workers

The urban working-class population, which has particularly great significance for the revolution both by virtue of its position and because of its relatively higher level of development, must attract serious attention from the party. The success of the initial assault depends entirely upon the conduct of the workers and the army. If in advance the party secures links with the working-class milieu such that at the moment of insurrection it can close down the plants and factories, rouse the masses and move them into the streets (provided, of course, they are favourably disposed to the insurrection) – this already goes half way to ensuring the success of the cause. Furthermore, the urban workers by virtue of their position are representatives of purely popular interests, and the whole character of the movement and degree of utility to the people of the revolution depends to a considerable extent upon their more or less active relationship to the insurrection, to the provisional government's measures and indeed to the very establishment of a provisional government.

So in the working-class milieu we must assiduously carry out *propaganda*: 1. for socialist ideas (the broader the better); 2. for political revolution and the creation of a democratic régime, as a first step to the realization of popular demands. Propaganda must be accompanied by *organization* of the working-class masses, with the aim of uniting them and developing within them an awareness of their unity and solidarity of interests. Organization of the working-class masses can be carried out on any basis, beginning from *artels*,[14] fellowships, self-improvement circles or strikes and finishing with purely revolutionary associations. Party members must organize more politically developed people (intellectuals or workers, it's all the same) into circles of the latter kind, then disperse the members of these circles around all the factories and plants to establish groups of the former kind, in order: 1. constantly to raise the level of consciousness of the working masses; 2. to select new individuals from their midst and recruit these to their own ranks; 3. to have the ability at the time of the insurrection to move the vast mass of workers. These revolutionary circles must be kept in the deepest secrecy from outsiders, but at the same time be linked among themselves and to the central organization.

(d) The Army

The importance of the army during the revolution is enormous. It may be said that if you have the army with you, it is possible to topple the régime even without any help from the people; but if you have the army against you, you will – alas! – achieve nothing even with the people's support. In present conditions, however, propaganda among the soldiers is hampered to such an extent that we can hardly place much hope in it. Influencing the *officer corps* is far easier: being more advanced and more free, it is also more accessible to influence. Meanwhile, of course, at the moment of the revolution no one can win over the soldiers to the side of the insurrection better than a popular officer who turns to his soldiers with appropriate instructions and proposals. In the last resort, should the mood of the company or battalion not allow any such appeal, its commander can still lead his soldiers not where they have been ordered but somewhere else; he can restrain them from firing, force them to retreat, demoralize them by aimless marching, and so on. In view of all this, the officer corps must be the object of our most assiduous influence. It is necessary to recruit the best, most advanced and energetic ones as conscious members of the party. So far as the remaining mass is concerned, it is necessary to raise their level of development, clarify for them their responsibilities to the people, destroy the government's prestige in their eyes and explain the aims of the revolutionaries. Officers who are party members must pursue two main aims: either 1. to win promotion and occupy important posts, or 2. to turn all their attention to acquiring popularity among the soldiers. Then, of course, they must raise the level of development of their comrades, and also of the soldiers; moreover, in connection with the latter, the forces of the former may incidentally be utilized. . . .[15]

Finally, we must make every effort to concentrate our best forces in the army at points which are important for the uprising, and as far as possible in such a way that there are specific units in which all important posts are occupied by our people.

(e) The Intelligentsia and the Youth

The intelligentsia and the youth, in particular, constitute spheres where any honest tendency only has to make itself felt in order to have supporters. Further comment on modes of activity in this milieu is not required. So far as the youth is concerned, it is important to support the revolutionary tendencies in its ranks: educating the new generation in a revolutionary spirit and offering it activity for which its forces are adequate – and which at the same time is useful to the revolutionary cause. Thus in their milieu, students can support the spirit of solidarity, steadfastness in struggle and civil courage, by striving for wider student rights; they can carry out propaganda among the workers, help the diffusion of revolutionary publications, and so on.

(f) Europe

In relation to Europe, party policy must aim to enlist the sympathy of *peoples* for the Russian revolution. Governments, with their fickle politics and diplomatic interests, cannot be stable allies for us. They cannot be particularly dangerous either, if we secure the sympathies of European public opinion. We saw the power of this force not long ago in the Hartmann affair.[16]

In order to accomplish this aim, the party must acquaint Europe with the whole ruinous significance of Russian absolutism for European civilization itself; with the true aims of the party; with the meaning of our revolutionary movement, as an expression of the whole nation's protest. The facts of the revolutionary struggle, the activity and aims of the party, the measures of the Russian government, its relationship to the people – if Europe were to know all this without distortion, her sympathy for us would be assured. With a view to this, it is essential we take steps to supply the European press with all information of this kind. Individuals residing in foreign countries must personally act in this same spirit at meetings and social gatherings, by giving lectures about Russia and so on. In cases like the Hartmann affair, it is essential to carry out lively agitation, taking full advantage of a moment when society's attention is turned to Russian affairs.

Programme of the Workers' Organization of People's Will[17] *(Extracts)*

A

The historical experience of humanity, and likewise study and observation of the lives of peoples, convincingly and clearly show that nations will only achieve their greatest happiness and strength, and that people will only become brothers, will only be free and equal, when they have constructed their lives in accordance with socialist teaching, i.e. in the following way:

1. the land and the implements of labour must belong to the whole people, with each worker using them as of right;
2. labour is produced not individually, but socially (through communes (*obshchina's*), cooperatives (*artel's*) associations);[18]

3. the products of common labour must be shared, by their own decision, among all workers, according to the needs of each;
4. the State system must be based on a federative alliance of all *obshchina*'s;
5. every *obshchina* is fully independent and free in its internal affairs;
6. every member of an *obshchina* is entirely free in his convictions and personal life; his freedom is only limited in those circumstances where it turns into violence against other members of his own or another *obshchina*. . . .

C

First of all, we must be clear about who our enemies are, who are our friends, and what changes in present-day practice we should strive for. We must know that:
1. All those who are today living at the people's expense, i.e. the government, the landlords, the manufacturers, the mill-owners and the kulaks, will never renounce their privileged position of their own free will, because it is far pleasanter for them to load all work onto the workers' back than it is to get down to it themselves. These gentlemen grasp the point that the working people will serve them only so long as it is ignorant, crushed by need and at loggerheads, and does not understand that its strength lies in the union of all workers. Hence it is fruitless to seek improvements in present-day practice from these gentlemen. It is true that they sometimes set up committees for improving the workers' lot in the factories and mills; but all their care and attention only recalls that of a landlord for the maintenance of his draught animals. They will never give a thought to improving popular education; they will never permit the working man to manage things so that he ceases to need them. Accordingly, the working people must rely on its own strength: its enemies will not help it.

But the people can always rely on its true ally – the party of social revolution. The members of this party are drawn from all classes in the Russian Empire, but they give up their lives to the people's cause, holding the view that all will become free and equal and achieve just conditions only when the labouring class – i.e. the peasantry and the urban workers – comes to manage the affairs of the country; for all other classes, even if they have striven for freedom and equality, have done so for themselves alone rather than for the people as a whole. Thus the social-revolutionary party is the best ally, and the working people can always stretch out a fraternal hand to it.

Apart from it, the people has no true allies. However, in many cases it will find support among particular individuals from other classes, educated people who would also like life to be freer and better in Russia. These people are not too worried by the fact that the Russian peasant is bound by debt to the landowner and kulak, since they are unfamiliar with such oppression. But they have had direct experience of the arbitrary rule of the police and bureaucracy, and would gladly help the people to put an end to these. The people, of course, would benefit from a weakening of governmental oppression: everyone would breathe more freely; every man's brain would work to better effect; learning would become more available to all; the number of well-wishers of the people would grow; but most important of all, the people would be able to agree and unite. So the working people must not reject these people; it is worthwhile to strive for an extension of freedom hand in hand with them. All that is necessary is for the workers not to forget that their cause does not end with this; that they will soon have to part company with these temporary friends and go on in alliance with the party of social revolution alone.

2. The change in conditions which we want to bring about must be understood by the people and accord with its demands, otherwise it will not introduce or support them. And as we have said, one cannot rely on other classes, because what they do is not what benefits the people but what benefits themselves.

3. Any changes in political arrangements must bring our existence closer to a socialist system.

D

Taking all this into account, we recognize that in the immediate future we can aim for the following changes in the State system and national life:

1. Tsarist power in Russia is replaced by a popular government, i.e. the government is made up of popular representatives (deputies). The people itself appoints and replaces these representatives; when

selecting them, it gives detailed instructions as to what they must strive for, and requires them to account for their activity.

2. The Russian State, in accordance with the local character and living conditions of the population, is divided into provinces (*oblast*'s), autonomous in their internal affairs but linked together in a single All-Russian Federation. The internal affairs of the *oblast*' are managed by a provincial administration; State-wide affairs by a Federal government.

3. Peoples who have been forcibly annexed to the Russian Empire are free to secede or to remain in the All-Russian Federation.

4. Communities (hamlets, villages, boroughs, factory *artels*, etc.) settle their business in assemblies, and implement it through their elected responsible officers – headmen, elders, managers, foremen, clerks, etc.

5. All land passes into the hands of the working people and is deemed national property. Each separate *oblast*' puts land at the disposal of *obshchinas* or private individuals – but only persons themselves engaged in its cultivation. No one has the right to receive more than the amount he himself is capable of cultivating. Reallotments of land are determined according to the requirements of the *obshchina*.

6. Mills and factories are deemed to be national property and put at the disposal of mill and factory cooperatives; the revenues belong to these cooperatives.

7. The popular representatives promulgate laws and statutes which indicate how factories and mills should be organized so that the health and lives of the workers are not damaged, fix the length of the working day for men and women, and so on.

8. The right to choose representatives (delegates), both for the Federal government and for the provincial administration, is held by every adult; in just the same way, every adult may be elected to the Federal government or provincial administration.

9. All Russian people have the right to adhere or convert to whatever doctrine they please (religious freedom); the right to disseminate, in oral or printed form, whatever ideas or teachings they please (freedom of speech and of the press); the right to gather together to discuss their affairs (freedom of assembly); the right to form associations (communities, *artels*, leagues, societies) to pursue whatever aims they please; the right to offer the people advice about their choice of representatives or any social issue (freedom of

electoral agitation).

10. Education of the people, in all lower and higher schools, is free of charge and accessible to all.

11. The present-day army and all armed services in general are replaced by a local (popular) militia. All are liable for military service and learn the military craft, without being cut off from their work or their family; they are called up only in the event of legally determined necessity.

12. A Russian State Bank is established, with branches in the various parts of Russia, for the maintenance and organization of factory, mill, agricultural and in general all industrial and educational communities, *artel*'s and leagues.

These, then, in our opinion, are the changes in national life that can be accomplished in the near future; we consider that the whole people – urban workers and peasantry – will understand all their utility and willingly stand up for them. All that is necessary is for the urban workers to understand that isolated from the peasantry they will always be crushed by the régime, the factory-owners and the kulaks, because the principal popular force resides not in them but in the peasantry. If they station themselves permanently at the peasantry's side, win it over and argue that the cause should be pursued in concert through their joint endeavours, then the whole working people will become an invincible force.

E

We shall still need to devote a lot of careful work to these questions, but we consider that the work should be carried out as follows.

(a) Those workers who have firmly made up their minds that it is necessary to change the present order and national lite as a whole, form small comradely associations (circles) of workers, clarify in common what they should strive for, and prepare themselves for the moment when we shall have to combine all our efforts and move to carry out the revolution. The circles must be secret and inaccessible to government blows.

(b) Members of the circles must explain to the people that there is only one way out of the present ruinous conditions – a forcible revolution – and that revolution is both imperative and possible. With this aim, members of the circles scatter through the mills, factories and villages and set up new circles of workers and peasants on various pretexts, mainly quite legal. (So, for instance, a circle may launch a mutual aid fund, a library, readings, hostels, and so on.) Enjoying the workers' trust and affection, the members of the circle sustain a spirit of rebelliousness in the working-class milieu, where necessary organize strikes against the factory-owners and prepare themselves for struggle against the police and State authorities – which always back the owners. Those individuals from the worker circles who give evidence of capability and determination in conducting the workers' action join the main worker circles, and in this way a secret league of workers becomes consolidated.

F

It is impossible to divine the precise conditions under which the worker leagues (the working-class organization) will have to operate. But whatever they may be, some general rules must constantly be borne in mind.

1. In order to achieve anything at all, the workers must establish a force capable of putting pressure on the government and, when necessary, ready to support their demands weapons in hand. Whether it comes to a bloody struggle or the enemies of the people concede without a fight – no matter: a force must be prepared, and the readier this force is to go into battle, the sooner our enemies will back down without any battle.

2. Only the entire party of social revolution can attack our enemies with any hope of victory, and the worker organization joins this as a section. The party musters forces within the people and throughout society for carrying out the revolution: it organizes leagues in the peasantry and the urban working-class milieu, the army and other social strata. From its own ranks the party details a combat organization, which attacks the régime, destabilizes it and throws it into confusion, thus making it easier for all the discontented – the people, the workers and all those individuals who wish them well – to rise up and carry through the universal revolution.

If a genuine revolt has broken out in some town or in the countryside, the party must support it with its own forces, introduce its own demands into it, provoke similar disturbances in other places and, if at all possible, unite these disturbances into a general uprising and extend this throughout Russia. At the same time, it is necessary to unsettle the régime and eliminate prominent officials (the more prominent the better), both civilian and military; it is necessary to win the army over to the people's side, then disband it and replace it with a popular militia drawn from peasants, workers, former soldiers and all honest citizens.

For the success of the cause, it is vitally important to win control of the biggest towns and hold them for ourselves. To this end, as soon as it has cleared a town of the enemy, the people in revolt must choose its Provisional Government, from workers or people known for their devotion to the popular cause. The Provisional Government, relying for support on the militia, defends the town from enemies and does all it can to help the uprising in other places, uniting and directing the insurgents. The workers keep a vigilant eye on the Provisional Government and compel it to act on behalf of the people. When the insurrection achieves victory throughout the country; when the land, mills and factories pass into the hands of the people, and in the villages, towns and provinces an elected popular administration is established; when there is no armed power in the State other than the militia – then the people at once sends its representatives to the Constituent Assembly (All-Union Government) which, after abolishing the Provisional Government, ratifies the popular conquests and establishes the new All-Union order. The representatives act under precise instructions, given them by their electors.

That is the party's general plan of activity at the time of the revolution.

There may, however, be a different situation. If the régime for fear of a general revolt should decide to make some concessions to society, i.e. grant a constitution, the workers' activity should not for that reason be modified. They must claim power for themselves; they must demand for themselves extensive concessions; they must introduce their representatives into parliament (i.e. the legislative assembly) and, if need be, back up these demands with mass petitions and disturbances. Putting pressure in this way on the government and accumulating forces during the struggle against it, the People's Will party awaits only an opportune moment – when the old, unfit order shows itself incapable of opposing the people's demands – then carries out the revolution with every hope of success.

Programme of the Military-Revolutionary Organization[19] *(Extracts)*

Fully agreeing with the party of social revolution that the present economic and political condition of the people is most unjust and humiliating to human dignity; that under the existing State order, basic reforms of any kind in the people's way of life are inconceivable; that the most innocent endeavours in this direction end in total failure and lead to persecution; that consequently, if one leaves things to the natural course of events, such a situation can be prolonged for a very long time yet, while escaping from it will be even harder – and in addition sharing the People's Will Party's belief that such a state of affairs in Russia is maintained exclusively by naked force (the army, bureaucracy and police), and finding for our part that the army is the main bulwark of the régime – we, as members of that army are deeply convinced that the role which we play in the Russian political order today, like that which we might play at the government's request in the future, is unworthy of an honest man, consider it our duty to link arms at once with the fighters for popular freedom. . . .

. . . . we adopt the following programme which we have elaborated ourselves, as binding upon every member joining our organization.

(a) The Role of the Military Organization in the General Revolutionary Movement.

1. As we have stated above, our organization recognizes itself as being in solidarity with the People's Will Party.
2. The organization agrees to participate actively in the struggle against the political and economic State system; i.e. agrees, in the event of a popular insurrection, to take part in it.
3. The members of the organization are ready for an exclusively military rising, designed to seize supreme power for the purpose of organizing popular representation. . . .

Last Will and Testament of Alexander Dimitrievich Mikhailov[20]

16 February 1882

I will and bequeath to you, brothers, not to waste your forces on our behalf, but to preserve them from every fruitless loss and use them only in direct efforts towards our goal.

I will and bequeath to you, brothers, to publish the decisions of the Executive Committee from Verdict A[21] to the announcement of our death inclusive (i.e. from 26 August 1879 to March '82). Add to them a short history of the organization's activity and short biographies of the members who have perished.

I will and bequeath to you, brothers, do not send people too young into the life-and-death struggle. Let their characters grow stronger, allow them time to develop all their spiritual forces.

I will and bequeath to you, brothers, to establish a uniform manner of giving testimony before the courts, and I recommend you to abjure all explanations during the investigative inquiry, however damning the slanders or criminal reports may be.

I will and bequeath to you, brothers, while still at liberty, to get to know each other's relatives, so that in the event of arrest and imprisonment you can maintain some kind of relationship with a comrade in solitary confinement. This procedure is in your direct interests. In many cases, it will preserve the dignity of the party in court. In closed courts, in my view, there is no need to refuse counsel for the defence.

I will and bequeath to you, brothers, to keep check on one another – in every practical activity, every trivial detail, every aspect of life. This will save you from blunders which no single individual can avoid, but which would be fatal to the entire organization. This mutual contact must enter consciousness as a principle and cease to be offensive, personal pride must be silenced by the requirements of reason. It is essential to know, concerning all your closest comrades: how a person lives; what he carries with him; how he takes notes, and what about; how careful, observant, quick-witted he is. Study one another. Therein lies power, therein lies perfection of the organization's performance.

I will and bequeath to you, brothers, to establish the most rigorous system of communications, which can save you from mass arrests.

I will and bequeath to you, brothers, to care for the moral satisfaction of every member of the organization. This will preserve peace and affection among you; it will make each of you happy; it will make the days spent in each other's company for ever memorable.

So I kiss you all, dear brothers, sweet sisters, I kiss you every one and clasp you tightly to my breast, which is filled with the same desire and passion that animate you. Please remember me kindly. If I have acted disagreeably to anyone, believe me it was not from personal motives, but only from a particular conception of our common good and from a personal trait of obstinacy.

And so farewell, dear friends! Yours truly and to the end,

Alexander Mikhailov

Last Will and Testament of Alexander Ivanovich Barannikov[22]

Comrades,

Just one step remains to the brink of the tomb. I shall leave the stage with deep faith in our sacred cause, firmly confident in its imminent triumph, fully conscious of having served it to the full extent of my limited capacity.

You are living through a great moment; make use of all its consequences. Remember that the power of the régime rests on a smaller number of sincere adherents than ever. It has succeeded in kindling hatred in all. One final effort – and it will cease to exist.

Are you ready? Do you have sufficient strength?

Remember that the right of the people to choose its own destiny will then appear on the scene.

Live and triumph! We triumph in our death!

Editor's Notes

1. For the discussion of Marx's contacts with People's Will, see Part

One and the biographical items in Part Two above.

2. This article was published in *Narodnaya Volya*, the clandestine journal of People's Will (No. 5, dated 5 February 1881) and was signed A. Doroshenko, a pseudonym of N. Kibalchich. For biographical details see page 174.
3. See 'The Civil War in France: Address to the General Council', K. Marx, *The First International and After*, Harmondsworth, 1981, p. 212.
4. P. Lavrov, *Parizhskaya Kommuna 18 Marta 1871 g.*, Leningrad, 1875, p. 216.
5. In 1877 the Land and Liberty organization (*Zemlya i Volya*) began to found 'colonies' amongst the peasant population of some areas, e.g. near Saratov, Voronezh, etc. The members of this were referred to humorously as the 'country-folk'. Plekhanov tried to mobilize them against the 'political orientation', i.e. the faction, that gave birth to People's Will.
6. The so-called old believers (*Starovery*) were the largest component of this schismatic movement (*Raskolniki*).
7. The author dates the commencement of Russian nobility from the granting of the Charter of Nobility by Catherine II in 1785.
8. For a definition of the Russian peasant commune, see pages 11-12.
9. *Kulak* (Russian 'fist') is an abusive description of a peasant exploiting his peasant neighbours and/or commune through usury, commerce, etc., and stressing the 'not properly peasant' (i.e. farming) main sources of income and/or personality traits of craftiness, stinginess, lack of neighbourliness. Often coupled with, or used synonymously with, *miroed*, i.e. 'a commune eater'. In the much later period of the 1920s, the word was adopted by the authorities as the equivalent of any 'rich peasant', defined by simple indices such as land held and horses owned.
10. The largest popular rebellion of cossacks and peasants which incorporated at its peak also many of the serf-miners, serf-workers of the Urals as well as Bashkir pastoral tribesmen. The rebellion was defeated in 1774.
11. The People's Will spoke of the 'social revolutionary party' (uncapitalized) as synonymous with themselves but often also as a broader concept, incorporating all of the radical camp within contemporary Russia.
12. This section was to define the role of the Executive Committee of the People's Will. In fact, the Executive Committee came to operate also as a centralizing force, overriding and directing the local organization while at the same time taking upon itself the most difficult task adopted by the 'combat organizations' – the killing of the tsar.
13. Among the special groups a particularly important role was played by the combat units, which took upon themselves armed operations.

14. See page 125, fn. 5.
15. An omission of a few words is indicated here by a row of dots; the words related to the technical aspect of gaining influence over soldiers.
16. In 1879 the French government refused to comply with a Russian request for the extradition of Lev Hartmann of the People's Will.
17. For Marx's particular reaction to the programme of the workers' organization of the People's Will, see page 61.
18. For discussion of peasant communes, see pages 11-12.
19. I.e. the organization of the People's Will operating within the army and consisting mainly of officers.
20. A.D. Mikhailov (1856-1884), member of the Executive Committee of the People's Will and one of its most prominent leaders. For biographical details, see page 175.
21. On 26 August 1879 the Executive Committee of the People's Will formally sentenced Tsar Alexander II to death.
22. A.I. Barannikov (1858-1883), member of the Executive Committee of the People's Will. For biographical details, see page 172.

Marxism and the vernacular revolutionary traditions

Teodor Shanin

A century ago marxists regardless of brand or interpretation were no more than one of the many competing groups of European radical dissent striving for social justice. In a major ideological change of scene, a single century has seen the global acceptance of marxism, by friend and foe alike, as the main socialist and revolutionary tradition, idiom and legitimation. To its followers it came also to equal science. This equation of marxism = socialism, revolution (and science), came to hide some major characteristics of a whole range of actual revolutionary and socialist movements and of theories, marxist and non-marxist; their real history and diversity, the original breadth of their questions and insights, the ways they related to spontaneous popular cravings and struggles for social change. As with all fetishisms, that simplification or concealment weakens the capacity of its socialist followers to use effectively social analysis. For the enemies of socialism it has served as a trick (or, again, as self-mystification) whereby any struggle for social change is dismissed as the outcome of 'marxist propaganda', 'Chinese agents' or Soviet 'moles'.

The analytical device underlying such deceptions and self-deceptions is the dualisation of all we know into 'us and ours' versus 'the bad and the ugly' with all else to the devil. Unilinear conceptions of history as 'progress', equated with the assimilation of all mankind to our own image (but possibly, even richer and wiser) served the same purpose. Bureaucrats and doctrinaires, the world over, love the simplicity of such models and historiographies and do their best to enforce them by all the massive powers at their command.

One way to breach that particular wall of deceptive simplicity and conscious manipulation is to question the relation between marxism and the indigenous revolutionary traditions and to look in this light at the parallels between marxism and science. That explains why Part I of this article will speak of science and of vernacular. Part II will consider aspects of 'false consciousness' within the types of marxist analysis relevant to the book's main theme. Finally, Part III will proceed to the interpretation of the input of the People's Will Party in Russia into socialist thought and consider Marx's own marxism in that light. The topic of the article due to conclude this book seems right, for that is the point where late Marx, his early interpreters and his Russian 'vernacular' connections offer some lessons which bridge past and present, opening out into the future.

Part I: Science and vernacular

Marxism: science and idols

Marxism is the science of revolution. Within the context of marxist thought that means also, and in its deepest sense – marxism is the science of society. Whether one agrees with these statements or not, they acquire major social significance by expressing correctly the aims and the self-image of the authors, interpreters and followers of that project, since its inception. To its followers, marxism has been many other things besides – a political credo, an applied ethic, a sanctioning device, etc., but it never relinquished its claim and its drive to be a science. The book and the programme of *Capital* have been treated as an ideal model of the content and style of the 'scientific socialism', to use the self-definition strongly favoured by Engels, and, albeit with some reluctance as to its positive scope, accepted by Marx.[1]

Behind that image, model or claim, lies a fundamental question: what is science? The contemporary self-images of its practitioners and explorers differ considerably from the sunny optimism of those nineteenth-century scientists, to whom their trade was the synonym of knowledge as well as of wisdom, untrammelled human creativity and liberty. It differs as much from the TV-infested laymen's images of science as a question-answering computer, or as modern witchcraft. Yet, the essential 'brief' and self-image of contemporary science at its inception still holds for most of those who look at it more closely: a universal language and method of exploration and exposition, a system of questions and questioning, a structured logic of laws, concepts and derivations tested by experience and productive of reasoned prediction, a store of accumulated information – the largest mankind has ever produced. The effectiveness of scientific 'problem solving' is by now universally acknowledged and its impact on the life of humanity massive and clear. What is new is the awareness of science's limits and limitations as well as of its Janus-like face, beneficial and dangerous, illuminating and foreclosing, exploring and mystifying, all at once.

The logical structure of a scientific discipline and its supportive technologies penetrates beneath appearances, but also restricts the fields of vision. It systematically selects aspects of reality deemed relevant and verifiable, often limiting investigation to the homogeneous and to the quantifiable (and thereby open to mathematical techniques). Extra-empirical tendencies, seldom recognised, suppositions of plausibility and relevance, intuitions, the selection of the questions accepted as legitimate (while others are invalidated 'at the threshold'), the 'tacit knowledge' underlying enquiry, etc. play a major role within ordinary scientific practice.[2] The quest for certainty and models assuming inevitability have usually defined the scientists' 'ideal solution'. History of science documented how much it was in fact not simply a process of accumulating more and more of the same, i.e. of the commodity called 'knowledge', but a matter of massive shifts in 'paradigms' defining the questions, in language and in style of the argument or of proof which, while opening new fields of enquiry, foreclosed others.[3] Also, besides its 'knowledge-producing' facility, science acted in turn as a major ideology defining norms and images of contemporary societies.[4] Nor were the extra-empirical determinants of science a matter of thought only; social pressures were exerted by bureaucrats, budgets and public opinion. Far from being ideologically and socially neutral – a blank sheet written on by nature via the scientist's hand – actual existing science is an active human/social endeavour and can be understood only as such.

All that holds true with particular vengeance where social sciences are concerned.[5] As with the natural sciences, systematic selectivity is built into every social theory. Once again, the fact that much of it is tacit makes its impact the more enduring, while the socio-political pressures are often stronger still. But there is more to it. A subject matter which is heterogeneous, contradictory, and which may transform itself through learning or by collective will, defies many of the methods transported from natural sciences. With laboratory verification being mostly out of the question, the basic way of validation must be reconsidered or else a major part of reality must be omitted as irrelevant to science. The frequent equating of science with necessity is particularly self-defying here.[6]

Does this all matter where marxism is concerned? Is it affected by the way people view knowledge? The political impact of ways of theorising and of collective cognition was brought to question mainly through two half-truths, themselves frequently presented as marxism (or else as the non-marxist political science, originating with Machiavelli). People act in accordance with their interests and *therefore* whatever they say should be treated only as propaganda, i.e. a cynically manipulative defence of what suits them best in any given moment. Thought does not dwell in the realm of eternal spirit, it is shaped by 'material' experience and class (or other group) conflict and *therefore* it is but a reflection of it with no momentum of its own. Both deductions are false logic. In the words of the great sociologist, 'Between consciousness and existence stand meanings and designs and communications which other men passed on – first in human speech itself and later, by the management of symbols' which together with the specific organisations and personnel involved, form a 'cultural apparatus . . . the lens of mankind through which men see'.[7] Patterns of systematic and collective thought have a consistency and dynamic of their own and while shaped by 'material' reality, shape it in turn. Thought alone cannot explain social power or collective action, but consistent cynicism and/or reduction to '*homo economicus*' models were never sufficient to explain them either. The understanding of patterns of cognition, of their discrete impact, of their realism and of their systematic distortions form a necessary part of studying societies and of the ability to influence their future. This was, of course, precisely what Marx did (also).

There has been nothing wrong with the ambition of marxist analysists to live up to the standards of scientific enquiry. What was often enough wrong was the misunderstanding by some of them of the structure, the limitations and the 'rules of the game' of actually existing science. The master-model of the science of society acts as a 'cultural apparatus' in the sense described, i.e. it serves cognition but also shapes it and limits it. Central to the functions of this 'apparatus' is the systematic selection of evidence deemed plausible or legitimate and of argument acceptable as logical – not a list of views but a process within which views are shaped and strategies adopted in accordance. This systematic selection of evidence is, of course, not simply an affliction of the human mind but the way analysis works – a necessary device of disciplined thought and scholarly endeavour. It helps us to see in greater depth and detail some interdependences. It also blinds us to others. We are dealing here neither with pure spirit nor solely with the reflection of class interests, significant as those may be. Thought patterns and thought producers must be understood (also) on their own terms. In the marxist camp it was Gramsci who laid the foundation for the study of the ways the 'cultural apparatus' finds its long-term history and its human agency in the 'intellectuals' – the specialised carriers, producers and transformers of what is accepted as scholarship.[8]

That is also why while 'people make their own history. . . they do not make it just as they please' – not only circumstances but concepts, symbols and images form a powerful structure influencing and controlling consciousness, or to quote-on Marx's words, 'the tradition of all the dead generations weighs like a nightmare on the brain of the living.'[9] Much of it is no doubt cynical exercise in social domination and/or manipulation of some humans by others, but the constant efforts of the monopolists of political and economic power to control cognition has had its limits. For one thing, the controllers themselves, their own understanding, misunderstanding and choice, are powerfully restricted by the ways of seeing they adopt and by the systematic distortion built into them.

That is also why and where socialism, which aims to be science, should profit by taking a leaf from the actual history of science. At the beginning of the seventeenth century, looking at the very inception of contemporary sciences, Francis Bacon spoke of the systematic biases of human cognition: the 'four species of idols [which] beset [the] human mind'.[10] He named and specified them, within individual perception, within collective thought and the standard practices of scholarship – a major step forward in knowledge about knowledge: the 'psychology of perception', the 'sociology of knowledge', and epistemology, to use the language of our own generation. It was the demystification of the biases of perception which formed for him a major part of knowledge as a process. The author of *Capital* has chosen to tackle that very issue at the threshold of his study – the 'fetishism of commodities' is discussed in Chapter 1 of Volume I, the explanation of why the truth is not self-evident coming before the consideration of what it is.[11] In studying the relations between Marx's theorising and the many unexpected results of the political practice it induced or guided, one must also establish, beneath the flow of the accidental, what are the patterns of bias and mystification that particular model of science is prone to produce. Or, to put it in the language of the masters: what are the specific 'fetishisms' of socialist theory and practice and which 'idols' make those conceptual 'lenses' systematically opaque. A century of experience offers considerable evidence to pose those questions squarely.

There appear to be two major types of patterned and systematic biases in question. The first finds its roots in the adopted standards of legitimation of beliefs and the consequent selection of questions and of evidence deemed relevant and plausible. It produces some genuine incapacities to perceive as well as extra-empirical invalidations of data and argument, i.e. 'idols' foreclosing debate. We shall devote Part II of this paper to the 'idols' prominent with Marx's more immediate interpreters. The other type of bias is rooted in an assumed historiography – a particular twist of invalidation which is expressed in the terms 'utopian' and 'vernacular'. We shall proceed to it directly.

The vernacular and the utopian

According to the Oxford English Dictionary, *vernacular* (of language, idiom, word) means 'native, indigenous, not of foreign origin or of learned formation'.[12] The etymology of the term is given as a derivation from the Latin word *verna*, i.e. a home-born slave. Mortals do not argue with the Oxford Dictionary, yet something fundamental is clearly missing from that definition. The term does not stand on its own, it finds its explanation in an implied binarity of two opposing concepts. While an actual word is missing, the content of the 'other pole', the antonym(s) of 'vernacular' can be defined with precision, the way 'darkness' simply means absence of light. The antonyms of vernacular are: cosmopolitan and worldly-wise, artificial and subtle, expert, official, universal and scientific. Moreover, vernacular means 'indigenous' *as defined by* a culture *which is not*. An influential anthropological theory has seemed to assign it all to the Grand Tradition of towns and *literati* (as against the Small Tradition of rural communities in the back of beyond).[13] Realistic etymology would have it derived, presumably, from the 'master race'.

The meanings which the term 'vernacular' carries in our time do not end at that. The world changes – that was always understood. The world's change has a direction, which is intrinsically necessary, linear and beneficial, corresponding particularly with the rise in material well-being – by the nineteenth century this idea of 'progress' came to be accepted as self-evident. Within that frame of reference the dual concept of vernacular/its antonym(s) turns into the stages of a necessary evolutionist scheme: the uplifting of men from the vernacular to the universal, the scientific and the sublime. Once that is fully appreciated, the 'vernacular' becomes, by a reverse implication, the equivalent of a language which is archaic, native and inferior, oral-only or incomplete, a peasant dialect maybe. This negative connotation links into a seventeenth-century usage of the word, when it also meant 'low-bred' and 'slavish'.[14]

One last step on the way thought travels and transforms – the meaning attached to the vernacular's binarity has been further extended and put to contemporary use through a metaphor, which broadened its meaning and turned its focus from the past/present to the present/future. In this derivation, the opposite to 'the vernacular' becomes: the mass-produced, the mechanised, the standardised, the streamlined, the cost-conscious and the efficient. Also, it may stand for centralised, bureaucratic and state-bound. The term 'vernacular' converts accordingly into unique, hand-made, informal, autonomous, self-generated or even 'native' in the sense of being 'un-European' (remembering always that North America is Europe, while Bulgaria is not). It is therefore a product or a situation which the mass market, price accounting and bureaucratic administration cannot handle to full effect. The directionality of progress becomes an official strategy of reforms due to bulldoze, replace in plastic and electronics or else to 'educate-out' any vernacular substances, i.e. the inadequate and archaic products, humans and ways. It is no accident that the term 'vernacular' has become a conceptual banner of the 'green', 'feminist' etc. movements of Europe and that old socialists so often mumble when meeting those phenomena.[15] On the other hand the pretence by many modern intellectuals to adore the vernacular and to oppose mass production should not mislead us here. Nine-tenths of those who talk thus prefer on choice to live within a context, nine-tenths of which is 'anti-vernacular' by their very standards.

The reason why the 'vernaculars' retreated and their defenders so often sounded hollow is clear and must be stated at the outset. Universal languages are convenient in global communication and useful for quantitative operations. Science as we know it is an effective way to get results, or to predict them or to speed them up and so are standardisation, mechanisation, bureaucratisation and mass production. Human history has seen a steady advance of universality, mass production and applied science because these offered more of what people have manifestly strived for, materially as well as spiritually. But once that is granted a major question remains. Within the grand streamlining of contemporary human history, does the eradication of 'vernaculars' deprive us of something of value? By gaining what we do, do we lose something else, and if so, what do we lose and what does it mean? And this is where the argument about the 'vernacular' truly begins. It is also where the issue becomes directly relevant to the understanding of 'scientific socialism' as a cognitive system.

To a consistent evolutionist, the answer to the first question posed is simple: we lose nothing. Advance is ascent and intrinsically good, tools must be replaced by better ones, universalisation of contacts and thought is natural, necessary and the very core of the civilisation and 'humanisation' of mankind. Industry, science and the advanced technologies of things and human relations are not only tools but positive values. Beside the many possible false starts lies a historical mainroad of humanity which is exclusively right, rational, necessary, scientific and beneficial. Social transformation must 'wipe the slate clean'. At the very opposite pole to that view, the appeals to mankind 'to go back for its own good' have been usually a hopeless task. The realistic alternative to contemporary evolutionism is not to preach this, but rather to consider social transformations in their full richness, i.e. to 'take on board' the possible multiplicity, multi-directionality and multi-quality of actual and potential social routes. Analytically, it means to accept that we cannot assume a scenario of unilinear evolution as 'natural', i.e. necessary. On the terms of the ideology of 'progress' itself, i.e. while treating as the major goal the efficiency of problem solving, the challenge to it is rooted in the increasing unease of some of the practitioners of sciences with the longer-term results of 'streamlining' and with the impoverishment consequent on the establishing of a theory, a paradigm, a cure, or a strand, by purging all others. Such scholarly practice often shuts the doors on unanswered questions and on unexpected developments, with the long-term probability of finding yourself in a conceptual cul-de-sac – a deeply conservative procedure masquerading as a scientific theory of social change.

The image of socialism as science, defended with considerable skill and zeal by the first generation of Marx's interpreters, has meant also the consequent structuring of the whole of the theoretical field in relation to Marx's intellectual breakthrough. The model of science, once adopted, has led to the construction of a related intellectual historiography, to the singling out of a field of naivety or superstition (i.e. of questions to be invalidated 'at the threshold', whatever the evidence) and to the definition of the sphere of 'vernacular'. To exemplify, Spinoza became a stepping-stone on the way from the Greek materialist philosophers via Hegel and Feuerbach to Marx, while Platonism was placed accordingly as an idealistic cul-de-sac. A variety of questions were dismissed as pre-scientific, e.g. the ethnic continuities which cross-cut 'modes of production'. A major new concept was adopted by Engels to generalise and express the world of vernacular socialist traditions. The concept is that of 'utopian socialism'.

The definitive work of Engels treats 'utopian socialists' from Morelly to Weitling as those governed by socialist ideals of a just society, but handicapped historically and conceptually, and thereby unrealistic in their stand.[16] They emerge in times when the proletarian revolution is not yet possible. They lack the class analysis necessary to reveal the objective conflicts of interests, i.e. to map out the political struggle leading necessarily towards socialism. Their theories are consequently a-historical involving a belief that a better shape for a society, once discovered, will be acclaimed by all (and could have been brought accordingly into life at any stage of human history). Marx's immediate interpreters, the 'scientific socialists' of the late nineteenth century, have often explored sympathetically such emotions, ideas and struggles of the past but assumed that only at an objectively defined stage of socio-economic development, (i.e. that of 'mature' capitalist 'mode of production'), and only as a result of class struggle of the proletariat, can the socialist transformation take place. The very emergence of 'scientific socialism', i.e. Marx's discovery of class analysis and the 'theory of surplus value', was itself subject to the historical stage of advanced capitalism and the first wave of proletarian struggles (Lyons 1831, The Chartists 1836-48, Paris 1848), for mankind 'always sets itself only such tasks as it may solve'.[17] Utopian socialism is pre-scientific, that is pre-marxism socialism, a product of the craving for social justice in a society objectively incapable of socialism, and thereby prone to mystifications.[18]

A closer look reveals phenomena of considerable distinction beneath the actual usage of this generic term. Marxist analysts have attached the term 'utopian' to the socialist critique and images of a better society produced by single authors of the past, beginning with Thomas More. The expression was also used for the plebeian gut reactions, traditions and revolutionary movements of the pre-industrial or early industrial era. Finally, a contemporary political movement for social justice could be so designated if following a path which is non-marxist (by self-definition or else in the eyes of a marxist observer), in a period when the 'scientific socialism' and the proletariat have already emerged. Such alternative theories of social dissent persisting beside marxist science came to be treated mostly as the intellectual reflection of the regressive social forces, e.g. Proudhon as representing the French pre-industrial craftsmen.

What bridged those different phenomena were the subjectively genuine and morally honourable ideals involved; indeed, it was the moralising tendency which was often branded as unscientific. Coming 'before their time', i.e. outside the objectively necessary circumstances for successful transformation of the society, utopian socialism was understandable and commendable.[19] But, within evolutionist terms of reference, such mistakes of the past became dangerous side-tracks to the socialists, once the stage of 'scientific socialism' was reached. They had to be eradicated absolutely and with all possible haste. To dispatch promptly any signs of 'utopian socialism' along with astrology and alchemy would indeed seem necessary to achieve socialism – the 'orthodox' marxists of the second International have fully followed Engels's views in that. The post-1904 Lenin has added here a characteristic amendment, combining a major change in strategy with the full acceptance of the general theory as it stood: the idea of a progressive utopia of the Russian peasants and the consequent call for a 'democratic dictatorship of workers and peasants'.[20] On the other side of the political barricade, to the 'socialism-bashers', the problem of utopian socialism has been simpler still. To them, the lonely theorists producing ideas of a better society are naive, corrupt or mad, while plebeian movements for social transformation express mindless violence triggered off by scoundrels and dreamers. The contemporary non-marxist or part-marxist socialists and revolutionaries, as long as they mean what they say, are thus written off as a bunch of foreign agents, stooges and dupes.

The nature of social theorising explains why the varying relationships between the concept of science and of vernacular is for the history of marxism not a far-fetched metaphor but a model of direct relevance. It is relevant for the implied binarity of science/vernacular. It brings into focus questions concerning the significance, and the eradication of the indigenous revolutionary traditions. It can also help to see the impact of the 'idols' i.e. 'fetishism' expressed in the 'extra-empirical' legitimation of evidence and of views. We shall devote Part II to the major quadrangle of legitimation adopted by the mainstream of the second International: purity, science, progress and state, or to put it in a language indicating the ideological aspect of our concern: purism, scientism, progressivism and statism. We shall then proceed to discuss the revolutionary vernacular of the People's Will party, its implications and its relation to Marx's own Marxism.

Part II: The four idols

Doctrinal purity and political power

At the core of the development of socialism as we know it lies the history of the three consecutive Internationals, the peaks of whose activity have represented three major periods in the history of the socialist movement: its 'infancy' in the 1860s, its seemingly solid and irreversibly growing power of the 1890s and 1900s, and the revolutionary upsurge of the post-1917 decade. There are two striking similarities between those very dissimilar organisations. First, each of them has propagated a universal analysis and programme of revolutionary socialist advance on a global scale.

The universal doctrine and social critique were marxist in their essence and, increasingly so, in self-definition. Second, each of the Internationals was a total failure in the achievement of its formal goals. Not even one successful socialist revolution and/or regime was initiated or led to success by one of the Internationals or their local branches. This triple failure is staggering considering the immensity of effort, the devotion of the followers and the resources mobilised. What makes it all the more surprising is the fact that during that period victorious revolutions led by marxists did take place, and that within less than a century self-defined revolutionary marxists have come to rule one-third of mankind, extending their influence also over the imagination of the socialists elsewhere. But all of that has happened outside the framework of the official power-houses of marxist theorising, the Internationals: first, second and third.[21]

Within the marxist camp the conventional explanation of those failures was the lack of purity of the marxist analysis used and the resulting failures of political effectiveness. Marxism is the truth. Knowledge is power. Deduction from the correct texts would have secured victory and a defeat must mean some weakness within the logical chains of deduction. To get things right one must next time get the deduction right (and in anticipation purge any deviations from it). Historical experience has flown time and time again in the face of that ever reproduced model of relegitimation. It was Lenin, the first marxist head of government, who was quick to bow to the theoretical purity, supreme marxist erudition and logic of Kautsky and Plekhanov and to call them masters (all that, of course, before being prevented from it by political confrontation). He was to be branded by both of them, quoting chapter and verse, for departing from marxism in its purity, and led his party to power in what Gramsci rightly dramatised as the 'revolution contrary to *Das Kapital*'.[22] Both Kautsky and Plekhanov failed the test of power, i.e. of transforming society in accordance to their own lights. Something similar, if less overt (for reasons due to the disciplinarian nature of the third International) happened with Mao in China and with a succession of other countries, parties and leading figures.

An alternative explanation for these failures, i.e. the explanation which is not that of 'lack of marxist purity' of everybody defeated, has been usually to point to the difference between theory and practical politics. At its extreme, and especially with the enemies of the socialist experiment, it meant the adoption of political cynicism as the equivalent of earthly wisdom, e.g. to regard Lenin as seeking power only, his marxism a window dressing, freely adjusted to his machiavellian designs. Such explanations fall to ground once you look at them more closely. To exemplify, both Lenin and Mao were major theoreticians of society and of political action, put aside considerable time for its study and wrote extensively. Both have revised some of the 'orthodox' marxist assumptions but left many major conceptual thresholds of marxist theorising uncrossed, regardless of the pressures of expedience and changes at the political scene (i.e. were 'dogmatic' to all those who disagreed with their stand). Both were ready to pay a heavy price of unpopularity for 'sticking' to their own principles. Always remembering that political failure is a matter of real powers in contest and not only of defeat in an argument, it was not the lack of theorising which promoted the political success of socialist revolutions, but rather a different type of theorising. In what way did it differ?

It is impossible to substantiate such matters in a short section, and the conclusion will be simply stated here. During the century in question, the purest forms of 'scientific socialism', i.e. those most strictly deduced from the masters, invariably proved politically impotent. On the other hand all of the pure 'vernacular' forms of revolutionary socialism have also ended with defeat. It has been the integration of marxism with the indigenous political traditions which has underlain all known cases of internally generated and politically effective revolutionary transformation of society by socialists. The polarity between the victories of Lenin, Mao, Ho and others on the one hand and, on the other hand, the defeats of Kautsky, the Mensheviks of Plekhanov or Martov or of the Asian marxists like Roy, bears testimony to the different sides of similar equations. While there is no way to understand political results in terms of the theoretical thinking of its participants only, marxism has derived specific strengths from the 'impurity', i.e. from its amalgamation with 'vernacular' traditions.

Why should it be so? The significance of the revolutionary vernacular for the political potency of the marxists is more straightforward in its causes. Overgeneralisation is a major hazard to any political theorists who try to work out effective strategy and tactics. Vernacular traditions are the product of native society, of its intellectuals or its plebeian strata. That is why they reflect specific conditions and carry, often tacitly, important elements of the knowledge of them. Also they appeal in a language of ideas, emotions and recollections which often 'ring a bell' relating directly to political experience and to circumstances known. The political successes of the socialists were ever subject to their ability to put together a broad and inter-class front of radical opposition to the forces which govern. The incorporation of vernacular traditions facilitates such broad social and political unity, which, indeed, cannot be formed in any other way. Also, the optimistic voluntarism, and the immediacy of appeal, usually present within the revolutionary vernacular may be unrealistic as the reflection of what 'is', yet it may act as a potent mobilising and energising force making new social circumstances come into being.

The significance of the vernacular ingredient increases the more the nature of the society in question differs from the western and central Europe of the nineteenth century, i.e. the socio-political experience on the basis of which classical marxism took shape. That is why the extent of vernacular admixture has been so significant for the successes and for the failures of the marxist movements of the so-called 'developing societies' of Asia, Africa and Latin America and, of course, for Russia.

Why the vitality of the marxist ingredient? A considerable number of analytical concepts/assumptions of marxist usage proved highly realistic, as long as these were treated not as absolutes, but within a given historical context: 'class analysis', 'mode of production', 'alienation', etc. Many of them were effective also as modes of mass mobilisation, e.g. the images of 'class war' in days of crisis. The tight conceptual system helped to maintain continuous intellectual-political presence and discipline, particularly impressive when compared to the relatively transient and erratic nature of its vernacular competitors. The fact that marxism carried major characteristics of science – a general system which organises and makes sense of massive experience and a logic which generates consistent interpretations in the face of unexpected social developments – aided political unity and action. (These very qualities have also helped, of course, to sustain bureaucratic structures.) Universalism of the theory promoted inter-group and international alliances. At the same time, marxist intellectual tradition has been significantly broader than the self-imposed confines of contemporary science, helping to draw strength also from the ethical convictions and offering an activist creed – a call for action. The catalytic force of such a mix of ingredients is not a matter of speculation – the history of socialism testifies to it well enough. The main danger of marxism as a logical system lies for its supporters in its very strengths – the paradigmatic character of its illuminations and the refusal to bring into analysis experience which does not fit. That is why the 'impurity' of amalgamation with the vernacular has played such a vital role in making it analytically and politically potent.

There are a few more comments to be made. First, the capacity to gain power by socialists does not automatically mean socialism in result; we shall presently consider the 'yardstick' for it. Second, many claims to marxist orthodoxy, beginning with Kautsky, are in fact based on partial and selective compilations as a way to establish 'the doctrine'. The claims of purity should therefore be taken with a pinch of salt even for the 'orthodox'. Third, a major division lies here between marxism as an 'ideological platform' of opposition and the official marxist self-images of the post-revolutionary regimes. Different social contexts, especially class and state contexts, facilitate different types of and different functions of theorising. As marxism becomes legitimation of a state policy, the claims of doctrinal purity increase, while the actual impact of marxist ideas is submerged by expedience.

We shall now proceed to discuss the 'idols' of science, progress and state. Readers who would rather avoid epistemological debate and keep to the single theme of 'revolutionary vernacular' may prefer to proceed directly to Part III (page 268). The text permits such a reading.

Science and will

The impact of the self-definition of marxism as science on the consequent mode of analysis has already been suggested. We shall return to it to consider how the image of science functions as an 'idol'. The more thoughtful scientists have increasingly acknowledged the inbuilt inhibitions of their trade.

The adherence of scientific 'establishments' to a particular view of reality has always censored un-orthodox views and humans. The Spinozan treatment of science as divine often developed into the unquestionable acceptance of the word of its official priests (also, importantly, in fields which have nothing to do with their expertise). 'Science' was also often used to justify unreasoning acceptance of technological solutions to all problems of humanity, past, present and future.

Yet the core of the idolising processes related to the ideal image of 'a science' is not simply the selectivity of the evidence, the rigidity and ideological use of interpretations but a view of human/social phenomena which disregards its specific characteristics. Moreover, that is the field where the self-correcting devices developed by the natural sciences are particularly feeble. Hegel has already suggested a fundamental division of interpretations of the humans within society in his categories of 'false consciousness': on the one hand, the assumption of a total and uncritical integration of 'the personal' within the social; on the other, the belief in the absolute independence from society of the 'Romantic Hero'. Both represent aspects of reality, overstated or caricatured as they may be. The conceptual models transported from natural sciences have facilitated a heavy bias towards the first, while forgetting the second. Such tendencies have also expressed at times the intellectuals' contempt for the particular and craving for the general and the absolute, or else, a technician's view of science as simply following a set of rules.

Central to this dilemma is that within the environment of social action determinism appears side by side, indeed, as 'another side of the coin' of individual and collective 'free choice', within the environment of social action. The nineteenth-century assumption that real science trades in necessities only, while anything less or or anything else is not acceptable as real knowledge, has meant purging from its subject matter of anything 'subjective', including moral judgment, individual preference, metaphysical philosophy, etc. – a 'positivistic' approach. According to this interpretation there is no difference between human reality and the rest of 'nature' and there should be none in their expressions within scholarship. Total human plasticity, i.e. the notion that human action as fully defined by an 'iron ring of necessity'[23] is taken for granted and therefore, also the absolute predictability of human reaction, will and choice. The term 'objective' is used to designate all of these. In the marxist idiom this reading of human history was usually expressed by a massive stress on the determining powers of the 'base' (especially technology) as against the 'superstructure'. The way Althusser interpreted 'modes of production' had similar effects.[24]

The practice of the social sciences constructed along these lines has inevitably meant a particular and very selective model presented as a 'strictly empirical' picture of human reality. By excluding the 'subjective' and also the heterogeneous, it substituted for the real human world a 'puppet-theatre' of extra-human determination, and then proceeded to study it with the full scientific ritual of symbols, mathematical formulae and computer techniques, masking the arbitrary nature of its fundamental assumptions. A particular Anglo-Saxon variation of this was to divide the realm of human thought into 'two cultures' – that of Science proper, concerned with things 'objective', and that of the Arts, i.e. 'all the rest' with aesthetics, ethics and other frills as major representatives of it. A good British compromise is struck thereby, assigning true knowledge to the divinity of science and leaving all the rest to the frivolous devils of subjectivity and of leisurely pursuits.

That line of interpretation was consistently challenged by a tradition which assumed a discrete dimension of human will and choice. Once again the lines of argument cut across the marxist/non-marxist division, however conceived.[25] Among the marxists they formed a major trend referring to Marx's reading of Hegel and Fichte, and represented by Lukács, Korsch and Gramsci. According to that view, the world of human action and interdependence is characterised by being intentional, goal-oriented and self-creative. It is not arbitrary but neither is it totally prefigured. It is also less homogeneous with higher propensity for the 'unexpected'. Typical to the human reality are 'laws of tendency' which can foresee a social situation or struggle but neither its full specificity nor its results. Most importantly, the contradictions between determinism and choice exist within the social reality, i.e. are not simple failures to comprehend it. Social sciences as well as political action differ thereby from the phenomena fully definable by the extra-human laws of determination. (Marx's *Capital* has assigned animals for that very reason to 'goal-less' nature, to single it out from the world of human action.[26]) Analytically, the individual and the collective will, choice and creativity are irreducible (i.e. not fully reducible) to extra-human causes and 'structural' determinations.

Also, accidents are a part of reality. A fundamental tragic dimension of human beings in society is therefore being implied (as against facile optimism and the 'cheerful robot' ideals of over-socialised humans), but also the liberating capacity for choice. That is why – following that line of thought – Gramsci attacked marxist positivist epistemology of his day as the 'degenerate tendency . . . which consists in reducing a conception of the world to mechanical formula which gives the impression of holding the whole of history in the palm of its hand' – a 'primitive infantilism'. He concluded that 'it is the very concept of "science" as it emerges [from Bukharin's textbook of marxist sociology] which requires to be critically destroyed for it has been taken root and branch from the natural sciences, as if this were the only science or science *par excellence*, as decreed by positivism.'[27]

As for Marx, he has challenged sharply the radical individualism which assumed the total independence of human from social frameworks and determinations, but had also some testy things to say about the 'mechanical' determinists and their fatalist interpretations of human action. He was aware of the fact that he is not here in tune with most of his philosophical allies; it was indeed the major area in which he suggested that materialists should learn from the idealists.[28] Marx's own emphasis on social determinism seemed to grow stronger and then to lessen at the end of his life, but he consistently held to his philosophical anthropology, i.e. a view about 'human nature' which assumed creativity, will and choice.[29]

A fundamental division of interpretations within the social sciences and in marxist discourse is anchored in philosophical assumptions concerning the nature of humans/society. Those philosophical 'underpinnings' are inexpressible in purely empirical terms, yet form a major part of any system of knowledge. The analytical schools which deny them such a status simply readmit them by stealth, assuming as 'taken for granted' some images of humans, of their consciousness and potentials (e.g. 'homo economicus'), and once this was done, bashfully looking the other way. To 'de-idolise' human sciences one must explore both their specificity and the philosophical preassumptions involved. The two most direct consequences are expressed in the diversity of approach to the historiography and to ethics.

Progress and choice

Directly linked with positivistic ideals of science as a legitimating device (and as an 'idol') is an evolutionist supra-historiography: the idea of progress. Within the liberal *Weltanschauung* it is the very advance of rationalism, with science at its peak, which forms the essence of human progress. The economic and social advances follow as a matter of course. In marxist idiom a similar idea appears, if more implicitly, with science providing a bridge between the accumulation of capital and the broader social scene. Applied science underscores industrialisation and thereby the extended reproduction of modern economy, while the accumulation of capital and industrialisation determines the contemporary rise of science. The rise of modern industry and of science lead necessarily to the creation of the revolutionary agency of change: of the proletariat and of the scientific socialism which naturally adopt each other. To both liberal and marxist 'progressists' the accumulation of riches, mechanisation and ascent of knowledge (which human choice simply 'reflects') have secured in the past and will secure, seemingly forever, further improvement of human welfare and liberty.

The reason why the marxist/non-marxist divisions are so often breached over the issues of science-and-progress, making often for strange political bedfellows and splitting old political friends, lies in the alternative approaches to the questions of human will and choice. Accepting the difference between the far-distant goals, the ever conspicuous similarities between marxist and non-marxist 'progressists' belong there. A recent book by W. Warren has brilliantly restated this view and that alliance.[30] To the author, the unavoidable, objective and positive economic advance of capitalism and of applied science, linked and wed, naturally produce and sustain parliamentary democracy, public wealth, health and education, i.e. what people need and want. The advance of capitalism produces as necessarily a working class and the socialist class-consciousness within it. Colonialism and imperialism are a price well worth paying for the speedier advance along that inevitable road. Nor is it in fact much of a price to pay, as the 'reciprocal advantages' make the relations between the 'first' and the 'Third' world good for all. Any attempts to resist it are Proudhon-like and/or populist, i.e. reactionary, anti-democratic and anti-scientific as well as 'a-historical' and unrealistic ('a-moral' becoming the synonym for 'objective' and 'scientific'). This triumphant legitimation of capitalism, on the pain of becoming a petty bourgeois populist, is no longer even the meeting-point between the academic ('legal' in tsarist Russia) marxists and the woolly liberals of old, but the acceptance of Rostow's *Stages of Economic Growth* (subtitled 'Anti-Communist Manifesto') as scientific, and thereby presumably marxist (before marxism became twisted by Lenin's post-1905 miscomprehensions of Asia and by the 'guilt feelings' of the Western intellectuals).

I believe Warren to be substantively wrong on points of fact and intepretation,[31] but what concerns us here is the idolatrous historiography of science-and-progress which those views exemplify. Contradictions, possible different outcomes, the human capacity for creative invention breaking social continuities, are substituted by a 'scientistic' image of history as inevitability, unilinearity, determinism and total human 'plasticity'. Also, whatever may be Warren's own socialist preferences, the idea of 'progress' has been paraded for a century and more as the chief legitimation of oppression, state elitism and priestcraft, taking over the functions of medieval catholicism in Europe. What is the socialist analysis of that political 'fact'?

As a rule, 'progressist' analysis was not even an effective book-accountancy of the 'objective' results dear to the admirers of science and progress. The long-term social results of mass repression and demoralisation of the 'native people' of the Americas on the indices of 'progress', the differential impact of the ways social structures transform (e.g. the impact of de-peasantisation on the post-peasant societies)[32] etc., are usually not even brought into consideration. Within a model in which everybody is bound to tread an essentially similar path which science has defined, all that becomes irrelevant. The consequent historiography is as unrealistic. Lassalle's attitude to the German peasant war exemplified it well: he declared that the defeat of the peasant rebels was 'objectively' progressive and thereby 'a good thing' for Germany and for mankind. The alternative road to capitalism taken by the Swiss smallholders who beat German nobles out of their valleys show how much that particular piece of 'evolutionism' is unrealistic in fact. Behind such misconceptions stands a misplaced pride in a 'cold mind', equated with scientificity but explaining nothing.

In socialist political theorising and prediction, the progressivist ideas have supported false optimism (often followed by blank despair, when 'progress' did not occur). Even more importantly, they have deeply trivialised the images and considerations of the future as much more of the same, to which the major attempt by Kautsky to describe the future socialist society bears immortal evidence of breath-taking narrow-mindedness.[33] Babel once described anti-Semitism as 'the socialism of fools'. Unilinearism is their history or at least their pet philosophy of it.

A direct derivation from the scientist/progressist outlook was the way the significance of the production of material goods has been interpreted as the supremacy of the industrial, the large-scale, and the technologically complex, not as possible methods to achieve some goals but as 'good things' in themselves, often in the face of massive evidence to the contrary. It has meant also the exclusiveness of 'objective' indeces, e.g. the equating of the number of factories with the advance of socialism or 'ascent of motherland'. Once again it was Gramsci who identified this type of sub-idolatry, declaring from the other side of the conceptual frontier that social analysis must centre, at least for marxists, not on 'economic facts' but on 'men, society of men, interdependence of men developing towards a society which . . . comes to rule [economic facts], to reconstruct them and to change objective reality.'[34] This brings us back to 'the subjective', i.e. to the specifically human. It must be looked at closely within realistic interpretations of society, especially so by those who wish to challenge and transform systems in which, as beautifully put by John Berger, 'all that exists becomes quantifiable – not simply because it can be reduced to a statistical fact, but also because it has been reduced to a commodity'.[35] To transgress it is, also, to attack conditions where 'All subjectivity is treated as private and the only (false) form of it which is socially allowed is that of individual consumers dream. From this primary supression of the social function of subjectivity, other supressions follow: of meaningful democracy . . . , of social conscience . . . , of history . . . , of hope – the most subjective and social of all energies (replaced by the sacralisation of Progress as Comfort)'.[36] Any consideration of human reality must face the issue of human choice. Within the positivist trend of thought, the ideal of 'objective science', the quest for 'truly scientific procedures' and the idea of 'inevitable progress' reflect panic fear of sounding sentimental or philanthropic by treating such matters at all. These moods were often expressed as scientific detachment, understood as a-morality and viewed as a particular marxist badge. The sociology of Bukharin, in the early days of Soviet rule, has simply declared the very notion of ethics to be the product of fetishism, due to vanish with the classless society. Nor is this a past tendency or a Russian overstatement. It was repeated for our own generation, in Paris, a short time ago.[37]

The retraction from the 'subjective', and especially from ethics, 'for science's sake', is ever doubtful when social interaction is considered. Within a marxist *Weltanschauung* which has invariably linked theory and the active pursuit of social justice, such an approach is particularly deceptive. At its worst it becomes stark justification of detachment from human suffering (of the masses of people) for the sake of some far and distant goals (defined by an elite) and a free hand for repressions and factional viciousness, all under a socialist banner. Its test and its ultimate conclusion were demonstrated equally in Stalin's 'purges' as by his favourite saying: 'When a forest is cut, splinters fly' – a suitable epitaph for Bukharin's grave, wherever it may be.

Not all of it need be as bloody to be as wrong. To return to the example already used, Warren's crusade against the 'petty bourgeois . . . feeling of guilt' of the Western socialist intellectuals towards the 'Third World' also belongs there. To him, the marxist, i.e. progressive approach, must retract from the a-scientific sentiments and from any concern with the 'price of progress'. The absolutely arbitrary nature of those assumptions presented as 'science' is breathtaking. Why 'petty bourgeois'? Were shopkeepers particularly prone to charity and solidarity with the poor and oppressed elsewhere, while industrial workers were not? Did proletarianisation actually produce socialism? Was it the feeling of guilt of the children of bourgeoisie which derailed it in actuality? What starts with hypothetical assumptions becomes a watertight prediction and then a justification one can challenge only at the peril of 'taking a reactionary posture' – a fine display of how fetishism works. If some of the conclusions and results do not look quite socialist, one must none the less remain 'scientific' and trust the unavoidable future.

'There must be more to the revolution than the question of

The possibility of personal choice (restricted as it must be physically, historically and socially), forms a necessary base to any meaningful ethic. Marx's socialism carried an irreducible moral component (and a related emotional one, for it was Marx who once remarked that 'shame is a revolutionary sentiment'). There can be no scientific proof of why social justice and 'the realm of freedom' should be fought for, yet without such a choice socialism mocks itself and loses its main yardstick of self-evaluation. Kautsky's lame explanation that people must support what is unavoidable, i.e. what is 'progressive' is a fair example of the intellectual sterility the other line of argument within marxism yields.

A 'social science' sterilised from subjectivity and ethics means that either marxism (and any other socialist creed) is not a science or else that such a concept of science must be changed. It means also that while the demand for 'objectivity' understood as an awareness of possible biases and of the need to counter them is admirable, this very concept used as synonymous with pure empiricism is false. As a moral prescription in its conventional usage, objectivity is indeed 'not a virtue', but an over-estimated dodge to avoid responsibility', to quote a comment of a wise 'non-scientific' observer of humans.[39]

To sum up, it was Albert Einstein who put best the case for a realistic attitude to science: 'We should be on our guard not to over-estimate science and scientific methods when it is a question of human problems. . . . Science . . . cannot create ends . . . at most [it may] supply the means by which to attain certain ends.'[40] As for realistic historiography, in the words of Antonio Gramsci: 'Utopianism consists, in fact, in not being able to conceive of history as a free development, in seeing the future as pre-fashioned commodity. . . . Utopianism in that sense of the word is a type of "philistinism" . . . [which has] degraded and soiled the socialist doctrine.'[41]

Tools and goals

One last step into the provinces where concepts turn into 'idols'. The fourth, and historically most recent, element of the 'quadrangle of legitimations' which turn into idols, is the revolutionary party/state. As the confidence in the power of conceptual purity, the certainty of the scientific prediction and the inevitability of progress eroded and the difficulties of realisation of the socialist dream mounted, the revolutionary party and/or state moved up in significance from a tool in a bag of tools to the decisive instrument of scientific progress and progressive scientificity. (Similar changes have been happening to the reformist ideals which produced the 'welfare state'.) The state was to force the gates of heaven, to break through the discrepancies between prediction and reality. As time went by, the deification of purity, science and progress 'rubbed off' on to the instrument of their realisation, making it seem as significant, admirable and transcendental as the goals it had to serve. As with later Hegel, the state and citizen discipline towards it became equivalent to rationality, virtue and higher civilisation. These assumptions linked to the ethos, self-image and legitimation of the bureaucratic structures, especially upon achieving state power. Once again, the larger the discrepancy between the West European presumptions of classical marxism and the social reality it actually encountered, the larger the role of the bridging instrument and the more powerful the pressure for its idolisation.

The main conceptual difficulty here was the considerable critical awareness of the oppressive nature of the state built into the analysis and writings of Marx and his followers.[42] That difficulty was bypassed mainly through the combination of the peculiar organicist metaphor of Engels, by which the state will simply 'wither away' under the proletarian rule, and by the growing canonisation of the revolutionary party, presented as a substitute for proletarian consciousness. The affirmation of marxism as the rule of science *represented* by the 'revolutionary intelligentsia' (later the 'party apparatus') and due to guide the working class to its destiny has already begun with Kautsky – its appeal to the potential 'guides' is obvious. Nothing has been said, indeed, about when 'the party' will 'wither away' and little was made of Marx's concern 'that the educator itself needs educating'.[43] The division between the state (not always a 'good thing') and the revolutionary party (representing all things positive), merged with the actual historical experience of the USSR. In the first post-revolutionary state led by the marxists, it was the party apparatus which came to act as the real locus of power. This arrangement, a polymorphic party structure with the 'state apparatus' as one of its expressions only, exported and came to be treated *ex post factum* as equivalent to a law of nature.

The appeal of the 'quadrangle of idolisation': purism, scientism, progressivism and statism, rest on some very real characteristics and achievements of human action and thought. The appreciation of the results of science and industry as much as the scorn for woolly-mindedness and ineffectuality are rooted in experience which cannot be discarded. Realistic inferences are, however, only one aspect of those matters, the other is the usage of purity, science, progress and state/party as legitimations which dismisses, without true examination, evidence and argument which do not fit its presuppositions. This aspect of analysis has been productive of 'false consciousness', censorship and self-censorship. The very invisibility of much of it, and its appeal to linguistic conventions, symbols and icons prompted idolatrous propensities, e.g. the use of 'purity' as a synonym for 'goodness', the legitimation by the personal authority of 'big men', etc. The four legitimations/idols are linked within a system of mutual support: progress is right for it represents science, state is right for it secures progress, the issues of doctrinal purity merge with those of the effectiveness of state and true science rests on doctrinal purity. When evidence flies in the face of one of those, the others are brought into play, together with the bureaucratic structures which reinforce them, to keep the whole chain steady.

Within the contemporary world in which an 'extended reproduction' of controlled communications and the corruption of language are a major political tool of domination, one must keep restating the essentials of what remains the main contemporary alternative to the *status quo*: the socialist creed relating directly to Marx (also). Socialism is not the equivalent of doctrinal purity, of industrial progress, of science or of state, the role of each of those for the socialist goals must be critically and constantly assessed and re-examined. Socialism is about abolishing the domination of people by other people, about collectivism which is nobody's prison, about social equality and justice, about making people conscious of their power and able to control their destinies here and now. Strategies, achievements and failures of socialism can be judged only by its goals, not by instruments. Tools turned goals become idols. Concepts used to rule out and to denigrate without examination views and facts, any views and any facts, are mystification from which somebody usually profits. That is where science does have a definite similarity with socialism, often unsaid.

It is the ethic of the scientific inquiry. One cannot lie for the sake of science, one practises. The result will not be science. One also cannot lie for the sake of the socialist revolution. Lies are counter-revolutionary.[44]

Part III The vernacular and Marx's marxism

The People's Will

In the words of a great historian, '. . . there is no true understanding without certain range of comparison, provided, of course, that the comparison is based upon different, and at the same time, related realities.'[45] Vernacular revolutionary traditions offer such a major range of comparison facilitating the understanding of the illuminations and limitations of marxist ways of analysis. They also present the explicit and tacit insights of many revolutionaries of thought and deed into the specific conditions in which they operated. These first presentations in English of the major theoretical documents of the People's Will party (*Narodnaya Volya*) offer occasion for such a reflection.

The revolutionary populists of the People's Will accepted goals fundamentally similar to those of the West European socialists and said so. They adopted different analysis and strategies – a 'different and at the same time related reality' of thought and action. Members of the People's Will knew and admired Marx's *Capital* without accepting it as fully relevant to Russia, and said so. Marx has, in fact, agreed with that view and, once again, said so, in no uncertain terms.[46] That does not make Marx into a populist or turn members of the People's Will into crypto-marxists. They were political allies, who supported and influenced each other. Some questions follow. What insights different from Marx's own did the People's Will offer to the understanding of Russia and its road towards socialism? How realistic were they? What, if anything, can their suggestions teach about Russia's past and about socialism's present, those who have at their disposal 'scientific socialism'? Or, to follow the general question concerning any vernacular, what, if any, are its uses for the world around us, and what do we lose by forgetting it?

A number of analytical achievements of the Russian populists have been discussed above in relation to late Marx's work: the particular attention to 'uneven' social change, the 'model' of multi-directional but combined societal roads, the specific character of 'backward capitalism' within a global and historical framework. The Russian revolutionary populists of the 1850s to the 1880s offered a critique of capitalist development (using Marx's *Capital* to strengthen their case), but went much further than simply to declare their distaste for it. They have systematically considered the ways and means for a major 'periphery of capitalism' to proceed along a road different from the experience of Western Europe, i.e. to bypass capitalism, moving into a socialist future. They under-estimated the potential of industrialisation, but also offered a very realistic 'environmental' analysis of its untrammelled development – an insight we are only now beginning to catch up with. They looked more closely at the *mutually* negative impacts of Western colonialism and its colonies. Herzen's discussion of *meschan'stvo*, i.e. the narrow-minded philistinism and cynical individualism linked with petty possessiveness; as the major ill of advanced capitalist societies, has initiated a socialist critique of 'consumerism', the 'mass society', etc. Those issues have grown in significance ever since, and most importantly, proved pertinent by self-admission also for post-revolutionary societies – witness the contemporary debate in the USSR, China, etc.[47]

Next, the Russian populists were more aware than the Western socialists of their age of the specific problems of state power, its class-creating capacity, economic expressions, relative autonomy of existence and patterns of bureaucratic reproduction. A century ago they also began to tackle the issue of 'the centre' versus the local power in a post-revolutionary society and of the dangers of the bureaucratic reforms 'from above' which, as Marcuse put it a hundred years later, are 'streamlining rather than abolishing the domination of men, both by men and by the products of their labour'.[48] Once again history seems to have caught up since with their concern and message.

While it was Marx (and Moses Hess) who produced the core of the argument we know today as the problem of 'alienation', it was further developed in the nineteenth century by the Russian populists rather than by the 'orthodox marxists'. The general issue of man versus society, the need for and the difficulty of combining individualism and collectivism under socialism, the place of ethics in socialist action and Marx's problem of 'educating the educators', i.e. of elitism, appear within what was misnamed 'subjective sociology' developed by the Russian populists as part of their ideological attack on the *status quo*. It has also made some steps toward the establishing of a realistic social psychology of political action, the absence of which still leaves the marxist and non-marxist analysis of phenomena like Khomeini so outstandingly inadequate. A major aspect of what they have called 'subjective' was, in fact, the explicit consideration by political activists of the 'tragic freedoms' of humans within oppresive society and of the problems of conscious political intervention in spontaneous social processes (which, if left to themselves, may well regress in terms of socialist goals). In the century to come it was the most effective marxist political organiser of Russia and its most outstanding political theorist in the West, Lenin and Gramsci respectively, who put into practice and in writing very similar ideas concerning the revolutionary party and revolutionary will. There has been little advance on it ever since.

The revolutionary vernacular expressed in the People's Will reflected a specifically Russian context and tradition. Was it utopian? Engels has defined as 'utopian' socialist revolutionary efforts in a society not yet capable of socialism, but then, he and Marx declared their belief that socialist-led revolution in Russia of the 1880s might definitely happen and succeed (subject to the Russian defeat in war, i.e. as it was actually to happen in 1905 and 1917, when Russia lost its next two wars). Engels has specified as 'utopian' political views which, while declaring for socialism, lacked the class analysis to show how it can be achieved and the proletariat to carry it out. Russian populists did produce a class analysis, if a different one from that of Engels, i.e. concluding that unlike France of 1848, or of 1871, the main forces due to face each other in Russia are the state and a state-bred squiredom and capitalists versus the 'labouring class,' i.e. a plebeian front of peasants, workers and intelligentsia, allied with the radical soldiers. In that frame of analysis Kibalchich had predicted in 1880 that for the socialists, power would be particularly hard to gain in Russia, but once that was achieved they would reach farther than Western Europe, i.e. there would be a combined political and social, anti-state and anti-capitalism revolution.[49] He suggested also that in

Russia the revolution would start in towns and spread into the countryside and that the revolutionary party should shape its tactics accordingly – clearly expecting not a proletarian rule but a major contribution of the proletariat to the uprising and the rule of the revolutionary party as an immediate result. Would you consult your history books, comrades living in the 1980s? Would you also consider the relevance of that scenario for the present and future of the so-called 'developing societies'?

To pre-empt a question and a misreading of what was said, does it all mean that it was Russian populism and not German marxism which 'got it right'? Did the revolutionary populists of Russia find the ultimate answer to the problems of socialism or at least a consistently better answer than the marxists did? I do not think so. The revolutionary populists of Russia did offer some important new answers to problems of 'Russia-like' societies. They have also added some important insights to the critique of the capitalist West, the significance of which proves considerable also for the more general scene today. The crux of the originality and illumination of the Russian revolutionary populist lies, however, not in those preliminary answers, but in the posing of a number of fundamental questions concerning capitalist society, its 'peripheries' and the socialist project. The attempts to disqualify those questions as belonging to the past only, i.e. representing Russian social backwardness in the 1880s or the petty bourgeoise nature of its peasantry, have been proved wrong by historical experience. The decline of peasant Russia did not make those questions disappear; quite on the contrary, most of them became increasingly global and pertinent also in super-industrial environments. Such questions left unanswered come back to haunt socialists time and time again, and will proceed to do so until faced, theoretically and politically. They can be avoided only at socialism's peril.

Something similar obtains for the general phenomena of the indigenous revolutionary and socialist traditions. The more so, for they have shown enough vitality to spark off constantly new intellectual and political developments; they are neither static, nor 'fit for museums only', nor else necessarily representative of defensive backwardness. To 'de-vernacularise' them in our understanding, i.e. to exchange their dismissal 'at the threshold' for critical appreciation of its scope, is to enrich both the socialist movement and the contemporary social sciences.

Two further issues of general significance should be recorded here in so far as the 'vernacular' revolutionary traditions are concerned. First, the universalised analysis typical of contemporary social sciences has achieved considerable results, but has often made us less aware of 'the particular'. That has been true with a vengeance where ethnic, cultural and conceptual continuities are concerned. Their importance for actual social sciences and socialist theories was generally neglected in the twentieth century, e.g. the 'historicity' and the attention given to the specific political sphere particular to Italian intellectual history: Machiavelli, Vico, Croce, Mosca, Pereto, Gramsci, etc. The other side of that coin is the way receptivity to socialist ideas differs within different local cultures (and not only in different social classes). Closer examination of the vernacular is a way to see more realistically intellectual histories and political prospects.

Finally, and to proceed further into the areas where the 'social sciences' and human reality differ from what chemistry or astronomy offer or can ever attempt, the ideas, models and 'utopias' of the human mind not only present social reality (correctly or mistakenly) but also generate it. For the human/social 'subject matter', the ability to choose, i.e. the existing degrees of freedom (its limitations accepted), is also an ability 'to emancipate oneself from the apparently overwhelming mental and physical dominance of the routine',[50], as expressed in invention, revolution, human creativity. Human action and thought do not simply express inevitable trends and laws but activate new, unexpected and unexpectable realities – a situation which neither positivistic science nor conservative politics can accept or even fully perceive. It is that potential of human creativity where the transformation of society and individual 'self' are concerned which has been the core of Marx's optimistic philosophical anthropology and his definition of the essence of 'general human nature' as creativity, capable of and striving for liberation. Without such assumptions the final goal and the limits of socialism are indeed simply a more efficient form of the 'welfare state' (not unlike what Kautsky has substantially suggested[51]). Different socialist traditions and utopias represent (also) conceptual experimentation, inventiveness and creativity without which a fundamentally different social world cannot come into being.

To 'make a hundred flowers bloom' is not simply nice for the flower-lovers, experts or amateurs. It is a way to produce more flowers, healthier flowers and to speed up the creation of new species of them. To keep the many vernacular insights 'on board', i.e. to be open to them without worshipping them either, is to have a clearer mind concerning actually existing science, actually existing socialism and some other important things besides.

Marx's marxism

None of the many attempts at definition, streamlining and/or purge have made actually existing marxism of one cloth. Its different faces and interpretations have indeed underscored and served its 'life-like' quality, its capacity to develop and transform. Few would have heard of it otherwise a hundred years since its inception in early Victorian England – a world which is mostly all over and done with.

The constant debate about various taxonomies of marxist thought has formed part of its development. Central to it, if often implicitly, has been the major debate over the nature of marxism as a system of knowledge, a division which can be expressed as that between deductivism and integrationism. A second argument, often related to but not fully overlapping with the first divides those who treat marxism as science understood in a positivist way and those who assume its essential characteristics to be much broader, incorporating what would be extra-scientific to the other camp, in particular an ethic rooted outside political expedience and utilitarian simplifications.

To those given to deduction, the essence of marxism as knowledge has been established in the works of the master(s) to which an obligatory extension by a specific interpreter is usually added, to form an enclosed axiomatic whole. The work of contemporary scholarship would be to establish and elaborate some 'mediating structures' of analysis which runs from the axiomatic general theory towards reality, but never back. The purer the deduction the better the explanation and the safer the prediction, while the failure of prediction proves weaknesses of interpretation but leaves forever untouched the axiomatic core. A major task of scholarship has been the militant defence of the axiomatic core from anything to anybody: people, thought or facts who challenge it. All of the major legitimating devices have been put to use to invalidate as illogical, unscientific, reactionary, anti-party and/or anti-state, in short, anti-marxist, any views to the contrary. Cases of possible ambivalence are 'vernacularised', that is, explained away as representing backwardness and due to disappear as the result of the natural course of history and science. The purity of deduction forms the index of truth in marxism of that type.

The marxists who adopt an integrationist view assume that the process described by Engels in which the achievements of German philosophy, French socialism, and British political economy fused and were advanced further in Marx's work, could not stop at that but proceeded and indeed must go on forever. New ideas and facts will ever challenge, integrate into and transform what is referred to as marxism, not only its outskirts but also its core. It means that the resulting impurities are often a major virtue, an enrichment which serves the realism of results, possibly a recognition of 'dialectic contradictions' which fuel necessary adjustment and change. There are no unchallengeable laws of science. Marxism is not about Marx but about truth. It is also, consequently, about the logic of untruth – about the rationale of the 'idols' and about 'fetishism', to use Marx's major concept also for his own words. The main heuristic danger of such an approach has been that of eclecticism – jumbling of analytical constructs unrelated by logical coherence. Such dangers exist, but in that view, are well worth risking, to open the theory to the breeze of 'external' evidence, thought and contradictions. It calls for discipline and vigilance towards theorising, but that is all.[52]

What was Marx's own marxism like in terms of these major divisions? He was manifestly aware of the ingredients of thought which were incorporated into the theoretical advance associated with his name – Hegel, Ricardo, etc. – but what was his view since his new theoretical design took formal shape in 1867 in *Capital*, Volume One? That is where Marx's relations with the People's Will offer major evidence of his own attitude to 'marxism', to the status of its possible revisions, to its scientificity, to its ethical composite as well as to the vernacular revolutionary traditions. In the late 1870s and 1880s Marx came face to face with massive evidence concerning a major society which did not fully fit with Volume One of *Capital*, and with an indigenous revolutionary movement there which was not 'marxist'. At that very time Plekhanov, the father-to-be of Russian marxism, adopted the view of Russia as a 'not-yet' Germany or England, on its way to catch up with the *Capital* Volume One model. That approach has necessarily 'vernacularised' the People's Will into a group of utopians, i.e. explained them away as people with honourable intentions but theoretically backward, analytically helpless and politically hopeless. That very line of thought produced in the 1890s Plekanov's treatment of Russian peasantry as a 'reactionary mass' and the belief that a prolonged period of capitalism under liberal bourgeois rule was for Russia a necessary preliminary to socialism.

In that major test, Marx had declared his belief that the People's Will party had a chance to win and his personal support for them.[53] Most importantly, Marx had clearly recognised behind Chernyshevskii's irony and the People's Will bombings, shrewd analytical thought and important insights into reality which was different from his own, as well as some strategic questions and considerations from which new illuminations could be drawn. Chernyshevskii had never read Marx, it was Marx who read Chernyshevskii, explicitly learned from him about Russia, and said so. Late Marx's writings show how much Marx adopted and developed new views concerning Russia – enriching his own analysis by that of others and ever self-critical of it.

It took the 1905-7 Revolution for some of it to dawn on the brightest strategists among Marx's followers in Russia. But the answer to our question about the nature of Marx's own marxism was clinched already by Marx himself in the last decade of his life. While the first generation of his interpreters fought unceasing battles for the purity of deduction from their master, Marx himself did the opposite. He refused to deduce social reality from his own books, to a point where some of his admirers have all but come to see his late work as feeble-minded.[54] The essence of his preferred epistemology was summed up by his very hand in the serious joke of his 'Confessions'[55]: *De omnibus debitandum* – 'doubt everything'. To Marx this joke clearly included his own work at the heights of its achievement. He chose as his favourite heroes Kepler and Spartacus, a scholar whose intellectual courage breached new grounds and a leader of the rebellion of slaves. He concluded by stating as his favourite maxim, 'nothing human is alien to me' – an ethical prescription.

Acknowledgments

Thanks are given to those whose comments improved this paper: Perry Anderson, Zygmunt Bauman, Ottar Brox, Noam Chomsky, Philip Corrigan, Boguslaw Galeski, Ernest Gellner, Iris Gillespie, Leopold Haimson, Andrzej Kaminski, Elfi Nunn, Ron Petrusha, Zillur Rahman, Shulamit Ramon, Raphael Samuel, Derek Sayer, Israel Shahak, Paul Sweezy, Daram Vir, Leon Zamosc.

Notes

1. Marx has noted (while disputing Bukanin's view in *Statehood and Utopia* about the marxist self-definition), '[The] words "learned socialism" were never used, while "scientific socialism" was used only to counterpose it to the utopian socialism which attempted to enforce on people new fantasies and illusions, instead of restricting its field to the study of social transformation of those very people; see my book against Proudhon.' See K. Marks i F. Engels, *Sochinneniya*, Moscow, 1961, vol. 18, p. 617. For the much more positive position of Engels on that matter see *ibid.*, vol. 19, pp. 105, 115, etc.
2. For discussion see, for example, W. Heisenberg, *Physics and Philosophy*, New York, 1958 (espcially pp. 194-206); A. Einstein, 'Consideration concerning the fundamentals of theoretical physics', *Science*, 1940, XCI, pp. 487-92; M. Polanyi, *The Tacit Dimension*, London, 1967; W.O. Hegstrom, *The Scientific Community*, New York, 1965; and, most recently, J.M. Smith, 'Understanding science', *London Review of Books*, 3-16 July 1982; etc. See also T. Shanin, *The Rules of the Game*, London, 1972.
3. See in particular T. Kuhn, *The Structure of Scientific Revolutions*, Chicago, 1970 (revised edition).
4. See in particular the work of the so-called Frankfurt School, e.g. the still very potent H. Marcuse, *One-Dimensional Man*, London, 1964.
5. For a good discussion of the issues involved see E. Cassirer, *An Essay on Men*, New Haven, Connecticut, 1944.
6. Further discussion of relevant aspects of science follows in the section entitled 'Science and will'.
7. C. Wright-Mills, *Power, Politics and People*, New York, 1963, pp. 405-6.
8. See A. Gramsci, *Selections from Prison Notebooks*, London, 1971, Part I.
9. K. Marx and F. Engels, *Selected Works*, Moscow, 1973, vol. 1, p. 398.
10. F. Bacon, *Novum Organon*, New York, 1900, pp. 319-27. (The book was first published in 1620.) Marx described Francis Bacon as the initiator of contemporary materialism and science. The manifest difference between Bacon's and Marx's approach to 'false consciousness' was Marx's powerful accentuation of the historicity of the 'idols'.

For discussion see D. Sayer, *Marx's Method*, London, 1979.

11. Unmistakably selecting the wrong end of the stick, Althusser suggested in his guide to the readers of *Capital*, vol. 1, to begin reading it at Chapter 2, and to proceed then to its very end, but not to go into Chapter 1 without the supervision of specialists, or else, to leave it out altogether. Althusser, *Lenin and Philosophy and Other Essays*, New York, 1971, p. 71.
12. *The Oxford English Dictionary*, Oxford, 1933, vol. 12, p. 137.
13. R. Redfield and M.B. Singer, 'The cultural role of cities', *Economic Development and Social Change*, 1954, vol. 3, pp. 53–73.
14. A. Shipley, *Dictionary of Early English*, London, 1957, pp. 705–6.
15. See, for instance, I. Illich, *Vernacular Gender*, Cuernavaca, 1981.
16. F. Engels, 'Socialism: utopia and scientific', Marx and Engels, *Selected Works*, op. cit., vol. 3.
17. Ibid., vol. 1, p. 504 (written in 1859).
18. The most significant Soviet analyst of the Utopian Socialist movements assigned them *in toto* to the period of 'primitive accumulation' as a specific cultural expression of it. See V. Volgin, *Ocherki istorii sotsialisticheskikh idei*, Moscow, 1975. For a contemporary 'Western' discussion of major relevance see Z. Bauman, *Socialism: The Active Utopia*, London, 1976.
19. For example, Engels has spoken harshly against Dühring's tendency to dismiss the Utopian Socialists as simply silly.
20. V.I. Lenin, 'The two tactics of social democracy' in 'Democratic Revolution' and 'The Two Utopias', *Collected Works*, 1963, vols 13 and 18 respectively.
21. Should one wish to keep that list precise there were of course two more Internationals; the 'two and a half' one of the Social Democratic Left and the fourth one of the Trotskyists.
22. A. Gramsci, 'The revolution against capital', *Selection from Political Writings*, 1910–20, London, 1977, pp. 34–7.
23. Cassirer, op. cit., p. 20.
24. L. Althusser and E. Balibar, *Reading Capital*, London, 1975.
25. Compare, for example, Cassirer, op. cit.; N. Chomsky, *Language and Mind*, New York, 1968; B. Kuznetsov, *Einstein and Dostoyevsky*, London, 1972 (initially Novosti Press Agency, Moscow, 1972).
26. 'But what distinguishes the worst architect from the best of bees is that the architect builds the cell in his mind before he constructs it in wax.' K. Marx, *Capital*, Harmondsworth, 1976, p. 284.
27. Gramsci, *Selection from Prison Notebooks*, op. cit., pp. 407, 428, 438.
28. The first of the 'Theses on Feuerbach', in Marx and Engels, *Selected Works*, op. cit., p. 13.
29. While working on *Capital* Marx was chiefly concerned with the social determination aspect of reality. Yet it is in *Capital* (Harmondsworth, 1976, vol. 1, p. 759) that Marx speaks again about human nature, both 'in general' and 'as historically modified in each epoch' – in direct continuity with concerns and views expressed in his 'Early Writings' and the content of the last decade of his work (see part I above).

30. Bill Warren, *Imperialism: Pioneer of Capitalism*, London 1980.
31. A considerable amount of critique of Warren's evidence and argument is by now in print; see, for example, A Lipietz, 'Marx or Rostow', *New Left Review*, 1982, no. 132. Whatever the conclusion about those matters, the issue of intellectual origins is more straightforward. Warren believed that his view was a return from later Lenin's position to those of Marx. It is not. It is a return to the 'progressist' interpretation of Marx by the generation of the second International, as discussed in this volume in 'Late Marx: gods and craftsmen'. In Russia precisely those views were expressed by the so-called 'legal marxists'.
32. See the thesis developed by Barrington-Moore, *Social Origins of Dictatorship and Democracy*, Harmondsworth, 1966, especially part 3.
33. K. Kautsky, 'The day after the Revolution', *The Social Revolution*, Chicago, 1913.
34. A. Gramsci, *Selection from Political Writings*, op. cit., p. 32.
35. J. Berger and J. Mohr, *Another Way of Telling*, London, 1982, p. 99.
36. Ibid., p. 100.
37. See above, p. 27.
38. Gramsci, *Selection from Political Writings*, op. cit., p. 28.
39. N. Freeling, *A Long Silence*, Harmondsworth, 1975, p. 39. The question was presented with all its philosophical and political sternness in the work of Sartre. For a major contribution by a Soviet scholar see Kuznetsov, op. cit., pp. 62-5, who traced the issue back as far as the debate about determinism and freedom by Epicurus in Ancient Rome and related it to the contemporary theoretical issues of physics and ethics.
40. A. Einstein, 'Why socialism', *Monthly Review*, 1951, vol. 1, no. 1, p. 5.
41. Gramsci, *Selection from Political Writings*, op. cit., pp. 28, 52-3. See also G. Lukács, 'Technology and social relations', *New Left Review*, 1966, no. 39.
42. K. Marx, *The Civil War in France*, Marx and Engels, *Selected Works*, op. cit., vol. 2, and its partial restatement in V. Lenin, *State and Revolution* (written in August 1971).
43. The third of the 'Theses on Feuerbach', Marx and Engels, *Selected Works*, op. cit., vol. 1, p. 13.
44. That is how L. Trepper (Domb), the chief of the legendary 'Red Orchestra' network in France of the First World War, has summed up all his lessons of forty years of service to the Communist movement and the experience of stalinism in it. For his life story see his *The Great Game*, London, 1979.
45. M. Bloch, *The Historian's Craft*, Manchester, 1964, p. 42.
46. See p. 101 (Western precedent).
47. The word *meschan'stvo* is indeed in constant use by the contemporary Soviet press and common speech when castigating the negative personal characteristics of the 'new middle classes' of the USSR.
48. H. Marcuse, *Reason and Revolution*, Boston, 1960, p. vii.

49. See pp. 212-18.
50. Bauman, op. cit., p. 11.
51. See note 33.
52. It is instructive to see how much that debate, once again, cuts across different periods and schools of thought, relating in each of them to their specific social context. Within the theological battles of the period of the Reformation, Erasmus has defended the view that 'wherever you encounter truth, look at it as Christianity' for 'truth is divine' as against Luther's demand 'to remain God's captive for ever' laced with German nationalism. See S. Zweig, *Erasmus and the Right to Heresy*, London, 1979.
53. See pp. 20-1, 61, 69.
54. See pp. 129, 133, fn. 6.
55. See p. 140.

Index